LANDSCAPE RECLAMATION PRACTICE

LANDSCAPE RECLAMATION PRACTICE

Edited by **Brian Hackett** MA, PPILA, RIBA, MRTPI

IPC Science and Technology Press

D
627·5
HAC

Published by IPC Science and Technology Press Limited, IPC House,
32 High Street, Guildford, Surrey, England GU1 3EW.

ISBN 0 902852 47 7

Photosetting by Thomson Press (India) Limited, New Delhi

Printed in England by
Whitstable Litho Ltd., Whitstable, Kent.

Contents

The authors

Ian S. Clark, FRICS   Douglas Macara, Groves and Associates, Chartered Quantity Surveyors.

Michael F. Downing, MSc, Adv Dip Landscape Arch, FILA   Lecturer in Landscape Design, University of Newcastle upon Tyne.

G. P. Doubleday, BSc, PhD   Grassland Officer, Durham County Council. Sometime Senior Research Associate in Soil Science, University of Newcastle upon Tyne.

Jill Foister, BSc, Dip LA   Landscape Architect, sometime Research Associate in Landscape Design, University of Newcastle upon Tyne.

Brian Hackett, MA, PPILA, RIBA, MRTPI, (also Editor)   Professor of Landscape Architecture, University of Newcastle upon Tyne.

B. R. Hutson, BSc, PhD   Division of Soils, CSIRO, Glen Osmond, Australia.

Mervyn A. Jones, BSc, FGS   Senior Research Associate, Department of Soil Science, University of Newcastle upon Tyne.

M. L. Luff, BSc, PhD, ARCS, DIC, FRES   Lecturer in Agricultural Zoology, University of Newcastle upon Tyne.

J. A. Richardson, MSc, PhD, M Inst P   Senior Lecturer in Plant Biology, University of Newcastle upon Tyne.

Foreword by the Secretary of State for the Environment, the Rt Hon. Peter Shore MP

I am glad to have the opportunity which the publication of this volume provides to stress the importance of reclaiming derelict land so that it can be put to some beneficial use. This is not simply a matter of improving the urban and rural scene, but also of helping to stimulate economic growth in less favoured areas and to meet the increasing demands made upon our limited land resources.

Over 12 000 acres of derelict land were reclaimed in England between 1 January 1972 and 31 March 1974. This good progress was primarily due to the efforts of local authorities, on whom the main executive burden falls, with the help of generous Government grants. But much still remains to be done and I trust that fresh impetus will be provided by the raising of the rate of grant to 100% in the assisted areas and derelict land clearance areas.

Reclamation work in a variety of locations and climatic conditions calls for the application of a wide range of expertise and there is a continuing need for the improvement of techniques. It is therefore essential that the experience which has been gained should be made widely available in works of reference such as this.

Peter Shore

(Peter Shore)

Introduction

Since the publication of the two volume report on the Landscape Reclamation Research Project of the University of Newcastle upon Tyne*, the national interest in the subject has not diminished, and there is an increasing number of persons and authorities carrying out the design and supervisory works necessary for reclaiming derelict landscapes. This has become evident in the announcement that the report had to be reprinted in 1974, and thus the occasion arose for a book which could be classed as a practical guide for practitioners and others involved in landscape reclamation, rather than a book based upon the results of experimental research. The publishers have been fortunate in securing the services of most of those concerned with the original research project as chapter authors, though some of them have now left the service of the University.

Eleven years have now passed since the research work commenced in the University and during this time it has become increasingly clear that there is still a lot of progress to be made in the management of reclaimed landscapes. Far too many examples come to mind where the initial reclamation has been well done, but deterioration has set in, often as a result of neglect, and sometimes from a lack of understanding about the way in which a reclaimed landscape requires further input over the years—maintenance of a different kind to the customary maintenance of a well-developed public park. In this book, we have referred from time to time in the specialist chapters to this continuation work, as well as in the chapter specially on the subject.

It is also necessary to emphasize again that the reclamation of derelict landscapes is a continuing research matter; each new project is likely to have its own special problems. Thus, the availability of specialist research facilities to the reclamation team will be of great advantage.

In producing a textbook of this kind, we have endeavoured to keep to basic principles and techniques, because it soon became evident that to cover such matters as the techniques used in the repair of a building of industrial or archaeological interest, or of a pair of canal lock gates, would not only be a mammoth task, but would in any case involve bringing in specialists for such matters. Rather have we kept to the reclamation of the landscape as generally understood.

Brian Hackett

*Landscape Reclamation,
Vol. 1 (1971), Vol. 2 (1972),
IPC Science and Technology
Press Limited.

1 Administrative procedures

Brian Hackett

1 Definitions of derelict land

There are many differing views on the physical state of an area of land which identifies it as being derelict. For example, there are gardens and parklands designed and laid out in the eighteenth century which have now become neglected paths, lawns, and flower beds, or dead trees and grassland invaded by bracken and wild shrubs. Some people see these as beautiful landscapes with a particular naturalistic quality; other people sense neglect and a deterioration in the fertility of the landscape. There is no specific statutory definition of 'derelict, neglected or unsightly' land used in the various Acts that enable grants to be made for reclamation; although a generally acceptable definition is 'land so damaged by industrial or other development that it is incapable of beneficial use without treatment' (Explanatory Memorandum (1973) on Grants for the Reclamation or Improvement of Derelict Land under the Local Employment Act 1972 and the Local Government Act 1966). But note that an adventure playground, which many people would consider to be a beneficial use, is almost ready made in some types of derelict land (see also Wallwork 1974).

2 Grant-aid

How does one decide whether it is worth applying for grant-aid? Let us examine examples of dereliction which are likely and unlikely to be approved, and examples of the kind of improvement works likely to qualify for grant-aid under the Local Employment Act 1972, the Local Government Act 1966, and the Industrial Development Act 1966.

2.1 Approved examples

These are likely to include disused spoil heaps, worked-out mineral excavations, derelict and abandoned industrial buildings and installations, abandoned military installations, and disused railway lines and canals when the objective is recreation rather than transportation or navigation. Adjacent land which is not derelict but is required for carrying out satisfactory reclamation works may be included for grant-aid.

Grant-aid is normally only given when a local authority owns the land, but exceptions can be made where no significant after-value is likely to be created and where there appears to be no need for the local authority to own the land. Whatever the circumstances, it is wise to consult the Government department concerned before starting work on the necessary investigation, survey and design processes.

2.2 Disapproved examples

Some areas of 'wild or natural landscape', such as marshlands, moorland and mudflats, degenerate woodlands and neglected farmland, which some people might consider derelict, are not eligible for this kind of grant-aid since they have not been damaged by industrial or other development.

2.3 Approved operations

The kinds of operation likely to qualify for grant are:

● expenditure incurred in the acquisition of approved land, including legal and professional expenses, and the expenses of investigation or survey fees; and

● expenditure, including professional fees and administration expenses properly chargeable to loan, incurred in carrying out approved works of reclamation. The works which are approved depend on the scheme. Provided that the Minister is satisfied that they are required primarily for reclamation the following works undertaken on approved land are eligible:

  (i)   demolition and removal of unwanted buildings and works;
  (ii) earth moving for levelling, filling, spreading and grading;
  (iii) land drainage essential to the reclamation works;
  (iv) importing and spreading of top soil and grassing for agricultural and amenity schemes;
  (v)   tree planting where necessary to stabilize slopes, prevent wind erosion, or act as a screen for structures or foundations where no other treatment is being carried out. A good case can be made for shrub planting where it serves similar purposes.

The amount of grant made by the central Government for reclaiming derelict land varies according to the location. At the time of writing, an approved scheme in a development area (Section 8 of the Local Employment Act 1972, or Section 20 of the Industrial Development Act 1966) qualifies for an 85% grant on the actual final cost of land acquisition, the contract works and professional fees. An approved scheme in an intermediate or derelict land clearance area (L.E. Act 1972 or the L.E. Act 1970) qualifies for a 75% grant, and a scheme approved under Section 9 of the Local Government Act 1966, qualifies for a 50% grant.

2.4 Other grant-aid sources

The Farm Capital Grant Scheme, as varied by Statutory Instrument 1972 No. 368, provides, for hill land areas only, a 40% grant towards the cost of clearance operations such as removal of roots and boulders and bracken eradication on derelict agricultural land. There is also a 70% grant under the scheme towards the cost of land drainage in hill land areas, and a 25% to 55% grant in lowland areas, assessed individually for each farm. These grants are intended to be limited to the estimated increase in the agricultural market value of the land. There are also grants of 60% for land drainage and 10% for land reclamation in both hill land and lowland areas, under the Farm and Horticultural Development Scheme, although this is unlikely to have a wide application.

The Forestry Commission is empowered to make grants for existing woodlands, including derelict ones, provided the owner agrees to continue to manage the woodlands in accordance with sound forestry practice. These grants amount to £45 per hectare (£18.21 per acre), with a supplementary grant of £125 per hectare (£50.59 per acre) for woodlands planted to establish a hardwood crop with a predominantly hardwood appearance over the greater part of the woodland's life. The normal minimum area for these grants is 1 hectare ($2\frac{1}{2}$ acres), but for areas of 10 hectares or more (25 acres), there is a legal instrument of dedication. Reclaimed landscapes, and also landscapes still retaining spoil heaps, are eligible for this kind of grant-aid.

Grants made by the Countryside Commission can sometimes be used for reclamation schemes. In National Parks and areas of outstanding natural beauty, grants of 75% of the cost can be made provided the work meets the objectives of the National Parks and Access to the Countryside Act 1949. The Commission can also make grants of from 25% to 50%, depending upon the priority of the locale, for reclaiming disused or derelict railway lines and canals which are not owned by the British Waterways Board if the result provides recreational facilities and opportunities. There have also been examples when the reclamation of disused or derelict railway lines has been assisted under the Local Employment Act 1972 and the Local Government Act 1966.

The removal of man-made eyesores, such as derelict buildings and scrap heaps, can also qualify for grants from the Countryside Commission of from 25% to 50%, depending upon the priority of the locale. There is a similar grant-aid arrangement to meet the compensation involved in a discontinuance order for removing objects disfiguring the countryside.

From time to time, reclamation schemes involve the preservation and reclamation or repair of derelict industrial artefacts, and large fixed machinery is regarded as an integral part of a derelict industrial structure. If a structure comes within the definition in Section 15 of the Ancient Monuments Act 1931, it is eligible for consideration for grant-aid; some structures might also come within the definition of buildings of outstanding historic or architectural interest in Section 4 of the Historic Buildings and Ancient Monuments Act 1953, and thus qualify for grant under that Act. Buildings within a conservation area can be considered for grant-aid under Section 10 of the Town and Country Planning (Amendment) Act 1972. There is also the Science Museum Fund of £150 000 a year to assist in restoring and preserving scientific and technological material.

Planning consent for the types of mining and industrial operation which led to dereliction in the past, often require reclamation of the site either during the operation or subsequently. For ironstone opencast mining, the Mineral Workings Act 1951 introduced a levy per tonne of ore extracted which is put into a restoration fund. With opencast coal mining operations by the Opencast Executive of the National Coal Board, the reclamation work is usually restoration of an agricultural landscape, rather than the removal of dereliction. The legal requirement for restoration is embodied in the Opencast Coal Act 1958.

3 Reclamation objectives and policies

The objectives for reclaiming derelict landscapes should be:

● the restoration of the health and fertility of the landscape, sometimes leading to an improvement on the original state of health and fertility;

● a result that either allows flexibility in future land uses or provides specifically for a planned land use;

● a landscape which is visually acceptable and fits into the surrounding landscape without discord;

● the removal and prevention of pollution, fire risk and danger.

An important additional objective is that of providing an agreeable habitat for wildlife in a balanced ecosystem.

There are also broad reclamation design policies which apply to

1

Figures 1 and 2. Before-and-after photographs of the reclamation project carried out at Trimdon Grange, Co. Durham, by the Reclamation Section of the Durham County Planning Department (courtesy County Planning Dept., Co. Durham).

particular types of dereliction; for a description of the operations producing the various types of dereliction, see *Derelict Land* by K. L. Wallwork (1974). An example of a reclamation policy for a particular type of dereliction is that stated in reports on derelict canals where the recommended aim was to restore the canal to a standard which could be maintained at the same level of expenditure as for similar canals already in the cruising network. Other aims were to improve the environment of the canal and its immediate surroundings, and to develop the canal's potential for supporting recreation (Leeds and Liverpool, Lower Peak Forest and Ashton Canals).

3.1 Types of dereliction

Deep mining

These operations usually produce spoil heaps, derelict buildings and equipment and subsidence on the surface. In a few cases, recommendations have been made to retain the spoil heaps as a feature in the landscape, either to add interest or to provide a viewing platform; the spoil heap is grassed or planted with trees. In general, however, the spoil heap is graded out to produce new contours which will, for example, give greater areas of southerly slopes than perhaps existed in the site's original condition; some problems of vegetation establishment have occurred however, especially on the steeper slopes. The new contours are usually better related to the topography of the surrounding landscape, and cost limitations are likely to restrict earth-moving operations to cut-and-fill works on the site or, at most, to spreading over adjoining land if this will produce a better result.

2

These operations should allow for the safe disposal of slurry and spoil which is prone to combustion or is toxic, and for the spreading of the available topsoil to develop the landscape as quickly as possible. Provisions for draining the surface water will have high priority in the design policy, since newly reclaimed landscape is so sensitive to erosion. When the future use of the site is clearly defined, the grading works can take account of this. But if it is unknown, the grading works should allow as much flexibility of land use as possible. Where there is a local demand at an economic distance for filling material (e.g. for motorway embankments), burnt shale or spoil, and more recently unburnt or black shale or spoil, have been removed from derelict sites, and have thus reduced the cost of reclamation. Similarly, some operators have found that spoil heaps can contain a sufficient percentage of coal to warrant screening it out.

The policy usually adopted for surface treatment is to develop a grass cover with tree planting on the steep slopes. But there have been some examples where the grant-aid allowed planting for wind-break and amenity purposes; the current situation, however, is as described in (v) on p. 2.

Many of the earlier deep-mining techniques practised in Britain produced sporadic vertical subsidence on the surface. Where this has produced a lake or 'flash', this feature can sometimes be developed as an amenity, if appropriate. When the subsidence is limited to small isolated pockets, they can be made up to the surrounding ground levels. When subsidence has produced a 'no-man's land' landscape, with numerous subsidence pockets and flashes, economical reclamation could be achieved by grading over the whole site to produce an even, although probably undulating, surface. There may be occasions when spoil can be brought in to such a site to

Brian Hackett

3

Figures 3 and 4. Before-and-after photographs of the sand and gravel pit restoration at Stillington, Co. Durham. The site is 32 ha (80 acres) in extent and was restored to agriculture (courtesy of the Sand and Gravel Association Ltd).

assist in achieving a smooth surface.

The horizontal effects of subsidence are more serious, especially in possible damage to buildings and subsequent dereliction. When a planned use requires a building on the site, and repairs to the existing building are no longer possible, the policy is likely to be the design of a new building on a raft foundation.

Deep-mining operations for iron ore have produced similar spoil heaps and subsidence, although the waste material is usually warmer in colour. But the mining of non-ferrous ores like copper, tin and lead, while producing lesser subsidence problems, often produced toxic waste, some-times of a spectacular colour. The mines in the past were often small, but distributed at frequent intervals over large areas of high-quality landscape. When the spoil has pockets of toxicity, a practical policy is to concentrate grassing and planting on the non-toxic areas, and to leave the toxic areas to recover gradually. Grading operations to cover the toxic areas are some-times possible, but there is a danger that this may lead to new areas of pollution of underground water.

Surface mining

Surface mining always results in a hole in the ground, which may be either a single large excavation or a series of ridges and hollows known as 'hill and dale' landscape. There may also be some mounding of overburden around the excavation, and derelict buildings and plant. When the floor of the excavation is impervious and there is no drainage outlet, or where there is a high water table, a body of water may be formed; this is seen in some areas of sand and gravel deposits.

The National Coal Board Opencast Executive's policy regarding open-

4

cast coal mining is straightforward reclamation to agricultural land on most sites, sometimes with shelter belt woodlands. One site, at Druridge Bay in Northumberland, was reclaimed as a country park instead. For other types of surface mining the policies are variable and often influenced by the nature of the site. Where the excavation is not deep and the exposed strata are pervious, producing a 'dry pit', it is often possible to replace the topsoil and use the site for agriculture or horticulture. Development in the form of housing, industry and roads is possible, although it will be necessary to ensure that there are places in the surrounding landscape where sewers exist at lower levels than the floor of the pit. Derelict landscapes of this type are also used for the deposit of waste, eventually bringing the site back to its original level, but existing water channels, above and below ground, will have to be maintained or diverted to avoid waterlogging.

Surface ironstone workings at one time left behind a hill-and-dale landscape that resulted from the earlier technique of distributing the overburden; these areas have sometimes been planted with trees, although the uneven nature of the ground makes forestry management difficult. Now, however, there is a scheme whereby the State pays part of the restoration cost and the rest is met by a levy on the ore extracted; under this scheme, restoration to an evenly graded site is achieved quickly (see also p. 20).

Where the excavation is bottomed with impervious strata or there is a high water table, a 'wet pit' results unless the unusual condition exists of a dip of the impervious strata away from the site. The result is a lake, and unless the excavation has vertical sides (and is thus inaccessible) or has dangerously deep water, it can often be developed as an amenity, especially with the growing popularity of water recreation. Deep wet pits are a particular problem if the reclamation policy is to fill them; town refuse is an unsuitable medium, although rubble and PFA (pulverized fuel ash) are suitable but likely to be expensive to transport.

Although some pits left by abandoned stone quarries have these dangerous conditions of deep water and steep banks, it is usually easier to terminate extraction with a better-looking result than for a sand or gravel pit, provided there are adequate conditions attached to the planning consent. One reason for this is that an exposed stone face, if left in a suitable form, is not dissimilar to natural exposed rock. But a successful result does depend upon the working plan of the quarry's taking due account of the landscape, and the end result's being conceived as a landscape design related to the surroundings.

The deep pits from which china clay is extracted have their own particular landscape problems. Those in production are dry, except for clay streams resulting from the hydraulic mining technique, while many of those not in production hold water; there are also the associated sandheaps formed from the waste material washed from the clay. Arguments have sometimes been put forward in favour of the dramatic appearance of these white sandheaps in the landscape, but these arguments often lose their force when one observes the resulting juxtaposition of heaps and pits. On the other hand, the sandheaps now being formed no longer follow the traditional conical shape, and if the excavation process can be carried out in accordance with a landscape plan, this particular argument is more easily supported because use and visual quality have been considered.

One of the dereliction problems faced by many deep- and surface-mining industries is the amount of waste compared with the amount of mineral extracted. In china clay workings, approximately eight tonnes of waste have to be placed somewhere for each tonne of clay produced. If the waste is put into previous excavations, it will sterilize the lower clay deposits which will be worked as the more accessible deposits are worked out; if the waste is placed on undisturbed land, it may sterilize good farmland or the working of further clay deposits underneath. Also, one cannot often find a market for the sand within an economic distance.

Unlike surface extraction of most other minerals, china clay workings are liable to have spoil heaps of the kind associated with deep coal mining.

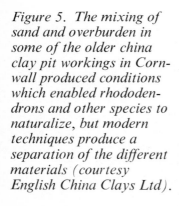

Figure 5. The mixing of sand and overburden in some of the older china clay pit workings in Cornwall produced conditions which enabled rhododendrons and other species to naturalize, but modern techniques produce a separation of the different materials (courtesy English China Clays Ltd).

If these heaps are formed by the single-point tipping method, a conical form is produced with new material constantly distributed on the surface; the result is that vegetation cover cannot be established. Other methods of forming the heaps leave completed areas behind the dumping process, making it possible to establish a 'creeping' cover of vegetation. Although it has proved difficult to establish vegetation on the waste from china clay working, research undertaken by Professor A. Bradshaw of Liverpool University and by English China Clays has produced encouraging results. Generally, of the eight tonnes of waste referred to previously, one tonne

6

7

Figures 6 and 7. Before-and-after photographs of the waste material from china clay workings in Cornwall. Grading and grassing operations were the techniques employed (courtesy English China Clays Ltd).

comprises overburden which is relatively easy to vegetate and is an important asset in the reclamation of the landscape.

Another facet of reclamation policy is tree planting around various parts of extraction sites for screening purposes; this is particularly true in the china clay industry.

Industry

The reclamation policies for industrial dereliction are as varied as the types of dereliction left behind by industry. Except in the cases where industry was established in remote areas or where the area is one of general decline, most reclamation policies are directed towards a new land use such as housing, open space or new industries. The work, more often than not, will involve demolishing old buildings and plant. Sometimes, however, the reclamation policy will include the revitalization of some of the buildings with grassing and planting on the areas between.

Areas once occupied by chemical, and some of the ore smelting, industries have problems of toxicity and fusion of material in waste heaps. A likely first step will be to ascertain whether there is any value in the waste; for example, basic slag from steel production has been used as a fertilizer. But with toxic conditions, a policy of isolation is likely, such as burying the material in a convenient excavation or surrounding it with a bund, leaving it to the passage of time to reduce the toxic effect.

Another feature often found on derelict industrial sites is the lagoon. This can take different forms, from an innocuous reserve of water, through washing ponds which may contain toxic elements, to slurry lagoons which are the most difficult to deal with. Where appropriate, the lagoons can form a feature in the reclaimed landscape.

There is currently much interest in industrial archaeology, and designers of reclamation projects now pay particular attention to any machinery or

Figure 8. This view of derelict buildings at Talbenny Airfield in Pembrokeshire is typical of the dereliction which can occur from disused industrial buildings (courtesy Central Office of Information via the Countryside Commission: Crown Copyright reserved).

Landscape Reclamation Practice

Figure 9. The area shown in this photograph of Dale Airfield in Pembrokeshire was the site of many derelict buildings until clearance and reclamation took place in December 1963 (courtesy Central Office of Information via the Countryside Commission: Crown Copyright reserved).

industrial artefacts left on a derelict site. Scarcity value, scientific and engineering interest, and the amenity and recreation aspects are often studied in order that a judgement may be made about the future of the artefact, and there is always special interest where they can be worked into the reclamation proposals.

Derelict housing

In most cases, this was referred to as slum clearance areas, but recognition of the snags inherent in high-rise housing as a replacement, and the basic structural quality and community potential in nineteenth-century high-density housing, have brought about a fresh look at what used to be termed 'derelict'. Thus, a policy now frequently adopted is that of revitalization; this is the province of the planner and the architect, rather than of those specifically engaged in derelict landscape reclamation. Nevertheless, where the policy is one of demolition and clearance, consideration should be given to the capital already invested in roads and services. There should also be an assessment of whether housing is now the best use of a particular site or whether the area fits better into the local plan as open space, industry or commerce.

A particularly bad effect of many derelict housing areas has been the protracted delay in reclaiming the site after the inhabitants have been moved to new areas; there is unlikely to be surrounding countryside in close proximity to mitigate the effect of dereliction, unlike the examples of the extractive industries.

It is always worthwhile to consider whether any elements from the derelict housing area might be preserved or incorporated in the reclamation proposals. Apart from the nostalgic and historical interest, reusing some of the materials and elements (e.g. granite setts for new paved areas, or retaining some of the original walling at possibly reduced levels) will take away the immature appearance.

Transport systems

For disused railway lines, dereliction is seen in the cinder foundation of the tracks, derelict stations and other buildings, bridges gradually becoming dangerous, broken fencing, and sometimes the regeneration of bordering hedges, shrubs and other plants. For roads, lack of use and maintenance soon leads to the gradual development of vegetation cover and hedgerow vegetation. In canals, the water sometimes becomes impassable with weed growth, or it drains out leaving a muddy exposed bottom; the canal locks deteriorate, as do the bridges and fencing.

The common feature of derelict railway lines, roads and canals is their linear character. This, together with the lands being under single ownership and small in area compared with the landscape traversed, makes them suitable propositions for reclamation and development for recreation. Complete restoration to agricultural use may involve removing embankments, filling in cuttings, taking down bridges and other structural works, but complete removal of all elements is only economic in urban areas where land values are high. On the other hand, restoration to agriculture, although small in area, could earn income indefinitely.

The problem that has faced the owners of derelict railway lines, roads and canals has been the responsibility for the structures and the heavy damages likely to arise from consequent accidents. If bridges are demolished, either the linear route is broken where it passed over a bridge or the users of a bridge over the route have to cross at grade; in both cases, unobstructed passage is affected.

Figure 10. This photograph of the derelict Ashton Canal in Manchester indicates the scale and nature of the reclamation task which faced the 600 volunteers who commenced cleaning refuse from the canal over a weekend in 1968. After further operations, the canal was reopened to boats in 1974 (Hugh McKnight Photography).

Figure 11. Typical old hardwood derelict woodland at Micheldever Forest in Hampshire. The coarse old trees will be felled for timber, and the crowded young trees, which include ash, sycamore and oak, will be thinned out to ensure the best growth of selected specimens (courtesy the Forestry Commission).

In urban areas, the value of the land occupied by disused railways, roads and canals will usually result in its acquisition for some other purpose—in itself likely to remove the dereliction. However, canal docks in urban areas can take on a modified use for pleasure craft and as an attractive environment for housing and restaurants.

Refuse tips

These vary from quarries and other excavations filled with town refuse under a controlled tipping programme to the dumping of car bodies and pieces of mechanism on sites which are sometimes deep in the countryside. Filling of quarries, if properly carried out, can finally result in a grass surface suitable for recreation; the proper answer for dumping areas is removal of the rubbish, although screening with tree planting would help in time.

Forestry and agriculture

It is not easy to define derelict forestry and agricultural land. To some people, woodland initially planted for commercial forestry may have charm

Brian Hackett

Figure 12. The outcome of fifty years of skilful tending for good timber form and linked scenic effects at Highmeadow in the Forest of Dean. The fine oak is neighboured by beech and larch trees spaced to reveal healthy foliage and grace and form (courtesy Frank Thompson, the Forestry Commission).

and amenity value if it is in a neglected and derelict state; it may even be considered an asset to the ecology of the locality. Similarly, grazing land invaded by bracken or gorse adds colour and texture to the landscape. Forestry and agricultural dereliction are largely a reflection of the economic situation, since the land is out of production.

Reclamation policy for derelict forestry and agricultural land usually makes use of the various grant aids (section 2) for clearance and land drainage (and management of woodlands). The real difficulty seems to be persuading the owners of small pockets of derelict land to go through the process of negotiation and sale (at probably unacceptable terms) to an adjoining landowner who might be prepared to reclaim the lands; this would almost certainly require a contribution by him over and above any available grants.

4 Legislation and reclamation

Section 2 refers to the legislation under which grant-aid can be made available for reclaiming various types of derelict landscape. Some of the

Figure 13. This expanse of derelict old oakwood at Flaxley in the Forest of Dean had become unprofitable following removal of all good timber stems in the 1939–45 war. It is being restored by planting rows of beech, oak and larch, seen emerging (centre) from amidst cleared coppice (foreground) (courtesy the Forestry Commission).

Acts referred to also govern the design and planning of reclamation projects. Nevertheless, although procedure may be clearly stated in the legislation, it is wise policy to discuss the proposals informally with the approval- and grant-awarding bodies at an early stage, and thus avoid subsequent disappointment and alterations due to misunderstanding on the precise interpretation of a clause.

4.1 Common law

The legal agreements under which the land is held by the person or authority initiating the reclamation should be studied, especially with regard to restrictive covenants, physical and land use restoration at the end or termination of a lease, commitments like the maintenance of a stream passing through the site, and wayleaves of services. There are also the more general matters like rights of way, damage from tree roots on the boundary, the maintenance of fencing, and the liability for damage which might result from an element in the design, such as grading works near a boundary which may lead to subsidence on adjoining land.

It is particularly important to reach agreement on the site boundaries and to have these marked in some way during the progress of the works, since grading operations may lead to the removal (planned or accidental) of existing markings like fences, hedges, trees and posts.

4.2 Planning legislation

It is advisable to consult the planning authority early, as well as other interested parties like the highways section of the local authority, before embarking upon the design work. Even when the planning authority itself is the applicant and client for a reclamation scheme, it has to go through the proper procedure of submission of plans, advertisement, notifying adjoining owners, etc, and complete the necessary forms (see also p. 31).

Compulsory purchase is possible for derelict land which it is considered should be reclaimed, but where an existing use operates, the compensation demanded can be very heavy. There may be cases when an application for reclaiming a derelict landscape is subjected to a public inquiry. The

Landscape Reclamation Practice

Brian Hackett

Figures 14 and 15. Before-and-after photographs of 'derelict' pasture at Pant-Hywel Ddu, Briton Ferry, W. Glamorgan, and the improved and reclaimed pasture after treatment (courtesy Mr J. Crook and Ministry of Agriculture, Fisheries and Food).

14

15

supporting evidence is likely to vary, but it is usually necessary to answer the charge that the likely new use after reclamation would be far more costly than developing the new use on a site which is not derelict, despite the fact that when a new use in a grant-aided scheme brings in a return it must be reimbursed to the Government. This will usually be so when the new use is agriculture or forestry, but there are the supporting arguments that the fertile land reserves of the nation are thus increased, that the cost should be amortized over many years (certainly as long as the use which caused the dereliction and prevented an 'amenable' use continuing), and that most of the cost will be grant-aided. The arguments in support of amenity improvement will also vary, but (if possible) evidence of the reduction of pollution from dust, smell, and water movement is likely to be more acceptable than an exploration of visual improvement.

2 Survey information

Michael F. Downing

1 Introduction

In recent years much time and effort has been put into developing ways to evaluate and appraise landscape. The problems of preparing development plans for counties, for highway development, or for recreation, have generated many attempts to arrive at ways to compare the visual qualities of landscape, and not least in this is the assessment of dereliction. Penning Rowsell (1973) conducted a brief analysis of the approaches in common use or under development, and found that of 33 methods he investigated only 5 were based directly on any response from the general public as landscape users. Most of the methods listed by Penning Rowsell are 'evaluative', in the sense that they depend on individual field workers' judgement of landscape quality for the assessment and comparative ranking of different landscapes. Penning Rowsell lists four examples of 'non-evaluative' approaches, but careful investigation of these shows that at least two depend heavily on the subjective judgement of the field worker (Clouston 1967; Land Use Consultants 1971). The third is a method of classifying landscapes simply according to types, and the fourth provides a completely unselective summary of common or unusual site features.

The important connection between the public's appreciation of landscape and the problems of the reclamation of derelict land is closer than one might think at first. This was clearly shown in the Pennsylvania Anthracite Refuse Report (MacCartney and Whaite 1969) which also drew attention to the subjective nature of the measurement of visual improvement. The following passage gives a good illustration.

'It is evident that anthracite refuse banks are unsightly; however, in contrast to water and air pollution, for which standards of tolerances have been established, comparative unsightliness must be judged subjectively owing to variations in locations, types of material, and sizes and shapes of the mounds. Many people in the anthracite region are inured to the sight of refuse banks in their communities: however, the casual visitor, tourist or industrialist from some distant point who is considering a site in the anthracite region for manufacturing purposes would find them annoying. To outsiders, and some residents, refuse banks are a blight.'

Public reaction to the visual qualities of landscape appears to be based on two things: tradition and association. The first is concerned with an essential conservatism of attitude; people commonly accept as beautiful or attractive that which they have learned in childhood or early life to regard in that light. The second is derived, perhaps, from that essentially Victorian division of objects into what was useful and what was beautiful with the suggestion that they were mutually exclusive. Although some artists and designers may see the relics of industry, pit heaps, or even active chemical plants and other industrial features as stimulating visual designs or abstract shapes, it is clear that the vast majority of people are principally conscious of these objects' association with nineteenth-century industry and its faults and discomforts. The associations make it difficult for people to view former industrial sites in a favourable light. The associations of active industry are also, for many people, a sufficiently strong deterrent to aesthetic appreciation. On the other hand, attitudes do not stand still; perhaps these scenes may come to be more widely accepted. It is the leadership of artists and designers that brings about changes in public attitude. However, the reclamation of derelict landscape is very much a practical response to existing public attitudes; this is clear from the way in which the programme of Government support was set up, and from the Government documents and Ministerial pronouncements published subsequently.

The concern to bring derelict land into beneficial use is clearly a serious aim; but a much wider responsibility has been identified. There can be no doubt that it is the malign influence on the surroundings exerted by 'despoiled' land that is uppermost in the minds of those concerned with the politics of landscape reclamation. The Rt Hon. Peter Walker in the foreword to *Landscape Reclamation* Volume 1 (1971) referred to the 'scars left behind by industrial development of the past, the abandoned wasteheaps, disused excavations and derelict installations' . . . being . . . 'an affront to our concept of an acceptable environment in the 1970s'. The general acceptance of the importance of public attitudes, although these had not been precisely defined or measured, was contained in the Ministry Circular 17/67, which stated in Paragraph 8: 'The first priority must be given to the treatment of derelict neglected or unsightly land in development areas where special measures are being taken to stimulate the growth and proper distribution of industry. It is important to improve the environment in these areas wherever possible so that the efforts which are being made in other directions to secure their well-being will not be prejudiced.'

The subsequent Circular 17/70 emphasized the need to 'get rid of eyesores' which would 'remove the blight on economic development arising from the inhibiting effects of a depressing environment' and referred to industrial dereliction 'disfiguring' the country. The intention 'in appropriate cases to put the land to useful purposes' was stated almost as an afterthought; the importance of this aspect with use as a means of maintaining the land in a healthy condition is developed in Chapter 4.

It is important to recognize the great significance of dereliction as an influence on the life of an area. Nevertheless, the Pennsylvania Anthracite Refuse Report (MacCartney and Whaite 1969) suggests that it is not possible to arrive at any really satisfactory basis for comparative study along these lines. This is why methods of analysis or evaluation of derelict land have so far attempted to avoid subjective, aesthetic or emotional criteria in classifying sites, or indeed making any qualitative judgement, save where a distinction has been made between areas which justify treatment and those which do not. The criteria for this distinction were set out in the Ministry of Housing and Local Government Circular 68/65 containing instructions to local authorities on carrying out the first national survey of derelict land. Land which was remote from public view and access, particularly in remote rural areas, was not considered to justify treatment; nor was land which had become substantially vegetated and hence was not visually prominent. It is interesting that the latter category, described as 'land damaged by development which has blended into the landscape in the process of time to the extent that it can reasonably be considered as part of the natural surroundings', is excluded entirely from the category of derelict land in the latest survey instructions (Department of the Environment 1974).

The interest in much industrial waste as a resource, and the increasing use of colliery shale (burned and unburned) as a low-grade construction material, provide some guidance for classification methods. The Transport and Road Research Laboratory have reported fully on the quality of both these (Lake 1968; Frazer and Lake 1967; Lake, Frazer and Burns 1966; Ministry of Transport 1969). The use of such materials as resources is constantly under review by many people.

The Pennsylvania Anthracite Refuse Report (MacCartney and Whaite 1969) surveyed mining wastes on the basis of location in relation to centres of population to give some measure of their influence in human terms. Additional information obtained included the area occupied by each deposit, the volume, and the type of the material in each. This survey gave information relating to individual sites, but otherwise its basis was broadly comparable to that adopted by the Ministry of Housing and Local Government.

No-one else has attempted qualitative distinction of derelict land; the logic of the quantitative approach is that, while aesthetic considerations are (to say the least) arguable, sites must be clarified according to precise and measurable differences. It is important, however, to retain a perspective in preparing classification methods for derelict sites, since the visual qualities of derelict land are so imprecisely defined. Reclamation is a response to the general view that any form of dereliction is visually objectionable and will have an adverse effect on the physical well-being of its surroundings. This is as true for the rest of Europe as it is for Great Britain, and probably also for most other parts of the world with industrial populations. Of course, some of the world's mineral extraction areas give rise to particular reclamation needs to ensure ecological stability.

It might be possible to grade different forms of dereliction on a scale judged by professionals, as with most landscape evaluation techniques, or by the general public, as in the five cases indicated by Penning Rowsell (1973). It might be more reasonable and less argumentative to ensure that the classification of derelict or despoiled land included reference to the positions of the sites in relation to population: either residential, travelling by road, rail or air, or making use for recreation or other purposes of adjoining land. Some method such as Hebblethwaite's (1973) 'zones of visual influence' might be used to indicate the importance of sites. In this way, the extent of the visual importance of a site and the number of people it affected could be estimated, and comparisons could be made on this basis rather than by trying to define whether one form of dereliction was more or less unpleasant to view or live with than another.

2 Existing despoilation

This chapter is primarily concerned with collecting and codifying survey information to carry out reclamation on individual sites. However, some more general aspects of survey are relevant: in particular, the definition of land which might become subject to such treatment. Classification of this land, on the sort of objective basis described in this chapter, could in the future provide a national, regional, or local picture of the distribution of what has elsewhere been described as 'spoiled' lands (Bush 1969). Various categories of despoilation can be distinguished and the divisions of this broad survey information can be used as the basis for the individual site surveys. The word 'derelict' itself needs to be used with some caution, as it has been defined in Britain in a somewhat narrow sense. The most recent surveys undertaken nationally (Department of the Environment 1974) embody some acceptance of the distorted picture of the visual importance of officially 'derelict' land compared with land which, though seemingly no different to the layman, is not derelict. The very large area of land in use for mineral workings and refuse tips, as yet only potentially derelict, justifies a continuing concern with the special problems of reclaiming sites of existing dereliction.

One might expect, nearly thirty years after the 1947 Town and Country Planning Act, that control of extractive and other industries would ensure that land is properly restored after industrial operations, and that effort would be concentrated on developing techniques for simultaneous operation and restoration. But this is not the case; some processes cycle so slowly that a number of sites predating the 1947 Act still have many years of active life. Other sites, subject to earlier and less adequate forms of planning control, have remained unrestored. A more fundamental problem is that one has to rely on individuals and companies to put aside the necessary finances for restoration at the end of, and beyond, the period of extraction. Many companies ceased to exist, as bodies that could be held responsible for restoration, on completion of extraction; others might well be prepared to gamble on the local planning authorities' not enforcing reclamation. They would frequently be justified in this, because pressure of work made the planning authorities loath to enter into enforcement procedures, with no certainty of righting the situation assuming a favourable judgement and with minimal penalties. Early experience has suggested to a number of those concerned with the problem that there should be a system involving financial sanctions to ensure that money is set aside from operating profits to pay for restoration of land—as for the Ironstone Restoration Fund (see also p. 7).

The Ministry of Housing and Local Government survey of 1964, and subsequently circulars and memoranda issued by the Ministry (later the Department of the Environment), led to the consideration of only very limited areas defined as derelict land in comparison with the areas which the layman might well think to be 'an affront to his concept of an acceptable environment' to echo Mr Walker's phrase.

Although the legislation allows for treatment of 'derelict, neglected or unsightly' land, in practice the familiar definition of derelict land as so damaged by industrial or other development that it is incapable of beneficial use without further treatment has limited the areas of land considered. The Ministry originally formulated the definition for the purpose of making annual returns, basing it on Professor Beaver's earlier (1946) work; they appended a list of six categories of land to be specifically excluded, limiting even further what was already a restricted survey. It is hardly surprising that, as the results began to appear, they omitted a great area of land visually indistinguishable from 'derelict' land. In September 1970 I drew attention to 'the pool of operational land which may become derelict almost at the stroke of a pen', while in the same year F. C. Baker, at the Countryside in 1970 Conference, referred to 'our stock of instant dereliction' and suggested that some other form of survey than merely of 'derelict' lands should be undertaken (Baker 1970). The 1974 survey undertaken for the Department of the Environment promises to give more detailed results and, in particular, to single out land which should have been reclaimed as a result of planning conditions. It also specifies separately areas of active mineral working and waste tipping, classed according to whether or not they have restoration conditions attached. If the survey undertaken in Denbighshire (Jacobs 1972) is taken as an indication, then the total area of land affected will double, though whether it would reach the suggested figure of 121 000 hectares (300 000 acres) is doubtful.

The Professional Institutes Council on Conservation undertook a comparison of statistics in 1974. It shows that, between 1965 and 1971, there was a net increase in derelict land justifying treatment, except for 1967 when the gross total decreased. In three of those seven years actual reclamation covered a smaller acreage than the net increase.

3 Classification of areas for regional planning and mapping purposes

The approach to classification begins the introduction of survey information which is important both in the broad context of the site in its landscape and for the internal understanding of its restoration. The most complete classification to be extensively tested is that of Collins and Bush (Table 1), designed for use with air surveys (Bush 1969). Wallwork (1974)

Table 1 Form of classification of spoiled lands: devised by Collins and Bush (1969).

I	II	III*		IV
A Heaps	1 Mineral working	1 i	Coal mining	Pictorial description
	2 Refuse	ii	Brick clay	
	3 Industry	iii	Lead	
	4 Transport	iv	Ironstone	a Tip
	5 Housing	v	Limestone	
	6 Others	vi	Chalk	b Dump
		vii	China clay	c Dry pit
B Excavations	1 Mineral working	viii	Sand and gravel	
	2 Refuse	ix	Tin	d Wet pit
	3 Industry	x	Slate	
	4 Transport	xi	Others	e Cleared land but still spoiled or degraded
	5 Housing			
	6 Others	2 i	Household waste	
		ii	Scrap	
C Ground level	1 Mineral working	iii	Cars	f Degraded land associated with the site
	2 Refuse	iv	Others	
	3 Industry			
	4 Transport	3 i	Brickworks	
	5 Housing	ii	Chemical works	g Degraded land peripheral to site
	6 Others	iii	Gasworks	
		iv	Iron and steel	
D Installations	1 Mineral working	v	Power stations	
	2 Refuse	vi	Sewage works	h Open cast workings, not yet pits
	3 Industry	vii	Others	
	4 Transport			
	5 Housing	4 i	Airfields	
	6 Others	ii	Canals	i Sludge
		iii	Railways	
		iv	Roads	
		v	Others	
		5 i	Terraced	
		ii	Semis	
		iii	Detached	
		iv	Others	

The numbered items 1–5 in this column refer to the classification as set out in column II.

has proposed a classification based on five levels of information (Table 2), the primary factor being the source of dereliction, and the secondary factor the form; this contrasts with the Collins and Bush classification which uses topography as the first level of distinction, with the source being identified at the second level. Collins and Bush include at the fourth level of their classification a pictorial description of sites which partially duplicates the first level. When it came to mapping on the basis of aerial survey information, the Collins and Bush colour coding was based on the source of dereliction; so this became the most prominent information on the survey. Certainly both Macdonald (1969) and Wallwork suggested that the source of dereliction should be in the first category to be determined.

Macdonald (see Table 3) suggested a progression from derelict land (level 1) to general cause (level 2) to particular cause (level 3), to general physical form (level 4), to particular physical form (level 5). He was concerned only with derelict land within the Ministry's strict definition. Wallwork suggested a similar structure of information level within three of his five listed categories, or levels;

1 source of dereliction, e.g. surface mineral working, deep mining, mineral processing or transport: this category also included reference to the mineral involved;

2 topography of dereliction;

Table 2 Form of classification of 'derelict' land proposed by Wallwork (1974).

	1	2	3	4	5
A Surface mineral working with type of mineral	Excavation waste plant	Form and depth Form and height Form			
B Deep mining with type of mineral	Subsidence waste plant	Form and depth Form and height Form	Surface and vegetation cover For *plant* record the state of repair	Alternative forms of restoration and after-use and alternative uses for plant
C Mineral-based industry with type of industry	Waste plant	Form and height Form			
D Transport with type of transport	Formation plant	Form			
		Extent is shown on each case at this level			

3 amplitude of dereliction, which included extents, form and relative relief.

Thus Wallwork's 1 corresponds approximately with Macdonald's levels 2 and 3, while his 2 and 3 are roughly comparable with Macdonald's levels 4 and 5. Wallwork also includes surface composition and vegetation cover as level 4 information; surface composition is unexplained, and does not appear in the examples he selects. Vegetational cover is a particularly useful class of information. Vegetation growth can sometimes be so good that the site does not need reclamation; and it is always otherwise a valuable indication of the site's reclamation potential. For his fifth level, Wallwork proposes that the potential use of reclaimed land should be noted; but again he does not show this in any of the examples he gives, probably because too many alternatives are commonly available. In reality, it is usually too early to make any meaningful contribution at this survey stage.

One could propose a further amended classification with cause as the primary level, and with the physical form as a subsequent matter. Such a classification could use the Department of the Environment's categories of surface mineral extraction and waste tipping and the other divisions which appear in the 1974 survey. The fact that the primary emphasis shifts from the DoE's simple division into excavations and other forms, as simply expressed for its national statistical survey, is justified by the classification's different purpose to distinguish individual sites or parts of sites by reference to air survey or other maps. The sequence from the general to the particular in the categories of both cause and form, following the sequence proposed by Macdonald, would be both practical and logical and provide four levels, while the fifth might usefully be concerned with vegetative cover. One could easily make a further distinction between areas which were operational or covered by planning conditions, as distinguished in the DoE circular, and areas which were no longer in use and thus derelict. For the general planning study it may be desirable to provide a little more specific information about the actual nature of the material, particularly dumped material, as hinted by Wallwork in his level 4. For example, it may be useful for planning purposes to record whether a colliery heap consists of unburnt or burnt shale, washery waste, or slurry.

Table 3 Macdonald's revised form of classification of derelict land (Macdonald 1969).

I	II Cause (general)	III Cause (particular)	IV Physical form (general)	V Physical form (particular)
Derelict land	Mineral working	Coal mining Brick clay Lead Ironstone Chalk Sand and gravel China clay Tin Slate Others	Each of the categories listed at III will give rise to one or more of the following generalized forms of degradation	
	Refuse	Household waste Scrap Cars Others	Heap	Ridge Cone Other shapes
	Industrial	Brickworks Chemical works Gasworks Iron and steel Power station Sewage works Others	Ground level (heaps and excavations not more than 10 ft (3 m) from original ground level)	Flat or hills and hollows
	Transport	Airfields Canals Railways Roads Others	Excavations	Rectangular Other shapes
	Others			Macdonald suggests inclusion of volume information for heaps and hollows

These distinctions must be treated with some caution, but they can give guidance as to the heap's resource value, degree of liability, or size of problem. The same simple distinctions may be possible in relation to other classes. However, it is important to limit information to what is simple, basic and important; detailed investigation will inevitably be needed before making specific reclamation proposals. The basic information at this level should be used to indicate general strategy for potential resources or liabilities and their overall effect. The main distinctions between different categories of dereliction or despoilation would thus be shown and some description of each site so distinguished could be given. A greater detail of information would only add confusion.

The amount of information required at the next level is so great that to add anything further without overcomplicating the detail would result in selecting one or two aspects from a wide range of things of equivalent or comparable significance. The classification suggested (Table 4) would, however, provide a useful framework for the further detailed investigations which form the bulk of the survey data necessary for development of individual sites.

Table 4 Derelict and despoiled land: revised classification adapted as a record form (to conform generally with DoE survey categories).

Site name	Location and map reference				
Cause of despoiation (general)	**Cause of despoilation (particular)**	**Physical form (general)**	**Physical form (particular)**	**Specify volume where appropriate**	**Vegetational cover**
1 Mineral working ☐	1 a Chalk ☐ b China clay ☐ c Clay and shale ☐ d Coal ☐ e Gypsum/ anhydrite ☐ f Igneous rock ☐ g Ironstone ☐ h Limestone ☐ j Sand and gravel ☐ k Sandstone ☐ l Silica and moulding sands ☐ m Slate ☐ n Vein mineral ☐ o Other minerals ☐	Each of categories in Column 2 gives rise to one or more of the following generalized forms: A Heap ☐ B Ground level (includes low heaps and shallow excavations not more than 3 m (10 ft) from original ground level) ☐	A 1 Ridge ☐ 2 Cone ☐ 3 Other shape ☐ B 1 Flat ☐ 2 Ground tainted by chemical wastes etc ☐ 3 Ground affected by derelict buildings, foundations, or other derelict artefacts ☐ 4 Hills or hollows ☐ Rectangular ☐ Other shape (wet or dry) ☐		1 None ☐ 2 Sparse ☐ 3 Ephemerals ☐ 4 Herbs only ☐ 5 Herbs and shrubs ☐ 6 Herbs and trees ☐ 7 Shrubs and trees only ☐
2 Tipping ☐					
3 Industry ☐					
4 Transport ☐					
5 Services (military etc) ☐	2 a Public waste ☐ b Commercial waste ☐ c Others ☐	C Excavation ☐	C Other shape (wet or dry)		
6 Others ☐	3 a Brickworks ☐ b Chemical works ☐ c Gasworks ☐ d Iron and steel ☐ e Power station ☐ f Sewage works ☐ g Others ☐				
	4 Airfields (private) ☐ Canals ☐ Railways (BR) ☐ Roads ☐ Others ☐				
	5 Airfields (military) ☐ Camps ☐ Defence establish- ments ☐ Others ☐				
	6 Others (specify) ☐		*Note: Separate forms would be used for individual sites or identifiable parts of sites*		

4 Detailed survey work

In *Landscape Reclamation* Volume 1 (1971) I proposed a checklist of required survey information categorized by the specific nature of the information, and gave the source from which it would be obtained when methods other than actual visual survey on site were to be adopted. Clouston (1974) inverted this method, preferring to list the sources first and indicate the information to be gained from the individual sources second. This has the drawback that there may be alternative sources for the same information; this then becomes difficult to indicate in such a checklist without creating considerable confusion. For example, information on site topography may be obtained from a number of sources, and it is easier to list these under the simple heading 'contours' than to list them separately and repeat the actual survey information sought under each heading.

If one follows the outline of Table 4, the following basic information about a site or a part of a site will have been recorded:

1 Cause of despoilation (general), e.g. 'mineral working';

2 Cause (particular), e.g. 'colliery (deepmine)';

3 Physical form (general), e.g. 'heap';

4 Physical form (particular), e.g. 'conical (black shale)';

5 Vegetational cover, e.g. 'none'.

The detailed survey will expand on this and consider the specific factors which might arise. There are, however, other areas of investigation which are common to all sites; these can be dealt with chronologically in accordance with the checklist given in Table 5 on p. 33. The main areas of separate investigation, which will be discussed in detail, are: topography; drainage—natural and artificial; geology—drift and solid; parent materials—natural soils and deposited material; vegetation—trees, shrubs and herbs on spoil and around site; artefacts.

4.1 Topography

It is, perhaps, almost too obvious to state the need to establish a precise representation of the topography of a site. From this information the designer can determine whether there is any need to regrade the material to provide a productive or useful contour pattern, and can calculate the required volume of material to be moved to achieve the desired result. He can then create a design relying on his calculations to help him achieve the maximum effect for the minimum movement of actual material.

The topographical survey should extend, at least in outline, well beyond the site to show the general topography of the surrounding area. This ensures that the design proposals take proper account of the prevailing topographic shapes, and the natural form of the landscape: equally important whether the designer intends to echo these forms in his design, or to propose a contrast.

4.2 Drainage

It is virtually impossible to consider topography and drainage separately. One of the most important reasons for setting any proposed reclamation site within its broader topographical context is to establish the natural drainage pattern of the area. This must be a primary consideration in preparing designs; if the design does not fit in with this natural pattern, then considerable expertise will be involved in the design and construction of water courses.

It is often difficult to assess the full importance of the drainage pattern for an area without the results of observations over a long period, so the information collected should include rainfall pattern statistics and should also take account of the watershed area supported by any water course likely to be affected by reclamation works. Seasonal variation may account for extensive changes in the water regime of an area and may reveal significant seasonal springs or changes in watertable. The depth of water-table, and any variations, are particularly important in connection with gravel pit restoration. The effects of pollutants in spoiled or disturbed land on water courses should also be borne in mind. Water courses and streams are frequently culverted near mine workings, and are not always readily visible. They can run under heaps, and sometimes carry water pumped from disused deep coal mines. One should look for indications of the presence of such features, as old mine records do not always reveal all the details.

In planning new drainage channels one should consider the possible effects of any changes within the watershed area, even outside the site area, to allow for any resulting increase in flow. One should also pay attention to any land drainage pipes which might be affected by reclamation; they may neither be readily visible, nor properly recorded.

4.3 Geology, drift and solid

Geology affects drainage, particularly where the rocks are aquifers, and the movement of overburden or spoil or the changing of a drainage pattern would result in the discharge of acid mine drainage waters or otherwise polluted water into the drinking water supply, or living streams and pools. It is also necessary to establish the geological pattern of a site and its environs, relating this not only to topography but also, ultimately, to proposals for the use of the site or parts of it.

4.4 Parent materials : natural soils

Natural soils (using the word soil to describe material which will sustain plant growth) are usually found only on small parts of sites in need of reclamation, or land required for spreading waste. When found, they are a valuable commodity and they should be accurately mapped and their details accurately recorded. The Ministry of Agriculture, in its advice on sand and gravel restoration (1971), enumerates the significant characteristics under the following headings, which provide a useful basis for preparing survey information.

Soil texture

The proportions of different size ranges of soil particles, described by terms such as 'loam', 'sandy clay', etc. Simple hand tests by rule of thumb are well known. Variations in soil texture result in differences in available water capacity, or the amount of water the plants can take from the soil. Course sands have a low capacity and this means that plants need to put down deep roots to get the water they need. Very fine sandy loams have a much greater capacity but, even so, crops on this soil in Southern England need to put roots down to a depth of about 300 mm (2 ft).

Soil structure

The way in which particles can be joined together into groups. This can be altered in a way that texture obviously cannot, and good soil structure is a basic aim of good husbandry. Terms such as 'fine tilth' and 'large clods' describe structure.

Soil drainage

The drainage condition of soil is important to plant growth; the soil should be neither too well drained and dry, nor too wet in which case there is inadequate air in the soil for the support of plant roots.

Soil depth

The depths are classified under the suggested headings:

Very shallow	—less than 150 mm (6 in)
Shallow	—150 mm (6 in) to 300 mm (12 in)
Moderately deep	—300 mm (12 in) to 525 mm (21 in)
Deep	—525 mm (21 in) to 900 mm (36 in)
Very deep	—over 900 mm (36 in)

Soil is divided into topsoil and subsoil; topsoil is usually between 150 mm and 250 mm deep and is distinguished from subsoil by structure and darker colour.

4.5 Parent materials: deposited material

A wide range of other materials may be met on reclamation sites and it is important to establish their properties. The detailed chemical investigation of materials is discussed later. The initial survey can be limited to the facts contained in the classification already suggested; the references to cause and form of dereliction will provide valuable information.

Colliery waste

Colliery spoil may be unburnt (black) shale in the process of burning, with the attendant problems this causes; or it may be burnt to a red shale, in which case the presence of fused lumps may add to the difficulties of reclamation. More modern colliery spoil heaps will consist of material which has passed through washeries and, besides being more uniform, will have a minimal coal and organic content. There is little or no danger of heating or burning occurring in such material. One may also find waste in the form of slurry, with a high moisture content tenaciously retained as the result of the use of flocculants. It is difficult to handle slurry, and to extract the moisture from it.

The original method of despoilation, which one can roughly guess at from the shape of the spoil heap, gives some guide as to the likely conditions. Tipping may have been by aerial ropeway or by wagon, both of which produce heaps 25–50 m high. Aerial ropeways result in ridge formations or, less frequently, cone shapes. Wagon tips, with the wagons raised to the top of a steeply inclined railway track to deposit their load, result in a heap which is tear shaped in plan view; the length results from the need to provide a satisfactory gradient for the loaded wagons' passage to the top. The other sides are much steeper, their slope being dictated by the angle of repose of the loose material—about $1 : 1\frac{1}{2}$ or $35°$ from the horizontal. The form of tips must, to a considerable extent, have been dictated by the area of land available for tipping and the volume to be placed on it.

Tipping in low ridges about 5 m high was probably the most common method up to the early twentieth century, when tipping land was not in such short supply. This tipping was usually by railway wagon and resulted in low compaction. More recently washery material is, where possible, deposited so as to raise ground level rather than build up a distinct spoil heap. A reasonable degree of consolidation results from the use of rubber-tyred vehicles and placing the material with a dozer. Where this is not possible, and there is no other means of disposal, washery material may be stacked in flat-topped rectangular heaps, perhaps 10 to 15 m high. The flat lagoon shapes of slurry ponds with their bund walls are easily discerned during survey.

As a result of this general survey, one can tentatively assess the use of the waste material as a resource. One should also note carefully the results and nature of any secondary exploitation on a site. The extraction of burned shale may result in very broken topography, leaving only material with high sulphate contents, other material toxic to plants, or large fused lumps. The extraction of black shale or washery shale areas might have occurred similarly. Less frequently, heaps may also have been worked for extraction of duff coal, and this usually involves selective excavation and the construction of settling ponds. These facts not only help to create a picture of the appearance of sites, but also give some clues as to the condition of the material to be reclaimed.

Other mineral workings

So far I have referred to wastes from the deep mining of coal; opencast or strip mining present similar problems of the chemical conditions of the shale materials excavated. Practically all other minerals extracted by surface methods give rise to relatively small quantities of waste. Chalk, clays, shales, igneous rocks, limestones, sandstone, sand and gravel all have relatively small wastage, and much that was previously regarded as waste is now utilized for such things as reconstituted stone, for sub-base material for construction, or even (in the case of soft sandstone waste) as hard surface for light traffic. The extraction of these minerals often results in deep chasms or even the removal of whole hillsides. Their reclamation provides an opportunity for depositing unwanted spoil or creates a setting for uses requiring screening or seclusion.

Slate mining results in very deep excavations and, though the actual overburden is usually quite thin, the wastage of slate itself (20 tonnes of waste to 1 tonne of saleable material) results in large heaps of waste. Because the working is in terraces to a considerable depth it is not possible to work progressively, returning the waste to the excavation; this has caused many problems. Slate waste is generally completely inert; it consists of particles of gravel to boulder sizes with very little fine material. A similar high percentage of waste is found in the china clay industry where, again, working is usually deep and where eight parts of waste are excavated for every one of useful material. The waste is sand and could be useful if the deposits were nearer a market. The sands are generally acid, as shown by the luxuriant growth of rhododendrons found on some old china clay spoil heaps (see May *et al.* 1973).

Ironstone extraction, historically, has resulted in a hill-and-dale formation of overburden but both these, and the more recent extractions carried out under the regulations of the Ironstone Restoration Fund 1951, have caused few insoluble problems of restoration. Ironstone seams are generally 30–35 m thick, while the overburden seldom exceeds 20 m.

The difficulties associated with the reclamation of metalliferous minerals are frequently evident from the preliminary recording phase of any inventory of sites. Plant growth is inhibited both mechanically and chemically. Complete absence of nutrients is common, as is the presence of chemicals, notably pyrites (resulting in excessive acidity), and metals in toxic concentrations. The development of genotypes of plants which are resistant to metal toxicity could obscure the nature of spoil and lead to assumptions about the reclamation potential of certain areas which eventually prove to be incorrect. In general, the difficulties of metalliferous minerals show that one must investigate most carefully the basic problems on any site before any design work. A full survey of a site in these circumstances would include detailed chemical analysis of both surface and deep samples, and would show the particle sizes and stability of the material; it might also extend to measurement of moisture and surface temperature.

Waste material from public refuse, and from industrial and commercial waste, will vary in nature; one must rely on detailed investigation of the deposits. One cannot make general assumptions as to what can be done with such areas; some industrial processes have in the past impregnated existing soil areas with chemical solutions which have effectively prevented plant growth even when no solid waste has been present.

One must ensure that deposited parent material is fully investigated, even for colliery wastes, in which the material is very heterogeneous. Samples taken on a measured grid over the site may be a satisfactory way of determining the nature of the site material, but one should couple this with some sampling at depth so as to make a comparison between the oxidized samples on the surface and those from depth. It is expensive to take samples by boring; nor is it very reliable on variable material, and the samples taken may be completely atypical. It thus becomes a matter of judgement just what lengths to go to in investigating the nature of the material, and it is perhaps wise to rely on the judgement of specialists in physical and chemical analysis who can advise on the relative costs, reliability and usefulness of different levels of investigation (see Krause 1973).

Vegetation

The designer must be interested in two things in relation to vegetation on sites for reclamation and development. The first is the retention and protection of as much of the existing vegetation, if any, on site which will enhance the appearance and condition of the site when reclaimed or developed. The second is to ascertain what species can be expected to grow in the physical conditions of the site. This extends not only to what will actually grow, but also to what is appropriate in design terms. It may not be necessary to record individual trees in copses or woodlands in the initial survey, but this sort of detail may soon become necessary when the siting of elements within a plan becomes critical. One should classify individual trees by species, height and spread, age and condition; one should give the same sort of information for groups, perhaps expressing the proportions of different species by percentages. One can adopt a broadly similar recording technique for shrubs, though these are less likely to occur as individual specimens. When recording herbaceous cover, one need not usually go to the extent of adopting standard botanists' methods, such as transects, to determine the plant population; but it may be helpful to record the plant communities with their component species, noting the dominants, and to record any changes in community which may be caused in different parts of a site by changes in parent material or any other factor.

For contract purposes one must usually record the trees that need to be removed by reference to their size; thus an initial survey which records the details of trees, even on areas where it is unlikely that they can remain, may not be an unduly wasteful exercise. This is particularly so if there is any likelihood of designing for the retention of specially valuable specimens. The decision may also be taken to move semi-mature trees or specimen shrubs from one part of a site to another. This is probably one of the few situations when one can really justify the use of machines such as the Michigan Tree Transplanter and the Vermeer Tree Spade, which bodily remove trees from place to place without any preparation. The high risk of this can be accepted for growing plants which would otherwise be lost, and which would in any case cost money to remove. It was on this basis that the Opencast Executive of the National Coal Board originally introduced the equipment to the UK.

Richardson (1956) and co-workers (1971) have shown the relationship of the natural colonization of pit heaps to the local flora. On heaps with vegetation established over a considerable time there was a good correlation between plant growth and those species which bear seed in the vicinity. This is why it is useful to investigate the vegetation in adjoining areas to gain some indication of the species which should be used for revegetating the site artificially.

Artefacts

A particular problem of all deep mine sites is the presence of concealed artefacts connected with former industrial use, especially when appreciable quantities of waste have accumulated over former activities. This may also be true for other minerals and industrial chemical sites. It is often difficult to obtain information about the presence of unseen artefacts on sites, since records are often of considerable age and variability, especially for some of the old colliery sites which considerably predate the National Coal Board. On these sites, there may be inaccurate or even non-existent records of the number and nature of pit shafts, the measures which have been taken to protect them and the positions of mineshaft staples, building foundations, conduited streams, etc.

In such cases geophysical test equipment may provide quite an accurate record of the presence, shape and depth of objects below the surface. The simplest equipment of this type depends on differences of electrical potential and resistivity in different materials. It will not show directly what the objects are, but this may often be inferred from the evidence. A whole range of testing methods have been developed during mineral explorations, relying on magnetic fields, acoustic waves, seismic shocks and even radioactivity. They should be used where there is reason to suspect the presence of such objects as pit shafts, especially where these may have been inadequately capped. Many such features represent a serious hazard. Records may often be of very limited use, only referring obscurely to the presence of a number of shafts; air vents may not be mentioned, nor indeed shafts which were begun, abandoned and subsequently roughly filled in.

Active service lines may also affect sites, and while any that may be on the surface or above it are readily visible to the surveyor, those below may not be. He must therefore carry out searches of a number of statutory undertakers and others, first to ascertain whether a site is in fact affected by services, and secondly to try to discover their exact position. The available information often fails to allow for differences in the actual position of service lines from the intended one. Ideally, the authorities should prepare drawings showing services 'as laid', but in practice this is uncommon. Extensive discrepancies are often met in the lateral alignment of services, and it is often impossible to get an accurate indication of the depth below ground level, even though some authorities have strict requirements for depths. This does not apply to sewers, except very old ones, as they are laid to critical falls and their position is carefully recorded.

The checklist at the end of this chapter lists the services likely to affect sites (Table 5, p. 33).

4.6 Legal and other constraints

So far this chapter has been concerned with physical features on site. The references to documents and searches have drawn attention to the fact that one must carry out investigation away from a site to obtain information on the position of objects buried by design, or by the passage of time and subsequent events. Further limitations may be placed on the site and its re-development by the effects of other constraints which may or may not give rise to visible results on the ground. One may have to consult a number of authorities to ascertain the possible effects of these limitations. Planning procedures may result in zoning which limits the use of land, though this is unlikely to affect reclamation. More likely, the limitations on the development or treatment of a site will result from the need to maintain highway control lines for widening or improving existing roads or developing future road lines of strategic importance, but this aspect should be very thoroughly investigated.

The aspect to consider is perhaps not so much that future proposals may prevent reclamation works, as that they may render them unnecessary. Where subsequent highway engineering works have largely negated the reclamation effort (as appears to be the case in the University of Newcastle upon Tyne Research Project's own proposals for Maria Colliery, Newburn, Tyne and Wear County), one must question whether the implications of the highway design were fully appreciated at the time the decision was made to go ahead with reclamation. Where a new road line is known to be proposed, one should pay attention to such questions as the likely level of its construction. This will provide some initial indications of the width of land taken up by embankment or cutting, the need for road fill, or excess of available spoil and the extent and nature of intersections where new roads cross existing ones. This information, while not final, may assist in deciding the extent of reclamation work for an area. It would allow one to minimize ultimately abortive work.

One should perhaps exercise the same care in investigating the actual minerals subject to reclamation as their nature and quality can give a lead to their likely future value, not only where they might be used in adjoining and current developments but also in more remote proposals. The values of minerals change, and there is the possibility that it may become possible to extract rare minerals from shale and waste heaps; hence the future may see the subsequent exploration of reclaimed landscapes, and this possibility should be borne in mind.

Less intractable problems, which nevertheless require attention to ensure that the legal position is properly dealt with, are the cases of rights over land, which may exist for a variety of reasons. They may be public rights of way, easements or rights associated with tenancies. In particular, agricultural tenancies confer rights of use and possession on their holders which require proper notice, and sometimes protracted negotiation, to extinguish. Legal problems can be caused by the holding of land on lease over long periods, as is often the case with land now devolving on the National Coal Board where the leasehold of the land results from an agreement between a private company and a landowner long prior to the establishment of the Coal Board. It has not been uncommon for the landowner to require that his land be restored to its condition prior to the industrial use, or to require adequate compensation *in lieu*. This can give rise to legal difficulties where an authority wishes to reclaim land and must acquire it with the existing lease unexpired. Some authorities have found it prudent not to proceed when their intervention was likely to place them between landowner and leaseholder and they might have incurred some responsibility for the payment of compensation.

Even the establishment of ownerships may give rise to problems. In many cases the acquisition of land, sometimes divided up among a number of ownerships, can give rise to a great deal of work including the difficulty of tracing the ownerships of small parcels, and hence cause excessive delays to the start of reclamation (see also p. 15).

All these matters must be recorded during the survey stage. It will then be possible to prepare a programme for the reclamation of a site which will make proper provision not only for the actual work on site but also for the preparation of drawings, contract documents, tendering and formal agreement of tenders. This should also take account of time necessary to acquire land, and extinguish or amend any rights which may be held over the land.

4.7 Climatic and microclimatic factors

In common with other landscape surveys, those for reclamation sites should include data on the local climatic conditions: rainfall (including its seasonal distribution), average temperatures including seasonal maxima and minima, hours of sunshine, prevailing winds, with seasonal variations. In addition the survey should include such local information as the likely cold-air drainage pattern of a site, and whether it would result in frost pockets which could be exacerbated by reclamation proposals. Much waste material is extremely sensitive to the influences of climate (Deely and Borden 1973). The surface temperature of materials is related to their colour; for example, because colliery shale is black it often retains a great deal of heat even when the sky is overcast, so that the temperature at the surface of a black coal shale heap is extremely high. Temperature levels for lighter-coloured materials with less heat retention are much lower in the same conditions; chalk, for example, will show a temperature not very much higher than ambient. This gives rise to problems of water availability, and in turn to difficulties about the establishment of vegetation, particularly on the warm south-facing slopes of many heaps which receive the most concentrated effects of the sun's rays. It may also be important to take note of the rainfall pattern, for example, in relation to the nature of the material deposited on site. Many deposited substances display a tendency to severe erosion in storm conditions even when these are of very limited duration or severity, and the design must allow for this.

4.8 Specialist geochemical investigations

The development of soil profiles, and the nature of much spoil as a parent material, are discussed in Chapter 8 of *Landscape Reclamation* (1971); and Dr Doubleday makes further observations on this aspect of soil in Chapter 6 of this book.

To understand fully what is likely to be involved in the reclamation of a site one may need to undertake extensive physical and chemical investigations of the site material, and a number of consultant firms now offer this service for local authorities. The measurement of pH, and the mineralogy of the spoil in question, investigations of salinity, nutrient deficiency and availability, the presence of pyrites or similar-acting substances or the general effects of weathering: all are important aspects of the chemical investigation of spoil as a soil-forming material. Local authorities or landscape consultants involved in reclamation are unlikely to have within their organizations the expertise or equipment necessary for investigations of this sort. Many would also need to obtain assistance in determining the civil engineering properties of materials to be reclaimed.

Particle size analysis, the dry density, moisture content, sulphate content, percentage of combustibles and state of compaction of the material *in situ* are all important factors. The last may be a particularly valuable piece of information because it can help to determine the ultimate volume to be replaced, if one knows what degree of consolidation is likely to be achieved by earth-moving machinery during regrading.

It is extremely difficult to ensure that the information is truly representative of the whole site, and this requires considerable experience of sampling on sites of an extremely heterogeneous nature. A number of firms are now prepared to offer a specialized service covering all these aspects, and additional investigations of, for example, the site history, if requested. This service was difficult to obtain only a few years ago, but a recent local authority advertisement elicited over 30 enquiries, and ultimately resulted in the submission of tenders from 17 firms to carry out the investigations which are likely to involve expenditure of between £5000 and £15 000 for an average-sized reclamation project; this is likely to represent between about 2% and 5% of the total cost of reclamation—a sum very much less than the savings that can result from the information gained.

5 Survey information

Table 5 gives a checklist of the survey facts required. It is with this information that the stages of programme of acquisition, design, and execution

Table 5 Checklist of survey information (the first five categories are an expansion of the revised classification of Table 4).

Information	Source
Site investigation	
1 *Cause of despoilation* (general)	Observation
2 *Cause of despoilation* (particular) with date of cessation of operations	Observation or local records
3 *Physical form* (general)	Observation
4 *Physical form* (particular) 1 Volume 2 Method of despoilation (where appropriate) 3 Precise nature of material desposited	Observation and local records
5 *Vegetational cover* 1 General vegetation; dominant and subdominant species, communities etc defined by plan area 2 Individual trees and tree groups: positions, width, species, age and condition	Detailed botanical survey
6 *Contoured plan of site and immediate surroundings* (*note:* in practice item 6 will be completed before item 5 is attempted as this plan is likely to provide the base plan for all working)	Aerial survey or Ordnance Survey Plan plus spot level survey or ground survey
7 *Geological information* 1 Drift 2 Aquifers, drainage and watertable 3 Commercial minerals	Geological Survey Maps and Memoirs, or Institute of Geological Sciences, Exhibition Road, South Kensington, London SW7 or specialist geographical survey
8 *Natural soils* (where present)	NAAS local office or simple field classification as outlined in section 4.4
9 *Surface water drainage pattern* of site and surrounding watershed area as affecting site, streams and ponds	Site observation and local advice for seasonal variation (see also *17* (8))
10 *Water quality*	Local Water Authority
11 *Aspects, shelter, exposure*	Site observation
12 *Position and description of artefacts on site* 1 Buildings, dimensions, materials, age, condition and use 2 Foundations, dimensions, material and condition 3 Other structures and installations, age, condition, visible services and service features. Note particularly items of historic interest	Site observation

Table 5 (continued)

Information	Source
13 Visual aspects 1 Views 2 Areas of containment 3 Ridges 4 Dominant features	Site observation

Archive and document searches for concealed features

Information	Source
14 Colliery sites Mine shafts, counter balance staple shafts coke ovens ⎫ structures ⎬ may be concealed foundations ⎭ beneath waste heaps	National Coal Board surveyors records
15 Other mines Shafts etc. Buried structures	Mining company records
16 Other industry	Plans in company's records or archives may help to locate different activities on separate parts of site as guide to problems, e.g. different chemical processes and resulting deposits
17 Services affecting site 1 Electricity, underground, overhead: voltage, line or abandoned depths or heights, special precautions	CEGB and Area Board
2 Gas (underground): pipe dimensions, mains or laterals, depths and live or abandoned, special precautions	Area Board
3 Water (underground): pipe dimensions, mains or laterals, depths and live or abandoned, special precautions	Area Water Authority
4 TV/Radio relay cables, underground: line and depth and method of cover	Local relay company
5 Telephone cables, overhead, underground: heights and depths	Post Office engineers
6 Main sewers: depth, dimensions, duplicate or mixed system, spare capacity	Local Authority
7 Other underground pipelines (oil, etc)	Local Planning Authority
8 Surface water culverts	Local Authority, National Coal Board, Area Chief Surveyor (see also 9)
18 Landownership etc 1 Landownership boundaries	Local Authority or Ministry of Agriculture Land Registry
2 Tenancies, leases and lettings, restrictive covenants, easements	Landowner
3 Public rights of way	Local Authority
4 Highway control lines Road improvement lines	Local Highway Authority

Table 5 (continued)

Information	Source
19 *General information* Development plan, including structure plan and local plan, proposals for site and its environment, planning limitations, e.g. green belts, areas of special scientific interest, nature reserves etc	Local Planning Authority

Specialist investigations

Information	Source
20 *Specialist investigation of geochemical aspects of site waste material* Compaction, physical nature and variations Particle sizes, chemical nature, temperature moisture content and WHC Development of soil profile	Specialist investigation by geochemical and soils experts. Surface sampling and boreholes
21 *Specialist investigation of soil fauna population* Stages of soil fauna development observed in colliery waste are set out in Chapter 7	Specialist investigation by zoological experts (an indication of the methods adopted is given in Chapter 7)

of a reclamation project can be appropriately organized within a critical-path-analysis summary or similar programme arrangement.

3 Design and layout influences

Brian Hackett

The design process proper to landscape reclamation is, of course, that of landscape design, which is based upon long-established principles and practice, and will not be dwelt on here. There are, however, certain factors and influences that are either peculiar to landscape reclamation or result from various after-uses which are generally established in these circumstances.

1 After-uses

When the initiating body (the 'client') makes the decision to embark on a landscape reclamation project, some thought will have been given to the use of the land after reclamation. In some cases, the after-use has been clearly defined and may well have been influenced by long-term proposals of the planning authority; nevertheless, the proposals should be reconsidered in the light of any physical difficulties which might arise from the reclamation proposals. For example, the removal of spoil from a site may prove too expensive and not qualify for grant-aid, while to distribute it evenly over a site might result in the reclaimed site's being very exposed and unsuitable for the original planned land use. In other cases, there may be no difficulty in providing a good basis for housing or agriculture.

However, there may well be occasions when the nature of the after-use cannot be decided, and the design should aim at providing a landscape which will not limit a large number of possible land uses. This would suggest that the orientation of parts of the site should not be restrictive, i.e. no large north-facing slopes of steep inclination, which are suggested for sites planned to receive agricultural uses, and that money should not be spent at this stage on setting in motion a policy of speedy soil formation, so long as the soil basis is adequate for future improvement. It would also be appropriate to design and plant a large-scale shelter-belt plan protecting large areas, rather than have a small-scale and 'overworked' plan.

1.1 Agriculture

The basic site factors which should be reviewed in relation to future agricultural use are:

- the potential for soil formation.

- The right balance between poor drainage and excessive drainage so that plant life is well watered, but not waterlogged or burnt up in hot weather.

- Orientations giving some variation between south-east, south and south-west, and restricting north orientations to steeper and narrower slopes.

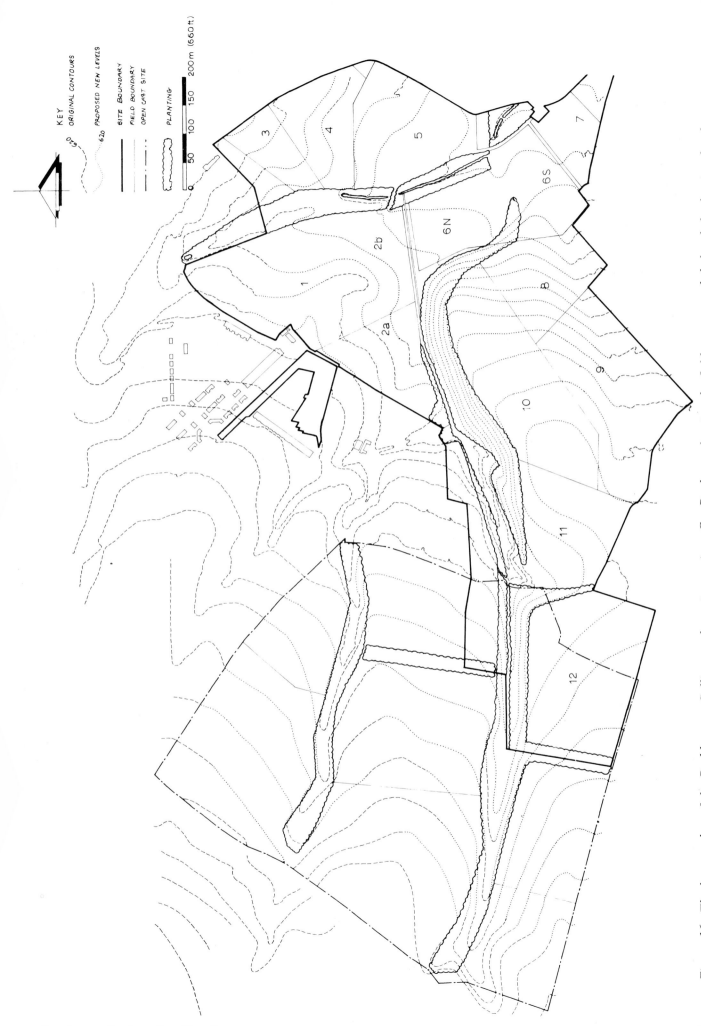

Figure 16. The layout plan of the Roddymoor Colliery reclamation project, Co. Durham, showing the field pattern and shelter belt planting for the agricultural use which commenced in 1968 after reclamation (courtesy Landscape Design Research, University of Newcastle upon Tyne).

17

Figures 17 and 18. Photographs showing (above) the Forest Park at Stoke on Trent when planting and construction were well advanced, but not complete; and (below) the same area before reclamation (courtesy Land Use Consultants).

- Gradients, apart from north-facing slopes and areas for shelter planting, limited to a maximum of 1:10. Note that, on slopes steeper than 1:40 or 1:50, erosion may occur on disturbed 'soils', while on slopes flatter than these gradients, natural drainage may be sluggish. If subsequent land drainage systems are to be installed, the flatter slopes will, of course, prove adequate (see also p. 58).

- Slope orientation and gradient proposals are also linked with areas planted as woodland for shelter belt and anti-erosion purposes.

- Access points that give a reasonable relationship with the local road system and enable a usable road pattern to be planned within the site.

- Avoidance of pollution in streams; this may be difficult to achieve on sites where the lower 'strata' of the graded material produces pollution in the underground water. This kind of situation suggests a land drainage system which is isolated from streams and especially where livestock will be using the streams for drinking.

Many of these factors are also important for most other uses. The precise arrangement of field boundaries and farm tracks is likely to be arrived at in collaboration with the farmer who will take over the reclaimed landscape and with local officers of the Ministry of Agriculture and Fisheries; the 'client', e.g. the planning department of the local authority, will also be involved. One should avoid a scheme which would make future modification difficult and expensive.

Details such as watering points and fencing should be adequate for the future use.

18

1.2 Forestry

Many of the landscape reclamation schemes before the 1960s were, in fact, small afforestation schemes on ungraded spoil heaps. Despite doubts about the economic viability of these schemes, the Forestry Commission sometimes made planting grants available. The likely inferior quality of the mature trees, and the large distances separating individual plantations, resulted in these schemes' being at a disadvantage compared with schemes which involved regrading and included areas of grassland as well as of tree planting, and thus had greater flexibility of land use. However, the scheme for a 'forest park' in Stoke on Trent, started in 1967, may presage more afforestation in reclamation schemes, especially where the proximity of several towns around a rural area brings problems for the farmer.

The basic site factors favourable to afforestation are certainly met by those required for agriculture (section 1.1), but the limitations on orientation and gradients are not so onerous; in fact, afforestation is more successful on north-facing slopes in the first years after planting because the burning effect of sunlight on dry south-facing slopes of spoil material is avoided (see also p. 59).

1.3 Horticulture

It is unlikely that market gardens or allotments will be developed on reclaimed landscapes until the surface soil has become reasonably fertile; but schemes based on dry gravel or refuse tips are a possibility. Favourable south-facing slopes with a gentle gradient are most suitable, except for orchards which can accept steeper gradients. Other important site factors are adequate natural or piped water supply, and sheltered conditions which can be improved or achieved with grading or planting.

1.4 Housing

Soil fertility is an advantage, because without it the inhabitants may find the conversion of the basic material into soil for domestic gardens too much of a problem. The green landscape areas of some housing estates are maintained by the local authority and can accept more difficult soil conditions. Grading operations which enable architects to design housing with favourable south, south-east or south-west facing aspects for the living rooms are an advantage, although variety in the grading should give the site planner greater potential for the avoidance of monotony. With housing, and other land uses involving building development, the stability of the final graded surface, and the likelihood of combustion occurring, will need to be taken into account. Also, the grading and planting should be related to the damaging winds.

1.5 Industry

The site factors favourable for most industrial uses are similar to those for housing land, except that orientation has less importance and a series of reasonably large and level areas are desirable (see also p. 57).

1.6 Recreation

If the recreation is the casual enjoyment of landscape, then the site factors applicable to agricultural uses, with some parts more specifically favourable to forestry, will be very suitable. If, however, playing fields are required, the site should be suitable for grading into several level areas at no more than 3 m height differences between them.

Figures 19 and 20. Layout plan, and artist's impression, of the reclamation scheme for the Forest Park at Stoke on Trent.

19

20

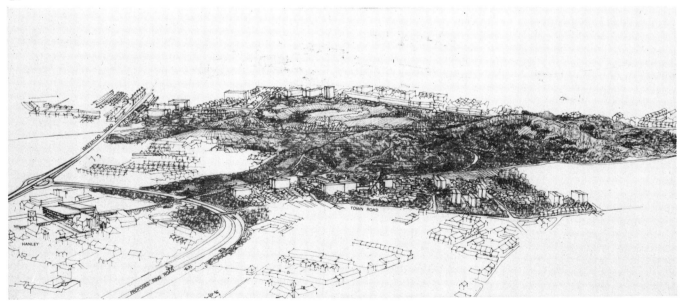

Protection from the wind is desirable and will influence the landform design where grading operations are included in a reclamation scheme. In particular, a design which will produce several small sheltered areas will be an advantage in most recreational open spaces. Grading operations can also contribute to the formation of water bodies which are always welcome in a recreational area.

Brian Hackett

ST. ANTHONY'S SITE B NEWCASTLE UPON TYNE.

SKETCH PLAN OF PROPOSED LANDSCAPE RECLAMATION.

SCALE 1:500

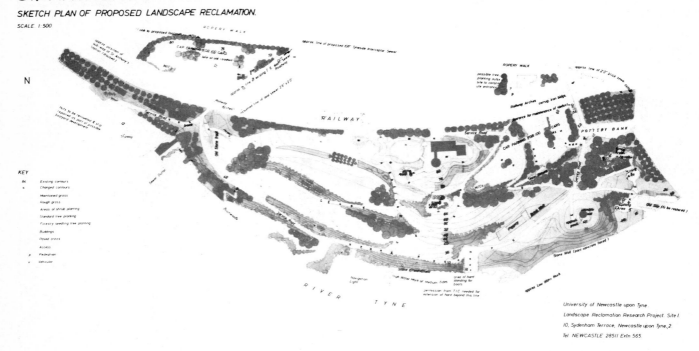

Figure 21. The general layout plan of the St Anthony's reclamation site, bordering the river at Newcastle upon Tyne, included provision in the future for a small boat harbour, a restaurant, a lookout point with a nautical museum, sitting and viewing places, casual games areas and car parks (courtesy Landscape Design Research, University of Newcastle upon Tyne).

1.7 Nature reserves

Many derelict sand and gravel extraction sites have proved very suitable for development as nature reserves, because the surface material usually favours vegetational development, and natural lakes have formed in the sites where the water table is high and the substrata impervious. In other examples, subsidence flashes from deep mining have attracted many bird species. Some important features which could be formed in a reclamation scheme for encouraging wildlife are islands, low-lying margins which will foster reeds and willow scrub and are difficult to traverse, and inaccessible terraces. However, all these suggestions depend on accompanying vegetation which provides food and shelter for wildlife. The potential for variety in the developed landscape should also be evaluated.

2 Continuing uses

The repair and restoration of canals, railway lines, and woollen and flour mills are examples of reclamation projects which revive a once active use. The design policy considered most appropriate to these examples has demonstrated meticulous attention to detail, and where new 'life' must be brought into an area, such as adapting canal wharfside buildings for community use, a respect for the vernacular has proved successful. The complete restoration of many of the uses which attract the public interest is usually a very expensive operation and various alternatives have been adopted which retain some of the advantages. For example, derelict canal locks can be replaced by a series of cascades, but this restricts the movement of boats. The modification of a canal profile by filling to reduce the water depth will not only reduce the accident factor, but help to sustain the stability of the banks; on the other hand, a reduction in depth has some-

22

Figures 22 and 23. Before-and-after photographs of the Big Waters reclamation site, near Newcastle upon Tyne. In addition to areas reclaimed for agriculture and recreation, a large part of the site was reclaimed as a nature reserve, with appropriate planting. In the particular part of the site shown here, experimental plantings of wild perennials proved to be very successful (courtesy Landscape Design Research, University of Newcastle upon Tyne).

23

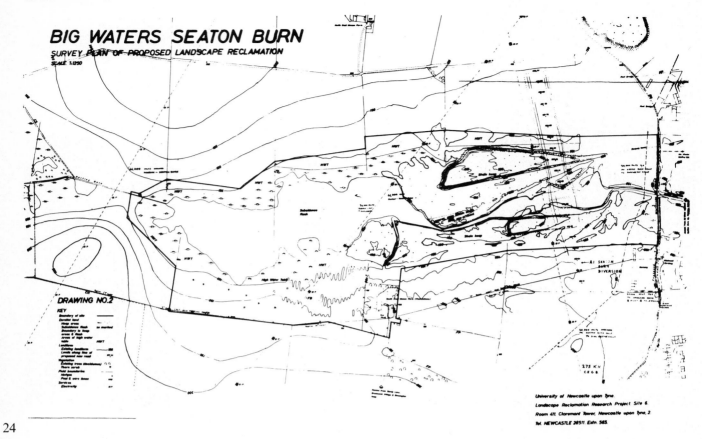

24

Figures 24 and 25. *The survey and layout plans of the Big Waters reclamation site, near Newcastle upon Tyne. The major nature reserve area is the lake and its surroundings. Other uses on this site are recreation in the form of angling and walking and agriculture (courtesy Landscape Reclamation Design Research, University of Newcastle upon Tyne).*

25

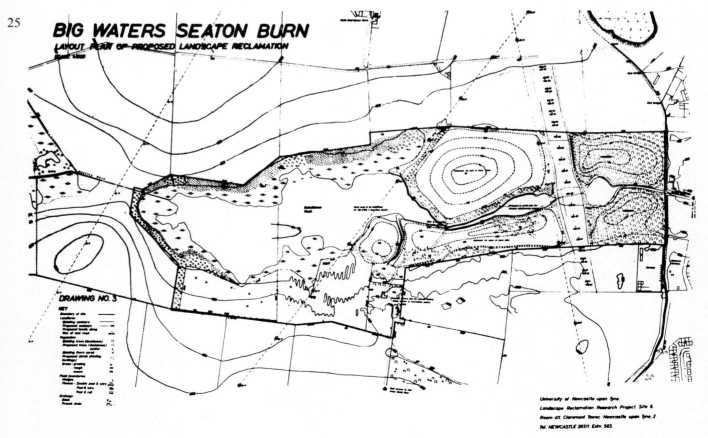

times encouraged the dumping of rubbish because the increased visibility emphasizes any precedent for dumping. Other repair and restoration techniques for derelict canals include sheet piling within the line of the original bank or wall, and balanced hinge or swing bridges replacing the rebuilding of a fixed bridge structure.

Derelict canals and railway lines are likely to have considerable vegetation growth which would not be acceptable on a commercial canal or railway line, but which adds to the quality of the landscape. It should be possible to thin out this vegetation to an extent which does not interfere with recreation, and satisfactory path surfaces can usually be achieved by balancing pedestrian use with an unmown grass cover, to avoid maintenance.

A contractual problem which can arise with the repair and restoration of canals and railway lines is that of access; embankments and cuttings cannot be easily negotiated, and the place where access is physically possible may be under other ownerships.

In addition to the references made to common law matters (Chapter 1, section 4.1), some canal towpaths are rights of way, and the position regarding railway crossing points should be investigated. There may also be fishing rights and drainage and water supply agreements which might affect a repair and restoration project. The legislation which affects the repair and restoration of a project aimed at bringing back or maintaining an existing use can be very wide ranging; for example, the replacement of a wooden crane jib with a jib of the same material is disallowed under the Factories Acts.

The repair and restoration of buildings is a specialist matter, but some change is likely to be required in the immediately surrounding landscape, which may have been the outdoor storing and dumping area of an industry. While circumstances will often dictate how the surroundings should be treated, simple grass lawns with trees, or the incidental open-space approach, are very satisfactory design solutions in repair and restoration projects.

3 Adjoining areas

Reference was made in Chapter 1 to the fact that land adjacent to derelict land may be included in a landscape reclamation scheme, and qualify for

Figure 26. The buildings and other artefacts of the canal system offer possibilities for restoration to new uses. This warehouse at the Dukinfield Junction of the Ashton and Lower Peak Forest Canals was unfortunately gutted by fire shortly after this photograph was taken; but for this, it could have formed a nucleus for recreational or residential conversion. The bridge could be the basis of an attractive urban landscape (Hugh McKnight Photography).

Figure 27. Compared with the earth-moving and vegetational works of the more familiar mining reclamation schemes, the reclamation of derelict canals often involves detailed repair and re-building work as in this view of the Stratford upon Avon Canal (Hugh McKnight Photography).

Figure 28. Mechanical earthmoving equipment has eased the technical problem of canal reclamation as shown in this view of Ladywood Locks on the Droitwich Canal (Hugh McKnight Photography).

grant-aid, if it can be shown that it is necessary or advantageous to the final result. There is always the fear that good-quality land is being tampered with, but the greater good usually prevails with the gentler grades achieved by spreading over the boundary of dereliction, and by the greater flexibility of orientation and availability of some topsoil from the adjacent land which might, by being spread thinly over the whole site, speed up the achievement of overall fertility.

Other advantages in having a larger area of land are the greater flexibility in design, the easier gradients on drainage channels and surfaces, thus reducing erosion, and the likelihood that a smoother marriage can be made with the surrounding landscape. It is clear, however, that a well-reasoned case must be presented before planning permission and grant-aid are likely to be given. In some situations, the weight of a spoil heap has affected the grade and drainage of adjoining land outside the formal boundary of dereliction; in this situation the inclusion of the affected area within the reclamation boundary is likely to be of general benefit.

4 Landscape of the locality

Many derelict sites occupy large areas of land which, apart from the prominence given by dereliction, will stand out in the local landscape if unsympathetically reclaimed. Unless there is some valid reason to design the reclamation in a way very different from the surrounding areas (for example, as a memorial park), the best solution is to take good account of the characteristic topography, types of vegetation, size and spacing of woodlands and tree groups, and details like hedge and fence treatment in the surrounding landscape. In many cases, the objective should be to make it difficult for anyone to identify the reclaimed area, once it begins to mature.

4.1 Topography

In order to achieve this objective of sympathy with the surrounding landscape, the new topography should merge in with that existing at the boundaries; within the site, it should relate to the particular undulating plateau, or to the 'long/gentle' or 'short/steep' topography in the locality, as the case may be. At the same time, the topographical limitations of a particular use, or of flexibility for future uses, should be kept in mind.

Occasionally, there may be a good case for the formation of an 'artificial' land form: for example, to create a viewing position, a ski slope, or to match up to an artificial form like a cooling tower in the locality. The design principles underlying modern sculpture are a valuable source for this kind of design exercise.

It is important to remember that the regrading of a derelict site may cause undue exposure to people whose homes were built in the shelter of a spoil mound; alternatively, the regrading may reduce effects of wind turbulence. A series of lesser mounds, instead of one large mound, may provide enough shelter, although this can be countered by the desire of nearby residents to set the gain from the newly exposed distant views against the loss of shelter.

The use of sand-tray models in the first stages of design of the new landform is most helpful, because it is possible for the sand, at first modelled on the existing situation, to be moved around to follow a number of design ideas, and to finish with the preferred design which will approximate to the final landform, though compaction and bulking are likely to bring some alterations.

4.2 Drainage

The recommended methods and techniques are discussed in Chapter 5, but the type of drainage provision is inevitably tied in with regrading. The drainage pattern will, naturally, be much influenced by the available outlets, and by the provisions in the locality, whether separate or combined sewers, or streams. As a general principle, the situation in nature should

Brian Hackett

Figures 29 and 30. Before-and-after photographs of the Roddymoor Colliery reclamation project, Co. Durham, showing the influence of the local topography upon the new landform of the reclamation (courtesy Landscape Design Research, University of Newcastle upon Tyne).

29

30

be followed where the high-altitude streams run steeply and the low-altitude streams run gradually; in other words a gradual slowing-up process as the smaller streams join to form larger streams. It is also visually (and probably functionally) appropriate to level out the landform in the lower reaches of the drainage pattern.

Drainage provisions in reclaimed landscapes are more satisfactory if they follow the usual natural drainage pattern of exposed water courses. This is not only cheaper than piped drains, but allows modifications and maintenance to be achieved with the least difficulty, and changes inevitably will take place in the early years of reclamation because of the 'juvenile' nature of the soil material.

4.3 Division of the landscape

Around most sites scheduled for reclamation there are likely to be areas of open countryside or rural landscape which have particular characteristics in the way that such features as hedgerows, walls, fences, roads and footpaths divide up the landscape. This may be in such a manner as to give elongated areas or more or less square parcels of land; also, these divisions may or may not be closely related to the topography. If these local characteristics can be followed in the design and layout of a reclaimed landscape, the result will stand a much better chance of becoming a part of the local landscape, and in principle this must be regarded as a worthy objective. Similarly, the divisions in the surrounding landscape will establish certain size or scale relationships which, if followed in the design of reclaimed landscape, will avoid a sudden change in the landscape pattern.

4.4 Vegetation

While decisions regarding the selection of trees, shrubs and groundcover vegetation should take into account the species in the surrounding landscape, there are two other influences which must have a bearing upon species selection. The soil material on some reclaimed sites may be basically different from the surrounding soils because it may have been extracted from geological strata at depths which have no influence as a parent material for the soils of the locality. Furthermore, the 'natural' ecology of the locality may constitute a different species complex from the species now existing under man's influence. The designer will need to find a compromise between these three guidelines on species selection; but, taking into account the principle that integrating the reclaimed landscape into the local landscape is normally the proper solution, the designer should also aim at achieving visual sympathy in the vegetation.

4.5 Land uses

There will probably be a land-use decision made under the planning procedures, and frequently this will match the surrounding land uses; for example, a return to agriculture where a derelict coal mine is located in the countryside, or a new residential use where an urban area has expanded all round. Frequently, however, a temporary use like grazing is established in order to improve the soil whilst at the same time maintaining the landscape until such time as the 'permanent' use is established.

In some reclamation projects, an adjoining land use may produce dust or smoke pollution or be visually offensive; these conditions would suggest the formation of mounds near the boundary or shelter planting. Conversely, the reclamation operations in themselves can create dust, and when the adjoining land uses involve many people or processes sensitive to dust, it may be necessary to restrict some operations when the winds are from certain directions or even to form temporary barrier mounds on the boundary.

5 Legal restrictions

- Easements and restrictive covenants may be written into the conveyances or leases under which the land is held. These might include access agreements and restrictions on use.

- Wayleaves and easements over or under the land granted to public utilities.

- Rights of way, drainage and water supply rights, and perhaps less frequently, ancient lights. There are also possibilities for achieving alternative routes for rights of way.

- Agreements on uses of the land for specified periods, for example, a concession to screen coal dust out of a spoil heap.

- Conditions attached to planning approval, tree and building preservation orders, by-law requirements, and proposals for new roads etc.

- The designer is usually given a plan which indicates the site boundaries, but experience suggests that, before reclamation works commence, the boundaries should be walked in company with the adjoining owners and the contractor, and a careful record kept of the agreements on the boundary markings. During the progress of the reclamation works, checks should be made frequently to ensure that these markings are not moved, destroyed or engulfed in the operations.

All these possibilities should be thoroughly searched by the legal representatives of the client but, at the preliminary sketch-plan stage, many of the restrictions can be ascertained by reference to previous users of the site and to the public utilities.

6 Existing elements

The retention of suitable existing elements of a derelict site has, on the one hand, the advantage of preserving the continuity of history and the sense of location and, on the other hand, can contribute to a speedier and perhaps better reclamation scheme. The current interest in industrial archaeology may lead to support for a proposal to preserve a piece of machinery, and there is often scope to turn preservation to good account: for example, using the track foundation of a railway which existed on the site as a footpath, and a signal box as a shelter from the weather.

Some elements, like existing streams, can form the basis of the drainage proposals and can be incorporated into a scheme to serve as an amenity. The slow growth of trees, particularly in northern latitudes, places consider-able value on existing trees, and their retention can be a strong influence in

Figure 31. The existence of a lake formed by a sub-sidence flash at the Big Waters reclamation site, near Newcastle upon Tyne, prompted the development of a nature reserve in this part of the site. A consider-able amount of planting was proposed around the lake to increase the range of habitat conditions and the supply of food for birds (courtesy Landscape Design Research, University of Newcastle upon Tyne).

the design of a reclamation scheme because existing trees not only influence the position of new elements on plan, but will dictate levels in some parts of the site.

When topsoil exists in certain places on a site, a decision may have to be made whether it should remain *in situ* and be given a vegetation cover commensurate with its fertility, or whether the topsoil should be spread thinly over a larger area to assist in the development of a fertile topsoil.

7 Climate

All landscape design projects are influenced very considerably by climate, from the point of view of both the types of vegetation proposed and the use of the site. In all probability, the reclamation operations will in the first instance lead to increased exposure because buildings and spoil heaps, which previously gave shelter, are likely to be removed or graded to more gentle slopes facilitating the flow of wind. Thus the designer will need to consider whether grading to form mounds or saucers for shelter will improve conditions on some parts of the site for certain uses, and likewise planting for shelter in the future. He will need to take note of the prevailing wind and other damaging winds, and such pitfalls as frost pocket effects. Also, the matters raised about orientation in section 1.1 are applicable to climatic variation.

Some design factors governing the climatic and noise situations on sites with mounds and saucers were stated in a study made in the Landscape Research Unit of the University of Newcastle upon Tyne (Daily, undated), and are summarized thus:

- The effectiveness of an earth bank for climatic and noise reduction purposes depends upon its height rather than upon its width and profile.

- Earth banks are effective for providing shelter from the wind and reducing noise, but tree belts, whilst effective in the former situation, are much less effective for reducing noise.

- Unless earth banks are at least 11.5 times as long as high, the airflow around the ends will have a marked effect upon the shelter at the centre.

- Gaps in earth banks can lead to wind speeds in excess of the unimpeded wind, and a similar result is experienced when valleys lie in the direction of the wind.

- The coldest winds are not always the prevailing wind.

- Mounds, as opposed to earth banks, are less effective obstacles for wind shelter because the wind can travel around a mound.

- Long earth banks, though effective for shelter, can produce a monotonous visual result, but a series or network of small mounds and banks can produce acceptable areas in sufficient number over a site.

8 Aesthetics

Aesthetic influences upon landscape reclamation projects include the landscape of the locality (section 4), traditional influences in landscape design, and various theoretical approaches (see Chapter 4, section 2).

The natural desire of many people to preserve the environment will sometimes introduce an aesthetic argument into the solution of the design problem; for example, opinions have from time to time favoured the retention of conical spoil heaps in flat landscapes because of the interest created. Also, the preservation of industrial archaeology artefacts may determine the grading level in certain parts of a site. Some types of dereliction, such as disused canals and railways, may take on their own particular charm from the lack of maintenance or wear and tear of the vegetation which thus becomes richer in species and greater in extent; these particular elements of the dereliction may have a considerable influence upon the design of the reclamation.

During the first years after reclamation, before the vegetation has become established, the effectiveness of the landform design will be very important visually; thus the landform design part of the design process, for this reason, and for the reasons of erosion control, land use and aspect, requires special care. In this respect, the relationship of the landforms to the path of the sun so that shadows are long and prominent is a matter for consideration.

In many large landscape projects the vegetation in the locality, both indigenous and exotic, is taken into account in designing the planting. Some degree of qualification often has to be made with reclamation projects in this respect because of the 'unnatural' soils; nevertheless the surrounding vegetation should as far as possible constitute a design influence.

9 Finance

The cost of any project is inevitably an influence upon most landscape design projects, but it is true to say that in many landscape reclamation schemes, in which the grading operations involve the major part of the cost, the cost is not a considerable design influence once a decision has been made to *grade* the site, rather than merely plant up the existing hills and valleys. This is due to the costing's being on the basis of the cubic capacity moved and the distances involved, rather than related to the kind of landform design. Also, the fact that many projects are largely financed by central government funds lessens the arguments which might be put forward locally. On the other hand, the central government has precise rules about what works will qualify for grant (see Chapter 1, section 2.1).

The costs of proper establishment and further development (sometimes for as long as ten years) are likely to require strong advocacy because many of these costs will have to be met at the local level; the fear that this will not happen sometimes influences designers to avoid elements requiring further work after the initial contract.

4 Landform design and grading

Michael F. Downing

1 Introduction: factors affecting design of regrading proposals

In *Landscape Reclamation* Volume 1 I discussed the factors governing designs under four headings: economics; aesthetics; topographical factors; and functional requirements of land use. While these divisions are helpful and reasonable, one can question both the order in which they were presented and the weight or value attributed to each aspect. Economics will clearly dominate decisions about financing reclamation, not only in the present severe conditions, but at all times when the expenditure of public funds is involved. Also, one must take a properly broad view of the cost implications of any reclamation exercise. There is a tendency to compartmentalize accounts, for example between capital expenditure on works and the responsibility for their maintenance, with the result that notional savings on capital works may be made at the expense of vast increases in the recurring costs for the ultimate maintenance. In the long term it is perhaps more valid to consider the functional requirements of land use as the major factor in the design of landform on reclaimed landscapes.

In Britain the most frequent aim of reclamation is to return to some useful function land which is unsightly and neglected, and cannot be put to use in its derelict condition. The Department of the Environment's* definition of the word 'derelict' relies on equating it with the word 'useless', rather than with the more traditional dictionary connotation of 'abandoned'. In other countries, and perhaps even in more remote situations in Britain, the emphasis may not be on putting land to good use, but more on ensuring that the state of the land is not such as to cause any danger to other areas adjoining or downstream. This is the case in the strip mine areas of the north-eastern United States, for example. In such regions it is soil and water conservation which is often the principal cause of active reclamation, in addition to a frequently stated concern with visual qualities.

Whether or not land is to be put to beneficial use, the functional aspects become very important; for land which is not going to be used profitably the design must aim to establish a landscape pattern that will be self-maintaining. The acceptable maintenance liability increases in proportion to the profitability of the land use, or its value to the community when direct profit is not involved. While it may not be possible to reduce maintenance liability to zero, there is virtually no land from which at least some profit and some social value cannot be attained. At the other end of the scale, land which is highly valued or provides high profits for its owner can be permitted (and indeed may positively require) a high level of maintenance. The design approach should be dominated by the need to achieve a level of maintenance liability which is compatible, in the vast majority of examples, with a comparatively low level of value or return. This also results in a need to create designs which are 'natural' in their inspiration (except in exceptional circumstances). The aesthetic idea of

Formerly Ministry of Housing and Local Government.

copying nature and fitting designs into the natural pattern of the landscape is not simply a matter of bucolic fancy, but should be more soundly based on the need to create a landscape which is stable, conforms to natural drainage requirements, is low in maintenance, and has a healthy plant community related to that of the adjoining landscape.

The original division into four categories was intended to define the functional aspects of land, as the specific limitations given by particular land uses, in terms of aspect, slope, elevation and area. I would suggest here that function should be considered as a more comprehensive term, embracing the whole healthy balance of the dynamic aspects of the land in question. This attention to the continuing health and equilibrium of newly designed areas was implicit in the presentation of the four divisions; and this concern will be extremely important to any designer. But it is quite fair to suggest that there are sometimes administrative reasons and external pressures on the designer which can militate against the best solution in terms of long-term maintenance. So the economic aspects are not in total conflict with functional requirements; rather, it is important to achieve a solution that is the best in economic terms and at the same time satisfactory in terms of the design, not merely as a finished product regardless of maintenance, but including the implications of continuing costs.

2 Classification of design constraints

A revised classification of constraints would involve the following:

2.1 Functioning of the site after reclamation
   (a) Economics
   (b) Topographical factors
   (c) Aesthetics
   (d) Constraints of land uses

2.2 Limitations imposed by materials found on site

2.3 Limitations imposed by the technical possibilities of machinery and known reclamation techniques.

The design solution is, in effect, the result of weighing the various constraints so as to find the optimum balance. It is unlikely that every aspect will be solved perfectly. Compromise is inevitable, but the compromise achieved must not disadvantage one aspect severely.

2.1 Functioning of the site after reclamation

(a) Economics :

The present grant system, despite allowing for five years' maintenance, may still predicate a reclamation approach which reduces capital expenditure at the construction phase but results in increased recurring costs in later years. This should be resisted as far as possible; but the problem can only be solved by eliminating the separation of responsibility for paying for capital works and short-term maintenance and paying for the continuing upkeep of sites.

(b) Topographical factors :

Regardless of land use there are certain topographical factors that must be taken into account in the design of regraded sites—basically, the angles of repose of the various materials. They are modified by the degree of consolidation of the material and are affected by the general topography and drainage pattern of the area. Angles of repose will very broadly be in line with those of the standard classification of soils adopted by civil engineers, dependent on particle sizes. Waste materials with particular particle size components will compare with similar-sized natural soils. Some spoil materials, notably chemical waste, steel and iron slag and fused colliery waste will form, by chemical fusion, what is the virtual equivalent of hard rock.

Drainage of reclaimed sites is dealt with in Chapter 5; but the point must be made here that the development of a satisfactory drainage pattern over the site requires attention to the topographical pattern of the surrounding area as well as that of the site. It is vital to achieve a stable and balanced topography to avoid erosion both of the surface and of drainage channels.

(c) Aesthetics

For almost all designers a main objective is the achievement of a good aesthetic result based on a sound technical foundation; so it may seem wrong to consider it as a subsidiary item. However, it is important that decisions of this nature are taken within the context of what is both practical and aesthetic. I have previously suggested that the aesthetic choice is between geometric forms and natural forms (Downing 1971). The term 'artificial' might be substituted for 'geometric'; or we might speak of 'man-made' and 'naturally formed' shapes. There are many ways to describe the basic difference between designs formed from shapes which stand out from the natural surroundings, and designs so self-effacing as to be indistinguishable from the predominant natural topography.

The choice of man-made forms is appropriate where one is attempting to introduce a high degree of sophistication; this is usually limited to situations where a large artefact dominates the landscape, or where a landscape setting is dominated by man-made structures. The creation of artificial forms in this way not only necessitates considerable ingenuity and work in their maintenance, because of the shapes involved, but also requires this level of care to uphold the aesthetic concept of a formal design.

Natural forms are likely to be chosen in most reclamation designs as providing the most appropriate aesthetic approach in relation to the surrounding landscape. Whereas the decision to design in an artificial manner presupposes particular efforts in drainage and slope stabilization, and (less importantly) control over vegetation, the decision to adopt a naturalistic approach accepts the tendency towards stability and soft gentle landforms which is inherent in all landscape. By meeting the natural criteria one can produce a landscape which is easier to hold in the chosen shape, because it results in fewer erosion problems. Nor should the division of landscape forms into 'natural' and 'artificial' suggest that the natural forms preclude any idea of dramatic manipulation. With suitable landform designs, views can be opened up or closed, spaces of different proportions can be created, or a footpath or some other route can be 'squeezed' by earth mounding or can debouch onto an open space of width. There are many detailed examples of how natural forms can be adapted to create significant visual effects. These arise from, and relate to, the practical aspects of the land use, but extend the problems that the design is intended to solve from the practical requirements into the purely visual area of symbolic or aesthetic perception.

However, the most dramatic effects can be created with geometric and artificial landforms. I have already pointed out the difficulties of long-term maintenance of this sort of feature, and the limited circumstances in which this approach is likely to be suitable. This is not the place for a lengthy discussion of the merits of different aesthetic approaches, but it is reasonable to suggest that the practical difficulties, great in themselves, do carry with them some philosophical presumptions about the nature of design.

Current theories of landscape design, as propounded by Hackett (1971), Simonds (1961), McHarg (1968) and others, involve the appreciation of the balance and working of natural ecology to create landscapes which may not actually reproduce this balance precisely, but make use of the understanding to create artificially similar arrangements of balanced plant communities, stable slopes, and even drainage patterns in tune with the natural drainage pattern of the area. The philosophical standpoint of this approach is to deny the historically dominant anthropocentric attitude and accept a position of partnership for the human designer, rather than to attempt to demonstrate human dominance or superiority. One could then argue that geometric and formal design solutions are quite out of keeping with the contemporary design approach and should not be undertaken, since they represent an outdated design philosophy. Bruno Zevi (1964) suggested that when landscape design was out of tune with fine art this resulted in a failure to create great design. But this view presupposes a stability in fine art movements which is lacking at present; fine art is searching for new forms of expression without apparently having found any that are really convincing. And when the main concern of artists is to ensure that their works cannot be commercially exploited, then it is fine art that is out of tune, the weakness is in the field of fine art—not landscape design. In recent years artistic interest has been shown in natural forms as abstract patterns, often relying on microscopic observation, but the egocentric attitudes of the pure creative artist are quite at variance with the humble collaborative approach of today's landscape designers. Ecologically conscious practical designers are hardly likely to look favourably on attempts at artistic self-expression which involve wrapping up mountains and cliffs in plastic!

Zevi based his comments on the historic relationships between the agricultural landscape and the pictorial landscape, and hence highlighted the importance of ensuring that practical designs (the agricultural landscape) should also be 'pictorial', and not be allowed to respond only to practical requirements. However, he was also at pains to point out the opportunities for landscape design to take the lead in creating a new aesthetic to respond to the requirements of modern planning—what he described as the 'informal or action city' where the blending of landscape and townscape offers the opportunity for an organic design approach. The same approach might well be adopted in many reclamation schemes.

(d) Constraints of land uses

Different land uses have different requirements for topography and its amendment. The creation of multipurpose designs has often been expressed as a desirable aim by those concerned with undertaking reclamation on sites where this work is set in motion before any clear idea of the final after-use of the site has been reached. The unhappy fact is that very often the degree of flexibility required to make a site suitable, without additional work, for a range of end uses tends to reduce its usefulness for any specific purpose. The dimensions of flat areas necessary for playing fields could also provide suitable land for industry; but to provide such planes may be a most expensive form of reclamation, unnecessary for casual recreation, housing or any other use. Indeed, housing may be positively advantaged by the creation of gently sloping topography, while sites for casual recreation, caravan sites or picnic areas may demand undulating topography to maximize the land's capacity to provide people with peace and quiet. Golf courses constructed on reclaimed land also require interesting topography for the most satisfying results—both for watchers and players.

If the alternatives are to produce a design specifically for one known end use of a reclaimed area or to produce a design which will be the least inhibitive as far as future uses are concerned, then the latter approach is definitely a second-class solution. Even minimal guidance as to possible after-use, as in a local plan or overall strategy plan, may help to give the design solution greater relevance. The designer of reclaimed landscapes can take some comfort in the fact that initial reclamation is the catalyst which results in a decision by an industrialist or developer to develop a piece of land. Although it seems regrettable that reclamation must be done in order to be altered, one must accept that it is part of the designer's art to visualize, and create from this, making use of his technical skill. He can see, and create, potential where others cannot. Others may need to see a healthy and pleasant landscape on which to base their developments, rather than being able to imagine a possibility.

Some common uses for reclaimed land are listed below together with some of the limitations.

Industrial development. Requires 'flat' land with a maximum fall in the case of large buildings not exceeding 1 : 50 (see also p. 40). Units may vary in size from less than 0.1 ha (0.25 acre) to hundreds of hectares. Small units below 0.1 ha are often built in blocks of six to twenty-four. On small industrial sites slopes of 1 : 30 may be acceptable. There is a presumption that for any factory development the whole site should be basically on the same level. While it will almost certainly be necessary to make special provision for the construction of industrial buildings on reclaimed land, this factor of topography becomes an important criterion in design where unit sizes for light industry or warehousing may commonly range from 0.8 to 2 ha (2–5 acres).

Housing development. Maximum slopes for house building on normal soils without special provision may be taken to be 1 : 20 (5%). There is some presumption against developing private housing on colliery shale because of reservations expressed by building societies over mortgage loans. However, there are a number of examples of satisfactory building of two-storey housing on special raft foundations on reclaimed land from colliery and other industrial wastes, and the importation of soil to provide suitable garden areas is scarcely different from what is often required on normal development sites where the main contractors have either damaged or removed the topsoil. It may well sometimes be possible to prepare plans for the development of high-quality housing on wooded sites as a long-term objective when the woodland has developed on the reclaimed material for perhaps twenty years. In such cases the development of soil, such as would support shrubs and grass, might well have occurred and it would only be necessary to provide pockets of topsoil where ornamental or productive planting was required by individual owners. In this sort of development slopes steeper than 1 : 20 could be accepted for individual houses in a woodland setting, though slopes steeper than 1 : 5 should be avoided.

Recreation. Land for active recreation and sports is usually associated with housing areas or industry and the design will depend on the uses to be accommodated. A single Association Football pitch will occupy nearly 1 hectare (2½ acres), a cricket field 1.49 hectares (3.65 acres). The common arrangement of summer and winter games to provide an efficient use of the land calls for a plane on which two winter games pitches are at the same level and are associated with a cricket square with slopes of a maximum of 1 : 40 across the field of play of winter games, while the longitudinal fall does not exceed 1 : 70. The fall on the square should be not greater than 1 : 80 and the plane will extend in size from 1.66 hectares to 1.95 hectares (from 4.1 to 4.78 acres). In some cases sports grounds will call for larger areas of flat ground, and allowance should particularly be made where hard wear is to be expected for longitudinal and latitudinal movement of pitches to avoid excessive wear occurring year by year in sensitive spots such as goal mouths. An individual Rugby Union pitch will occupy an area of 1 hectare (2.47 acres) so that rugby in an association of summer and winter games will necessitate a suitable increase in the dimensions. It may well be that a suitable use for reclaimed land will be the development of a running track, in which advantage can be taken of spoil to create mounding around the central running track area. The 'flat' area of this will extend over 1.8 hectares (4.4 acres) and will call for careful attention to drainage because of the very fine requirements of slopes for running tracks themselves.

For passive recreation there is no generalized set of space requirements which can be set down as clearly as those for games areas. Landforms are manipulated to provide visual effects, to contain, open up, or direct views, and to provide shelter and seclusion. The design of broken topography for this purpose may be an objective in contrast to active recreation and other uses. Daily (undated) in his work on the size and shape of spaces in the landscape for passive use was unable to make any general observations on ideal dimensions of spaces. He was able to point out the importance of a barrier long enough to provide adequate shelter to allow for eddying effects around its ends. He also was able to demonstrate that a long bank only 1.5 m (5 ft) high provided some shelter for at least 15 m (50 ft) on the lee side of the prevailing wind; the profile of wind reduction was broadly similar to that of a shelter belt. For design reasons related to the capacity of recreation sites, it is unlikely that areas for exercise and picnicking will need to exceed 100 m (330 ft) in both dimensions. The same is true of caravan sites, where the dimensions of the site and placing of embankment spoil will be related to the dimensions of roads and the minimum area necessary to park a caravan with reasonable shelter and screening, and with an individual space for the enjoyment of the occupants of the van. Caravans may be parked in individual bays separated by embankments or planting, or both, or more economically in land-use terms may be arranged in small groups which are separated in a similar way from the whole site and, most importantly, from the surrounding landscape.

Agriculture. The main limitations on the use of reclaimed land for agriculture will be placed on it by the nature of the material involved. The use of land will be very limited without the addition of topsoil, which usually involves placing a top layer or (in certain cases) its admixture, or the addition of a suitable ameliorant.

Estimates of the timescale for the development of a soil profile which can be cultivated without becoming seriously broken down vary considerably. It has been suggested that 70 years may be required to achieve this aim with suitably treated land. It remains to be seen whether current investigations will provide alternative solutions which give quicker development of cultivable soil, but it is clear that arable farming on reclaimed land is not a short-term prospect without very expensive soiling operations. Nevertheless, there are other factors to be taken into consideration, as shown in the range of criteria used in the land-use capability classification of land for agricultural purposes (Bibby and Mackney 1969).

Grazing and fodder cropping for hay, dried grass and silage all play an important part in modern agriculture and for the operation of machines without difficulties the angle of slope should not exceed 7° (1 : 6) (see also p. 38). Where it is hoped that ploughing may eventually be possible a maximum slope of 11° should be adopted as the recommended maximum for ploughing in two directions. Aspect, shelter and drainage are all factors which will influence suitability of land. There are often apparently conflicting short- and long-term views concerning a southerly aspect. On shales, in particular, which as a result of their black colour are retentive of heat and become excessively dry, it is often extremely difficult to establish vegetation; seeds are unable to germinate or if they do are quickly parched, and shallow-rooting plants are unable to survive. However, if a good vegetation has become established, it provides advantages of mesoclimate to both flora and fauna. Coupled with controlled drainage and adequate provision of shelter this clearly has agricultural advantages.

The use of land for agriculture will also obviously depend on the economic organization of the surrounding farm units. It is most unlikely that an area of reclaimed land could form a farm unit by itself, and it therefore needs to be linked to adjoining or convenient farms—perhaps the very farm from which it was originally appropriated. In such cases it is important to establish that the additional area can make a useful and positive contribution to the farm unit. It has been suggested (Hackett 1971) that in the light of modern agricultural techniques field sizes in Britain may increase from an existing average of 5 hectares (12 acres) to 10 hectares (24 acres). The tendency to increased field sizes will naturally need to be considered in the design of agricultural units.

Forestry. Much reclamation land is devoted to woodland solely for amenity purposes, but even where there is no intention of commercial exploitation the criteria for the selection of land for economic forestry should be borne in mind. Otherwise, the removal of dead timbers, and other maintenance operations, may become unreasonably expensive and difficult. For commercial forestry, below the height ceiling of 365 m (1200 ft) in Britain which is unlikely to be exceeded for reclaimed sites, the maximum slope should be 25% (1 : 4); roadways, certainly not steeper than 7° (1 : 6), and with a preferred maximum gradient of 1 : 10, should be provided to give access to all the blocks. Because of the very high cost of providing suitable rabbit-proof fencing, attention should be paid in a cost-conscious operation to the shape of the area to be planted, with a strong preference for rectangular plantings. The viability of forestry as a commercial operation on reclaimed land must depend on the species it is possible to grow successfully, as many of the species which can be guaranteed to grow well have very limited commercial possibilities (see also p. 40).

Maintenance. Agriculture and forestry are two examples of the use of land in which the actual use is, in itself, a means of maintaining sites in the required condition. Forestry involves the smallest outlay for activities of management not concerned with the actual removal of saleable timber, in the form of weeding, maintenance of fencing and accesses, and control of pests. Agriculture involves virtually no operations which are not part of the profitable business of farming, though perhaps the point should be made that there are some differences of attitude between profitable short-term farming and good husbandry. It is assumed that the latter is the paramount aim for reclaimed areas, as it should be for all agricultural land. With regard to recreational use for formal activities, the maintenance necessary for the use is virtually what is required to keep the land in trim, though there is often some element of additional work involved with incidental areas requiring special attention for purposes of appearance.

There is some evidence to suggest that, in contrast to agriculture and forestry where good practices will tend to improve land condition on both natural and reclaimed soils, there is a danger that normal playing-field maintenance may result in deterioration of reclaimed surfaces. This was observed at Whalleys Basin, Lancs in 1967 where a playing field had been created on industrial wastes comprising black colliery shale, chemical wastes and domestic refuse (Downing 1967). The soil of the site displayed symptoms of severe compaction at depth, some of which was attributable to mechanical compaction. At the same time inadequate drainage had resulted in severe surface waterlogging. Proper drainage is, of course, necessary for all playing fields and this problem might not have arisen if a reasonable level of subsoil drainage provision had been installed. Other uses of reclaimed land result in maintenance problems unconnected with the central activity on the site, and it is in such cases that the cost implications of particular design solutions must be very carefully evaluated.

2.2 Limitations imposed by materials found on site

I have already indicated the limitations which may result from the nature of materials on site. Materials on derelict land will obviously vary widely in both their chemical and physical composition, and the angle of repose may be one of the more important limiting factors. For the designer seeking to produce a new landform for the greatest operational advantage and the best visual results, the nature of the waste material and its relative position are also important. He must aim for the smallest amount of regrading, and will rely on detailed knowledge of the variations in both physical and chemical properties of site materials in addition to the topographical survey information. To summarize:

- Landform design will need to attempt the preparation of a new plan to conform to the natural drainage pattern, and most likely with the general natural landscape pattern with the minimum displacement of spoil.

- A modifying factor in the new plan will be a knowledge of the ease or difficulty with which certain materials will be handled. Also important will be the knowledge of what difficult materials must be dealt with. This category includes slurry materials, associated with colliery waste, which need to be spread and mixed with other shales to counteract their particular physical properties: also wastes which contain chemical elements or substances unfavourable to plant growth and hence must be placed well beneath the regraded surface.

Note that the limitations imposed on the site by the nature of the materials may be reviewed in relation to the four individual criteria for judgement enumerated for site functioning. The same is true of limitations imposed by machinery and techniques.

2.3 Limitations imposed by machinery and known reclamation techniques

Set down in print it seems a truism that the designer should frame his proposals so as to be sure that he can get them carried out economically and efficiently. This implies a knowledge of the machinery available to carry out major earth-moving works, and an understanding of machine operation. Particularly important is knowledge of what can be done easily and cheaply, and what will require lengthy and highly skilled operations and hence be very costly.

(a) Machinery in use

There are two basic processes for removing material from one part of a site to another. The first is to push it about, as is done with comparatively small volumes and distances with a dozer blade. The blade grader is an adaptation of this process to achieve smooth flat profiles. The most important development in this direction, and the most important introduction in modern earthmoving, is the scraper in which the soil, instead of being pushed along in front of the blade, is scraped off the surface and into a box-like container in which it is retained until the appropriate point on the site where it is to be dispersed. The extension of the blading technique to carry rather than push the material vastly extends the range and volumes with which it is possible to operate. The second basic method is physical digging using machinery which operates like a spade. Here again two basic types can be identified, at least in relation to larger operations: the dragline, familiarly operating from the highest level in relation to the area of excavation, and the face shovel which works from the excavated floor upwards and into the face to be cut away.

Modern hydraulic techniques have resulted in a series of small-scale machines which may be used on particular reclamation operations and which combine the features of both of these two classical types of earth-moving equipment. With only very special exceptions the size of draglines is larger than that of face shovels, and their relative use is illustrated very well in the role they play in opencast or strip mine operations. The dragline operating on original ground surface level is used to remove overburden and expose the surface of the mineral. This is then normally taken out by the face shovel working from an excavated platform at the base of the mineral itself. In this operation the dragline generally picks up loose material and replaces it, still loose (and in fact a great deal less well-compacted than its original condition), within a distance limited by the length of the beam of the machine. The face shovel frequently works in much harder material, such as most coal seams, and lifts this into other vehicles for removal to the point of use or sale, or perhaps mere redispersal. Except for the excavation of minerals and similar items of commercial value, it is clear that the operation of draglines and face shovels has considerable limitations.

The distance through which these machines can move material is limited to the length of their beam, and the material they move is deposited loosely without any compaction. For more extensive operations they require the addition of trucks to cart the material to the site of deposition; furthermore, it is necessary to deal adequately with this spoil when it is deposited from the trucks in heaps, spreading it out with a bulldozer blade and running over it to consolidate it. This means that earth moving using draglines or shovels as the basic digging tool must involve at least two other types of machine, and this usually requires a fleet of trucks and a tracked dozer. This sort of arrangement becomes necessary when carriage of material from site on public roads is unavoidable, though that in itself is undesirable from a number of points of view.

The advent of the wheeled scraper, either towed behind a tracked vehicle as a separate unit or powered by its own engine, has revolutionized the possibilities for the movement of material for motorways and airfields (for which they were originally developed) and for the regrading of derelict sites. At the simplest level of the box scraper towed by a tracked vehicle the advantage is obvious; by the operation of a single machine, with only one operator, material can be picked up in one place, transported, and laid down again where required in reasonably compacted layers, rather than loosely dumped. Performance statistics are very satisfactory also, in comparison with other methods of working. The capacity of the Caterpillar 435 box was approximately 10 m³ (13 yd³) requiring the use of a D8H (now superseded by a D8K). The top speed of this type of vehicle is comparatively low; the D8H was given by the manufacturers as 6.2 mi/h (approx. 10 km/h). This led to the conclusion (Scoular 1966) that the maximum distance of economic operation of tractor-towed scrapers was 400 yd (366 m). This would mean that the haul phase of an operation might last only three minutes in each direction, and this relates satisfactorily with the loading and deposition times within the whole cycle. It is obviously uneconomic to tie up this sort of machinery in excessively long hauls, as the time element is the one variable which can be controlled to affect the output figures.

Studies of demand on a worldwide basis have led manufacturers to cease production of tractor-towed box scrapers. This suggests that short-haul work is a comparatively insignificant part of earthworks on an international scale. Manufacturers suggest that the use of elevator scrapers for small jobs, where perhaps only one machine is required, will be the most satisfactory means of operating. The Caterpillar 613 with an 8.4 m³ capacity is an example of this type of machine (Figure 32). On the other hand, there is a suggestion that at a local level there is a demand for box scrapers at second hand, perhaps from operators who are unable to make full use of the much more expensive elevator equipment, or who do not have the capital to acquire it. Whether there will be a return to independent box manufacture no doubt depends on the economic force that such operators are able to wield within the industry.

When wheeled scrapers are used there is a dramatic change in speed of operation and volumes of material carried. Scoular (1966) suggested that

Figure 32. Caterpillar 613 elevator scraper with 8.4 m³ (11yd³) capacity (courtesy L. Leverton and Company Ltd).

wheeled scrapers operated efficiently over distances of from 400 yd (366 m) to 1 mile (1.60 km). There will be a marginal increase of unit cost within this distance at the higher end, but it will be insignificant because it generally represents a low proportion of operating costs. Above one mile distance there will be a progressively greater unit cost increase attributable to distance. Although it may still be the most economical way of moving earth above this distance, this does provide some guidance as to the sort of design limitations that should be adopted. This sort of problem is comparatively rare on reclamation sites, where such haul lengths are unlikely to be encountered; it is more likely on road works where the haul of material should, as far as possible, be limited to what are reasonably economic lengths. The balance of cut and fill along a road should take account of the limitations on haul length necessary to keep the operation within economic bounds.

Those who are less familiar with the operation of different forms of earthmoving plant will find a simplified description of the basic equipment in the appendix to Johnson (1966). This deals with the operating pattern of various machines and includes reference to the types of material in which they can each best operate. The point which must be made here is that scrapers presume a material which can be described as 'freeflowed', implying small texture. Material must also be dry. Rock-like material will need to be moved by shovel, if some form of explosive is not required; exceptionally wet material, slurry for example, may need to be excavated from the edge using a dragline. The treatment of slurry is at present the subject of a two-year programme of investigations at the Warren Springs Research Laboratory, where methods of drying and handling are under scrutiny. This includes the possibility of electrolysis as a method of drying the material. Also, several authorities have found it possible to move slurry making use of the lighter weight per square inch of tractors towing box scrapers in situations when wheeled scrapers could not be used.

The Caterpillar range of scrapers is representative of performance of standard scrapers. They range from the smallest, the 621, which has a capacity of 15.3 m³ (20 yd³) and a top speed of 50 km/h (31 mi/h), to the 666B with a capacity of 41.3 m³ (54 yd³) and a top speed quoted at 69 km/h (43 mi/h). The 666B is not found in operation in Britain,

Figure 33. Caterpillar 657 operating on the Roddymoor site of the University of Newcastle Reclamation project. The maximum capacity is 33 m³ (43 yd³) and top speed 50 km/h (31 mi/h) (courtesy H. Leverton and Company Ltd).

where the largest machine used is the 657 (Figure 33). A number of models of different capacity are available either in a version with two engines or with a single front-mounted engine. It is clear from the data that the slopes up which it is necessary to operate can be very critical in terms of the gear ratios that can be used, and hence the speeds that can be achieved. Twin-engined machines can, it is claimed, work fully loaded up comparatively steep gradients, and at steeper gradients and higher speeds than single-engined machines. Gradients of 28% (steeper than 1 : 4) have been suggested as workable for twin-engined machines, although those with single engines will fail at this angle. However, it is the speed of operation which is perhaps more critical; for scrapers it may only be when the angle of elevation remains at 1% or below that the highest gear, and top speed, may be reached.

So limitation of gradient can be a factor in the design of earthworks, though it may not contribute too significantly to cost. I have already referred to the need to design in accordance with rounded and natural forms for aesthetic and practical reasons, and this is supported by study of the operation of earthmoving plant. Smooth and rounded shapes and gently flowing curves are the most simply carried out by scrapers, since they can easily be produced by these machines operating in an unbroken cycle. Strongly geometric shapes, steep angled banks, or sharp angular forms can be expensive to form and may require not only careful manoeuvring of the scraper, but also additional shaping-up with other equipment. Most scrapers can turn round in less than their total length, giving turning widths of between approximately 8.5 and 14.5 m (27.9–47.6 ft). This dimension might be critical where stepped banks or some other intricate form of earth shaping is attempted, but the dimensions quoted do not appear likely to be unduly inhibitive in design terms.

(b) Compaction

Compaction is an aspect of mechanical earthmoving which needs careful attention. Calculation of volumes for regrading designs, which will be discussed later, depends on the state of compaction of the material *in situ* before regrading and the subsequent compaction achieved by earthmoving machinery. Where reclaimed land is to be used for open space a high degree of precision in achieving compaction may be unnecessary. Nevertheless, this problem must be carefully considered if differential settlement is to be avoided. Scrapers generally exert sufficient weight to achieve the sort of accuracy of levels recommended by the Transport and Road Research Laboratory for mass fill on road construction. This is the equivalent of a 12 tonne roller with pneumatic wheels making four passes, and produces compaction down to only 10% voids. Note in this context the RRL's observation that moving equipment results in effective compaction down to a depth of only 150 mm (6 in); this points clearly to a need to ensure that material is laid down in suitably thin layers. It may be possible to control the operation of the plant on site to make use of it to achieve the best compaction.

Scrapers provide a degree of compaction which can with care be adequate for most non-specialist land uses; but the operation of tracked vehicles does not. In their investigation of compaction, the Transport and Road Research Laboratory studied the effect of tracked vehicles compared with pneumatic-tyred rollers. They found that between 15 and 20 passes of the tracked vehicle would be required to achieve the same degree of compaction attained by four passes of the roller. Although these vehicles vary considerably in weight and horsepower the area of track is proportioned to the size of the vehicle, so that the pressure exerted does not vary very much and probably ranges from about 0.5 kg/cm² (7 lb/in²) to 0.7 kg/cm² (10 lb/in²). A scraper will probably exert a pressure of four times that amount. The use of vibratory rollers may be called for where it is necessary to attain a high, and controlled, level of compaction.

It has recently been suggested that this work can be more effectively and quickly undertaken by large self-propelled compactors of which the American Ray-Go Ram 75 and the Caterpillar 815 compactor (Figure 34) are examples. A Ram 75 is in use at Aberman near Aberdare in South Wales where colliery waste is being regraded for industrial use. The civil engineer's specification for the contract called for compaction by eight passes of an approved vibratory roller. This was to be undertaken in layers. It has subsequently been accepted that two passes of the Ram 75

Figure 34. Caterpillar 815 compactor operating on a refuse tip, both moving and compacting refuse (courtesy H. Leverton and Company Ltd).

may be used to replace six passes of the vibratory roller (Stothert and
Pitt 727). This has meant time saving; not only are fewer passes needed but
also the machine operates at higher speed. Hence earthmoving work can
now go ahead at unabated speed, whereas before it was delayed by the
layer-by-layer passages of the roller.

3 Computation of volumes

Chapter 5 of *Landscape Reclamation* Volume 1 contains description and
comment on the standard methods of earthworks calculation, and of course
these methods are fully described in standard volumes on surveying such as
Clarke (1949), Middleton and Chadwick (1955) or Whyte (1969). They are
the grid of levels, the measurement of areas and hence volumes between
successive contours, and the measurement of cross-sections at parallel
intervals. Each method has its particular application.

3.1 The grid method

The grid method is generally unsuitable where the ground surface is
exceptionally broken, but it may be the least taxing to operate and provide
a perfectly adequate result where the existing ground level is not too
unevenly graded. Roberts and Stothard (1968) produced a table of grid
spacings which would give results for earthworks with an acceptable level
of accuracy. This was reproduced in *Landscape Reclamation* Volume 1
(1971) and is repeated here (Table 6). This table is appropriate for most
if not all natural conditions, but many pit-heap areas and the waste
deposits resulting from other industries are very much more broken than
the very irregular areas defined by Roberts and Stothard and have average
slopes very much in excess of 1 : 10. The result is that many such sites
would need very much more frequent spacing of grid intervals. A grid may
provide a useful initial design approach when only a rough indication of
volumes is required—for example, where the merits of two alternative
design solutions need to be compared. Before embarking on a full-scale
use of this approach the designer is well advised to assess the number of
grid points which will be necessary to give an adequate level of accuracy
over the area for the calculation.

3.2 The contour method

The contour method has always been accepted as having only limited
application. It is particularly convenient where simply shaped heaps or
excavations are concerned or where contour lines are closed. The area of
successive contours can be measured by planimeter and the volume

Table 6 Grid point spacing related to ground and
contour shape (after Roberts and Stothard 1968).

Contour shape	General ground shape (average slopes)			
	1 : 100	1 : 50	1 : 25	1 : 10
Regular	150	100	75	50
	(50)	(35)	(25)	(20)
Uneven	100	75	50	25
	(35)	(25)	(20)	(10)
Very irregular	75	50	25	25
	(25)	(20)	(10)	(10)

Table originally published in feet; SI equivalents (m) in
brackets.

between them thus calculated. In this way the volume of spoil in a heap can be calculated, as could the volume in a newly formed ground shape. It is clear, however, that this method is only really appropriate where a small number of measurements need to be made with the planimeter, though it would be advantageous where the outline is itself complex.

3.3 The cross-section method

The cross-section method appears to be favoured by a number of those involved in earthworks calculations, both for highways (a principal area of earth moving) and reclamation. The use of the end area formula for this work is usually regarded as sufficiently accurate, though there may be occasions when the prismoidal formula is adopted. While it is obviously important to achieve a degree of accuracy in the balance of before-and-after volumes in the process of earth moving, it is as well to remember that differences in compaction may play some part in affecting this balance. One cannot always be certain about the state of compaction of the material *in situ*, nor can one without costly precautions be sure of the degree of final compaction. This tends to negate the accuracy of the measurement of before and after volumes.

The cross-section method can be used with a planimeter to take off the volumes of cut and fill at the cross-sections and, although there is some-thing to be said for selecting the sections at regular intervals, this is not essential. The flexibility of the system gives a high degree of accuracy with the minimum number of measurement points, both in the section itself where the measurement points along the section can be chosen to give the best representation of the ground on existing and new landform, and in the careful selection of representative intervals between sections.

3.4 Use of computers

The grid method and the cross-section method are both readily adaptable to the computer. A simple method for working with cross-sections based on a road program and used in the University of Newcastle upon Tyne Landscape Reclamation Research Project was described in *Landscape Reclamation* Volume 1 (1971). In the same volume some reference was made to the computer application of the grid method. The decision to make use of a computer to calculate volumes depends on a number of factors. The first of these relates to the use of a program. The ideal situation is that where a program has already been written and is entirely suitable for reclamation, as was that described in *Landscape Reclamation*. Otherwise it is necessary to consider very carefully the cost of writing such a program or adapting an existing one, in relation both to the advantage to be gained by the use of the computer over hand methods and to the number of occasions on which the program can be used. Availability of time may also become a critical factor, because if it is not possible to gain access to the computer to run the program or to re-run parts of it when it has been necessary to make design changes, this could seriously affect progress of the design and subsequent contract.

At present, it appears that most local authorities find it satisfactory to carry out their calculations by hand. This is certainly so for Tyne and Wear County and Co. Durham, both of which have a high degree of experience. It is, after all, only the largest and most complex sites that fully justify the computer approach; many of the smallest and most simple certainly do not, and many in the middle range will depend on the particular circumstances prevailing at the time of their reclamation.

Naturally there has been considerable interest in the use of computers, more particularly where they might be used as a design aid rather than merely to assist in the calculation. The Transport and Road Research

Laboratory is currently working, under the title Highway Optimization Program System (HOPS), on the optimization of vertical and horizontal road alignments in order to reduce the costs of earth moving. The design of major highways is, of course, subject to much more precise criteria than would be necessary for most landform proposals for reclaimed areas, and so nothing so complex in the form of input instructions to control the vertical and horizontal geometry of the final shape would be necessary for reclamation. It should be possible to substitute for that part of the system a program which ensured that maximum and minimum slope angles were not exceeded, and produce designs on that basis. The adaptation of programs so that they can be displayed in cross-section on television tubes to show the visual impact of different design solutions is another area of current interest in landscape reclamation. Such costly methods can only be justified for landscape reclamation where the volume and complexity of outstanding work will justify it.

3.5 Changes in volume of moved material

There is no satisfactory solution to the problem of allowing for changes in bulk of material in the process of earth moving. Actual bulk density depends on the specific gravity of the material under consideration, the degree to which it has been compressed to pack particles together and eliminate voids, and the amount of moisture present in the sample. In the process of movement of a material from one place to another, the only one of these which is unchangeable is the specific gravity of the solid material. Disturbance will cause considerable variations both in the degree of consolidation and the moisture content, and these will result in changes in volume. This change can be estimated where the bulk density of a material on a site is uniform or an accurate average figure can be obtained, and the deposition of the material in its new position can be undertaken by a predetermined and controlled method. However, the material derived from mineral extraction and industrial processes is often extremely variable in bulk density and moisture content. Just as natural soils vary in particle size and organic content and are thus classified by engineers as cohesive or non-cohesive and of low or high compressibility, so these deposited wastes will vary considerably in condition and behaviour. A good example of this variation is colliery waste, which may range from slurry with an exceptionally high adsorbed moisture content to fused material formed into solid boulders of considerable size. For most waste heaps one might expect sampling to reveal considerable variation in particle size, consolidation, moisture content, and the degree of compressibility of each sample under standard conditions. When it is difficult to exercise control over the degree of compaction in regrading, it becomes virtually impossible to predict the final volume the material will occupy in its new position.

Experience in the excavation of overburden in opencast or strip mining operations, both in the UK and elsewhere, has shown that where overburden is taken off and tipped without any attempt at compaction other than through the weight of the material itself and natural settlement, the new ground level would be expected to be higher than the original and the material would bulk by at least 10%. Although some further settlement would be expected to take place with the passage of time, the period that should be allowed for the land to return to original ground level cannot be guessed at.

In contrast, regrading of derelict land results most commonly in compaction. Prior to regrading, the material *in situ* is frequently very loosely packed and is comparable to the material deposited from strip mining. The action of tyred scrapers has already been discussed. Using normal methods and without any special precautions it is quite possible to find that the material reduces in bulk by up to 25% on the movement. The figure usually used for colliery waste in the north-east of England is 15%, and a check of figures at the Windynook/Whitehills site carried out by the University of Newcastle upon Tyne Landscape Research Team for the former Felling Council (now part of Gateshead Metropolitan Borough) showed that the final contour pattern achieved showed a shortfall of 31 729 m³ (41 500 yd³), against the planned finished levels. No prior allowance was made for compaction, the design being based on a straight replacement of volumes, but being designed to be sufficiently flexible to allow for some variability. The total billed volume of spoil movement was 210 803 m³ (275 721 yd³) but the replaced volume was 190 543 m³ (249 221 yd³), and this represents a compaction factor of almost exactly 14% assuming that the exact billed amount of material was excavated. A check of bulk density taken on part of the *in situ* material suggested that this sort of average could be expected, with some material compacting by 25%.

The same situation will be met with other waste materials and it may be desirable to undertake civil engineering tests on the bulk density of the material *in situ* to ascertain the likely degree of compaction. Where this may be critical a level of compaction may be stipulated in contract documents, or some restriction may be made in the type of plant to be used which could control the level of compaction within certain limits.

4 Information for contractors

An important part of the process of creating a design on the ground is to ensure that the information is conveyed in the simplest and most direct manner to the contractor undertaking the work. This is also important at the tender stage, when broadly speaking the more clearly and precisely the contractor is able to interpret what is required of him the more keenly and competitively will he be able to price his tender. This means supplying the best information about the nature of the material to be worked, particularly volumes and depths of materials that are difficult to handle. Plans will naturally be provided for the contractor with cross-sections; the results of specialist surveys and investigations should also be made available and problem areas located on the plans. The precise requirements for the movement of material should not be left in doubt; for example, some material will need to be buried whereas other material will be used as a surface material, perhaps being dug out and spread over a wide area. Even where no special provision of this sort is to be made some indication should be given of the lengths of haul likely to be anticipated. Where cross-sections are employed the disposition of material, cross-section by cross-section, can be a helpful indication of the extent of earthworks, though it is probably wise to include this as advisory material only and not as a binding part of the contract documents because of the strong potential for variation. It is not usually necessary to provide any further information of this sort for the contractor.

5 Summary of design criteria

The criteria for landform design and regrading of derelict landscapes may be summarized in brief:

● Take account of the functioning of the land in future.

● Do not contradict the general drainage pattern of the area in which they are set.

- Take account of the topographical limitations imposed by natural forces if not those of actual land uses.

- Always attempt the maximum achievement of effect for the minimum of spoil movement and as a general rule build on existing forms within the site and reinforce those outside it to achieve this end.

- Always balance cut and fill, allowing for bulking or compaction, within the site. Do not take material from, or bring it onto, the site in the interests of economy.

- Take account of the limitations and potentialities of machinery in use for earth moving in considering design solutions.

5 Drainage

Michael F. Downing

1 Introduction

Everyone who is familiar with land management will be aware of the importance of controlling surface and soil water for good production and efficient farming, and designers will appreciate the need to take particular care of drainage matters in preparing plans for the regrading of sites.

Two chapters in the two volumes of *Landscape Reclamation* (1971, 1972) described the basic problems of drainage of colliery spoil lands, with the emphasis on the physical aspects of water control. This discussion is recapitulated here, together with fuller coverage of the chemical factors affecting site water.

2 Water quality

The problems of water quality have so far not been taken very seriously in Britain, and other similarly densely populated countries where dereliction is generally associated with centres of population. Often, the influence of derelict areas on water quality pales into insignificance beside that of active industries. But attitudes towards the control of pollution are changing, and perhaps the creation of the new water authorities will see greater control of this aspect. The significance of derelict waste heaps as a source of water pollution may then be seen more clearly, and another reason for reclamation will become obvious. In many parts of the world where extensive mineral extraction has taken place in areas remote from the mass of population the principal purpose of reclamation has been to ensure the stability of land. This has been achieved principally by covering the area with vegetation in order to reduce the run-off of surface water, thus minimizing the leaching of pollutants into water courses and in watershed areas influenced by the disturbed lands. The control of water quality, not only for human purposes but also for the protection of natural fauna and flora, can in itself be a very important objective for landscape reclamation.

Because the waste material from mineral extraction operations is natural, it does not immediately strike the casual observer that it could well be a considerable source of pollution. Nevertheless this is so, and the chemicals it contains may be easily soluble and thus can be expected to leach out quite rapidly. The use of draining techniques to accelerate this process may therefore be appropriate. Alternatively, they may only become soluble as a result of oxidation or some other reaction, in which case the process may not become obvious for several years after the material has been exposed to the atmosphere, and may continue for an indeterminable period of time. This condition is susceptible neither to drainage nor to planting and amendment.

This is why the site investigations must include specialist soils matters, such as are discussed in Chapters 2 and 6, so that the full effect of different materials on water quality can be appreciated, and so that the appropriate steps can be taken. This could sometimes involve providing special drains to leach out excessive salts as rapidly as possible. This method was initially proposed at the University of Newcastle upon Tyne Research Project site at Windynook, Felling (now part of Gateshead Metropolitan Borough), where it was suggested that tile drains should be installed at intervals rather greater than normally adopted for agricultural or playing-field drainage. In the event, circumstances resulted in the method's not being used, and a large volume of material was found to have characteristics which made it necessary to bury it to prevent oxidation of pyrites. In the Landscape Reclamation Research Project written report (Downing 1970) submitted to Felling Urban District Council (now part of Gateshead Metropolitan Borough), it was stated that surface and borehole sample investigation had shown the material to have a potential for extreme acidity which would develop at or near the surface due to oxidation. This would result in a build-up of acidity over five to ten years. The process could be expected to continue into the foreseeable future.

The two possible solutions to this problem, which have been discussed elsewhere, can be considered here in relation to water quality. The first involved blanketting the material with a depth of 450 mm (18 in) of material, since virtually no oxidation occurs below this depth. In his preliminary report Doubleday (1970) emphasized the need in these circumstances to install an efficient drainage system to prevent acid- or iron-rich groundwater from reaching the rooting zone, or seeping out over the vegetated surface. Such a drainage solution is, of course, only acceptable where drainage is to closed mains, and not to open watercourses. Even then it can only be accepted under particular circumstances, where the effluent can be adequately handled and will not adversely affect the whole system.

The second possible solution was continual ameliorant treatment to attempt to rectify the excessive acidity. This would have involved adding high concentrations of basic slag, lime and pure chemical fertilizers for a great number of years. Although this was dismissed primarily on grounds of cost, it was undesirable on other grounds. First, the continual addition of high quantities of artificial fertilizers and other additives could result in a disturbance of the nutrient status of the soil which would be difficult and costly to correct. Secondly, the addition of these materials with inevitable leaching could result in serious problems of water quality. Even where drainage was to municipal mains this would be an unacceptable commitment. The effects of the leaching of fertilizers into natural or other open water bodies are too familiar to require any elaboration here.

The extent of the problem of acid mine drainage in the USA was dramatically illustrated in a paper by McNay (1970a). He stated that chemical and physical pollutants from the processing of minerals and fossil fuels had contributed to the degradation of more than 14 500 km (9000 mi) of streams. He added that statistics showed that during 1962 more than 16×10^6 dm^3 (4.2×10^6 gallons) of effluent were discharged straight from bituminous and lignite preparation plants into streams. This waste water (known colloquially as 'black water') contains, in addition to chemicals in solution, fine coal and refuse material in suspension.

The same author (McNay 1970b) writing in a Bureau of Mines Information circular discussed investigations made of the Muddy Creek, a main stream flowing through the Moraine State Park Area of Western Pennsylvania. Reclamation of past surface and underground mining was undertaken in two main areas of the 6000 hectare (15 000 acres) recreation facility of Moraine State Park. It was proposed to develop a lake over 1300 hectares (3200 acres) with water from Muddy Creek, but this was found to be polluted by acid mine drainage, mainly from underground mining;

surface extraction was only responsible for 20% of the total pollutant. In periods of high run-off the acid load of Muddy Creek, which drains a watershed of 150 km² (58 mi²), was 286 kg (630 lb) a day. There were 66 mines involved, with some additional surface excavations which added indirectly to the pollution by exposing some of the underground working and allowing polluted water to escape. The greatest concentrations of acid water occur at times of high precipitation and surface-water run-off. The acidity of the mine water was measured at between pH 3 and 4, and an iron precipitate known as 'yellow boy', deriving from mine drainage, was extensively present on stream beds where it smothered flora and fauna.

The effects of acid mine drainage on aquatic life are dealt with in greater detail by Warner (1973). Curtis (1973) has studied the changes that take place in streams before, during and after mining, and the subsequent rate of recovery. He quotes a number of sources of information about the effects of opencast or strip mining on stream discharge, erosion and sedimentation, and stream chemistry. He also confirms that acid drainage occurs in the highest concentrations at times of 'flush out', i.e. when large volumes of water are running. During and after mining operations a great deal of material is carried into streams where it may be quickly deposited at weirs, or on the stream bed, or may be carried for a considerable distance as suspended solids.

To summarize:

● Water quality is affected by disturbance of the surface, whether for mining or reclamation, by the increase in suspended solids, and by the concentration of minerals in the water.

● It is important to include proper safeguards when drainage is into mains, and vital when natural streams are likely to be affected.

● Advice should be sought from an hydrologist in difficult cases.

● The effects of high acidity are associated with periods of high run-off. Agnew and Corbett (1973) have suggested that management techniques involving impounding and releasing water to dilute particular acid spates may be used to counter this problem.

● The effects of the disturbance are usually fairly shortlived, particularly as far as physical transport of particles is concerned.

● The problems of water quality seem to be principally associated with coal extraction. Many minerals create no problems, though some (notably iron ore) may result in problems due to spoil bank erosion and drainage. Iron mining (in the United States at least) has low levels of pollution and appears to be controllable.

3 Run-off

In addition to changes in water quality, the disturbance to the surface will also affect the volume of run-off to be expected. In *Landscape Reclamation* Volume 1 I described two stages of development of sites requiring different levels of drainage provision. A particularly high drainage provision is required to cope adequately with the very high rate of run-off experienced in the first and probably second year after the completion of regrading. The rates of run-off normally expected on roads and footpaths are between 90 and 95% of the total precipitation; for areas of grass the run-off is usually only 10% of the total precipitation. As grass swards and other vegetation develop, the run-off characteristics change from being similar to those of roads and paths to something approaching that of natural grass areas. The need for particularly high-capacity drainage provision is thus only shortlived, and attention should be paid to ways in which short-term drainage can be achieved without excessive cost. This high rate of run-off on recently disturbed reclamation sites is paralleled by Curtis' (1973) observations on the greatly increased storm-water peaks that occur in watersheds subject to strip mining compared to those which have not been affected by this activity. He showed that in comparison with an unmined water shed, where storm-water flow produced a peak volume of 226 dm³ (8 ft³) per second for a 25 mm (1 in) precipitation, the same rainfall resulted in a peak flow of 1188 dm³ (42 ft³) per second on a strip-mined area.

4 Calculation of rainfall run-off and capacity of drainage system

The required capacity of drainage systems is calculated from a number of factors:

Rate of run-off or impermeability factor. Also expressed as coefficient of run-off, this has been discussed in section 3, and a number of authorities have provided values for a range of different types of ground surface including the British Standard code of practice on drainage (BSCP 301 : 1971). One of the most detailed of these is that of Seelye (1963).

Rainfall, intensity and duration. The Transport and Road Research Laboratory (Young 1973) has recently produced a new book of tables of rainfall computed on the basis of the Bilham formula, from which the expectation of rainfall in terms of intensity and duration can be estimated over given periods of time. This may be necessary where large areas and precise calculations are involved: for example, where it is necessary to make use of existing sewers of limited capacity. In many cases, however, the calculation of drainage is based on a simple assumption that the worst conditions that should be expected are those of the precipitation of 37.5 mm (1.5 in) of rain in 1 hour, and that the drains should be designed to have sufficient capacity to deal with the product of this rainfall, allowing for impermeability and for the time of collection of the surface water from the watershed area. Storms of exceptional duration or great intensity occur only very infrequently, the most severe perhaps only happening once in 100 years. It is thus possible to design on the basis of the worst anticipated storm over a selected period of time. It is not normal practice for engineers to design surface-water drainage systems to allow for the sort of conditions that are to be expected only once in 100 years. Precipitation of 37.5 mm (1.5 in) per hour is generally accepted to be the worst anticipated storm over a seven year period. This period of years has been taken by engineers as a reasonable compromise, with the acceptance that more serious and infrequent storms may cause some problems of temporary standing water, flooding on a limited basis, or surcharging of the surface water sewers. The BS Code No. 301 allows a figure of 50 mm per hour for most sites as the basis for calculation of pipe sizes, with a suggestion that special calculations should be undertaken for larger sites.

The area of the watershed from which surface water run-off is to be collected

These factors are all brought together in what is known as the rational formula, which is designed to determine the run-off in ft³ per second, this being the product of the measurement of the area of watershed in ft², a, the coefficient of run-off, c, and the rainfall intensity in inches per hour, i; thus $Q = Aci$.* Other formulae are in operation but this one illustrates the means of obtaining information on the required capacity of pipes or ditches. It also demonstrates very clearly the importance of the coefficient of run-off (alternatively the impermeability factor) in the calculation of sewerage capacity.

*1 ft³ = 28.32 dm³ ;
1 ft² = 0.093 m² ;
1 inch = 25.4 mm.

5 Design of the drainage system

The need to design a system which is capable of dealing with a high level of run-off from the surface in the early stages has resulted in the installation of some extremely costly schemes in relation to the final drainage requirements of sites.

The provision of this system so that the mains can carry away the peak flows when the coefficient of run-off is high is not, however, the whole of the problem. It is important to use some means to prevent the build-up of large volumes of water running over the surface at high speed because both of these phenomena will give rise to erosion of the surface, disturbance of germinating seed or growing plants, and the deposition of silt in ditches, drains and watercourses. It may also sometimes be possible to make use of temporary intermediate ditches, not only to prevent the build-up of volumes of water moving over the soil surface, but also to hold up the flow of water into the main drainage system of pipes or channels. An alternative to this might be the provision of special bunds to hold surface water to be released at a slower pace into a main drainage system of a more limited capacity than required for efficient and speedy removal of the maximum anticipated surface water volumes. A second alternative might be a design which would allow a certain area to flood should a particularly bad storm take place. All these would allow expenditure on expensive permanent drainage to be kept to the minimum necessary for the long-term requirements of the site.

It may be that on a number of sites some form of urban residential or industrial use is ultimately anticipated on some part. There the inclusion of the full drainage provision required for the short-term drainage of the site can be justified on the ground that it can ultimately be brought into use to provide the main drainage system. At the Landscape Reclamation Research Project Felling Site, it was necessary to provide storm-water sewers to connect the field drains and the existing main sewers on this 56 hectare (140 acres) site extending over a length of 1200 m (3940 yd). The pipe sizes were between 375 mm (15 in) and 675 mm (27 in) to cater for the volume of storm water likely to be encountered in the early stages of the site development, and to provide the basis of a main drainage system in the event of comprehensive development of part of the area for low-density housing. The cost of this was very high, and this does sometimes have to be accepted as inevitable, but where this sort of provision is necessary to solve short-term problems the design and layout must take into account the longer-term potential use of the site so that the investment in drainage is not completely wasted.

6 Permanent drainage pattern

Although I have so far emphasized the problems of the period immediately following regrading, the design of the drainage pattern must be based primarily on the future development of the site, and must as far as possible allow that development to take place without interference. This implies that permanent drainage should not be undertaken until the permanent use of a site has been established. It may be possible to determine use zones on a site and plan the main drainage system so as to follow the boundaries of these zones leaving their centres intact and uncompromised.

If the procedures set down in the BS Code No. 301 : 1971 are followed, the preliminary information necessary for the design of a system will have been gathered. This will include the items relevant to drainage in the general survey checklist included in Chapter 3. It is particularly important to note carefully the ease of accessibility of sewers, internal dimensions, falls and capacity, as well as the difficulties which may be faced when excavating trenches for drains where support of structures or reinstatement of particular surfaces either within or outside the defined site may be involved. Sometimes connections to mains may involve special wayleaves, or interruption to traffic on the public highway. Discharge of water into watercourses will almost certainly involve agreement with water authorities and control by them of the methods of construction. The BS Code No. 301 : 1971 lists a considerable volume of legislation in Great Britain covering the duties and responsibilities of local and public authorities, which may control the design of drainage on reclamation sites.

To recapitulate, the objectives of drainage are : to prevent waterlogging or excessive soil moisture; to prevent and remove standing water; to control erosion and other damage as a result of sudden storms; and to ensure that the soil has an adequate supply of water to support plant growth in most circumstances for which provision can be made. The drainage system therefore has the dual function of dealing with the problems created by sudden storms when the run-off from the surface of the ground must be contained without causing damage, and with the control of groundwater in such a way that a correct level of water table is maintained for the development of healthy plant communities.

The function of the components of the drainage system can likewise be divided into two: the collection of water from surface and ground, and its transport into main drainage channels or water courses. Traditionally, the use of ditches has been the primary method of water control but, even on agricultural land, current farming techniques suggest the elimination of ditches as far as possible. Open ditches interfere with land uses and reduce available land. In most conditions, and particularly on shales, they have a great tendency to instability and result in considerable maintenance problems. The objective in most drainage designs must, therefore, be to eliminate ditches as far as possible, although they may be necessary where interception of surface water or storage for long or short term is involved. The part they have to play in the short term is discussed in section 7.

The instability of main watercourses was illustrated in *Landscape Reclamation* Volumes 1 and 2 in relation particularly to colliery shale. The design of ditches, where necessary, should take account of the flow of water, and it is probably wise to ensure that slopes are not steeper than 1 : 80 to reduce the danger of erosion. Even then, it may be necessary to provide some form of stabilization for the ditch. Large watercourses may need to be lined with gabions for their length or at sensitive points, corners or junctions. Smaller ditches might be protected by the use of poly-propylene mats (Figure 35) or even by placing stones in the bed or walls of the ditch by hand, though this is costly. Smaller laterals in the drainage system, whose principal function is the interception of surface water run-off, may well be more appropriately set at shallower grades and may be between 1 : 100 and 1 : 125 for best effect. For ditches which are required to deal only with occasional spates of storm water and will not normally carry a continuous flow, the use of a wide shallow section with the incorporation of grass and herbaceous plants in the bed will provide a suitable means of collecting storm water, and will release it slowly to the drainage system. The presence of the vegetation, which will only be seri-ously damaged by extended submersion, will ensure the reduction of speed of flow as well as the protection of the ditch against erosion. Such a feature might be from 1 to 3 m (3.3 to 10 ft) in width, and anything from only 0.25 m to 1 m (0.8 to 3.3 ft) in depth according to width.

For most permanent systems of drains the objective will be to provide a pattern of french drains: excavated ditches with a porous pipe at the bottom and filled with rubble to the surface. These will allow for the percolation of surface water run-off and will be placed at reasonable intervals to do this, depending on the topography and land use of the site. They will act as both interceptors and transporters of water and, in addition to dealing with surface water, will regulate the ground water of

Figure 35. An open water-course showing gently angled banks. Some erosion on the right bank (picture right) has been arrested by the use of polypropylene matting.

the site. On many sites it will be sufficient to arrange the pattern of these drains to coincide with the heads and foots of banks dividing different levels of the site, and rely on natural surface falls to carry surface water from one drain to the next. On flatter areas the arrangement of french drains should coincide with boundaries of field units, and avoid crossing open and usable areas. Where there is an excessive distance between drains, or where the falls required for adequate drainage over the surface cannot be achieved, it may be necessary to include a pattern of underground tile or plastic pipe drains to remove water which first of all stands and then percolates through the ground into these drains. Such a system will be necessary in designing a playing field area.

There appears to be considerable advantage in finishing the surface of the rubble drain, when this is done (see section 7), so that the rubble does not come up quite flush with the surrounding surface, and creates a slightly dished effect that retains the surface water momentarily. Even on established grass areas there is some tendency to minor erosion which can result in silting up of the rubble fill of the ditches at the surface. The water then runs over the ditch and on to the lower ground. When the flow is checked by the shallow depression of the ditch this appears to be sufficient to allow the water to percolate into the rubble medium and thus into the pipe. It is important, too, that the rubble medium is of a satisfactory nature; the stone should be hard and not subject to mechanical or chemical effects which might cause it to break down into smaller particles and thus clog the voids. Resistance to the effects of weather conditions (which notoriously result in the breakdown of shales) is important, and the specification for the rubble backfill should be quite unequivocal on this point; it should also give directions as to size, which will be likely to be between 40 mm (1.6 in) and 75 mm (3.0 in) for individual pieces.

I have already referred to the falls on ditches, necessary to retain them as self-cleansing and yet not subject to erosion; the same criteria apply to the design of piped drains. There are standard ranges of gradient for piped drains, dependent on pipe size in order that they may operate efficiently.

A velocity of 750 mm/s (30 in/s) has been suggested as the minimum for self-cleansing pipes. It has also been suggested, where land may be subject to subsidence as is the case with regraded land, that the laying of pipes should be at the steepest end of the acceptable range of gradients (BS Code No. 301 : 1971). This is to prevent the subsidence causing backfall on the pipe where water would stand and sediment collect for a section. Because of the dangers of uneven subsidence of this sort, many authorities recommend delaying the completion of a piped system for as long as possible.

The introduction of plastics into drainage has resulted in more flexibility, much longer lengths of drain and less danger of projections and unevenness which can trap sediment, and hence has lessened the problems in comparison with old-fashioned tile drains.

On embankments, the distance between drains placed across the slope to intercept the flow of water will be largely dependent on the slope. It has been suggested elsewhere that slopes of more than 1 : 5 should be avoided wherever possible. Above this angle there may be a need to provide angled drains or 'grips' placed up the bank at a 45° angle to the slope, or to put interceptors running across the slope at intervals of 6–7 m. At 1 : 5 or above, the intervals might be from 10 m to 20 m apart (33–66 ft). At the Landscape Reclamation Research Project Felling site a distance of 35 m (115 ft) between laterals along the embankment, planted with trees, was selected where the slope was of the order of 1 : 6. Where it was shallower a distance of 40 m (131 ft) was adopted and this has proved perfectly satisfactory. These interceptors were actually laid at a gradient of 1 : 55 to 1 : 50, the maximum slope recommended by Conover (1953). When this system is adopted the principal problem becomes the method of bringing the water down the slope vertically. To do this successfully without the danger of causing erosion to the bank involves carrying the water down in a sealed pipe system and this must be stable.

The use of such items as flumes (as discussed in *Landscape Reclamation* Volumes 1 and 2) is a poor alternative as it seems to be attended by problems of spilling, undermining and subsidence, rather more than properly constructed piped drains. The latter may be constructed even up to the angle of 45° (1 : 1) though this is not really advisable, nor in fact likely on reclamation sites. It is necessary to provide proper manholes at the junction of interceptors with these carriers and these should be designed with silt traps. It is particularly important to be able to trap the silt at the base of the embankment, where the change of rate of flow from the steeply angled drain to a much gentler gradient could result in depositing large quantities of silt where the flow reduces suddenly. It is worth noting in relation to silt that where ditches and water courses are used the provision of check dams may be used to help clear the water of suspended solids. This is a legal requirement for the reclamation of strip mine sites in some states in the USA: Pennsylvania, for example (Curtis 1973).

7 Temporary drainage provision during establishment

It is now established practice to leave open the parts of the permanent pattern of the reclamation sites which act as collector drains for at least one season after the sowing of grass or planting (Figure 36). It has been found that, in addition to the question of subsidence of drains, already mentioned, the high proportion of silt carried along in surface water run-off (particularly during the first season) requires this. The ditches should then be cleaned prior to the laying of pipes and backfilling with rubble. Unless this precaution is taken the silt will fill the interstices of the rubble and may even enter the pipes themselves. The rubble drains, if they are affected in this way, cannot be cleansed and the only solution is to throw the material away and replace it with clean rubble. Whereas open ditches of a

Figure 36. A cut-off ditch at the lower end of a gentle slope before back filling.

more permanent nature should be constructed with sides at angles not exceeding 45° (1 : 1) (Figure 35), steeper sides may be acceptable, depending on ground conditions, for the trenches that are to be subsequently back-filled. Here the angle of the side slope should not normally exceed 60°. The dimensions of these ditches will be of the order of 600 mm (24 in) bed width and 750 mm (30 in) depth.

In addition to the permanent system it will be necessary to provide a series of intermediate drains to deal with the high run-off rate that has already been discussed at some length in this chapter. The opening up of contour ditches, which may simply consist in some cases of furrows ploughed across the slope of the embankment at reasonable intervals, will help to protect the surface from excessive volumes of water. The contour ditches may be set out at distances of between 10 and 20 m (33–66 ft) and will be arranged to debouch into main ditches which have an intercepting as well as carrying function. These cut-off ditches can be specified as 75 mm (3 in) depth, 100 mm (4 in) bed and 60° batter, which is a commonly used dimension. When the ditches into which they flow are filled in and piped they can themselves be filled in with soil; they may already be quite extensively silted up in any case.

This sort of drain is used widely in Pennsylvania, where it is described as a diversion ditch. It is recommended that it should be laid to a continuous grade of 1°–2° to prevent the impounding of water and it should be excavated to between 375 mm (15 in) and 750 mm (30 in). In an area of the world where the greatest difficulty is found in getting herbaceous material to grow at all on mining wastes, it is recommended that these diversion ditches should be sown with a suitable grass, or grass–legume seed mix. It is recommended that these features should be introduced where the slope exceeds 60 m (approx 200 ft) as erosion can become serious above this dimension.

While it is obviously necessary to fill in such temporary features crossing open areas as the site develops and uses begin to take place, where land is to be retained as woodland they can be allowed to remain open. In woodland one would also not normally attempt to provide french drains but would leave open ditches. Piped drains are susceptible to damage by tree roots; the advantages claimed for agriculture, and the necessity to avoid the use of open ditches when the recreation of the public is concerned, do not apply for woodland.

It is very important to make the fullest provision for cleaning-out of drains during the maintenance period and before the piping and filling because of the high concentration of silt that can be met. The high percentage of run-off as a proportion of precipitation is a primary problem of the early years of site reclamation. Both to reduce this problem, and to improve conditions for plant growth, attempts must be made to improve the permeability of the material. Opening up the surface of the material with tynes should be specified and, although this process would not perhaps really be considered as part of the drainage operations, its contribution towards the improved water conditions of a site might well be considerable. Heavy equipment seems to be frequently necessary to carry out this work, and a specification calling for the use of tynes at 600 mm (24 in) intervals and rooting to a similar depth may well be adopted. This may give rise to the need to remove some stones brought to the surface and carry out minor regrading. It may well be desirable to undertake this operation in two cross-directions, or to undertake the second at some remove in time from the first. Whatever the precise requirement the direction of operation should be such as to minimize the danger of erosion by operating, at worst, diagonally to the slope. There does appear to be a tendency for much of this sort of material to recompact to a marked extent where vegetation is sparse or absent, and it may be desirable to undertake further operations after the sward has begun to develop, using a standard aerator.

8 Other points on drainage

There are two further aspects of drainage which merit attention. The first is the problem of underdrainage prior to regrading. It is most important that any survey of the site includes careful recording of any damp areas or standing water on parts of the site which are to be covered by additional depths of material as part of the grading process. Where such effects are observed these must be carefully and fully investigated. If they are found to result from a source of moving water it is most important that this is controlled by piping leading to an appropriate outfall. Placing material on top of such emissions could result in serious instability and danger in the future. The tragic Aberfan disaster of 1967 was an extreme example of this phenomenon, unique both in scale and effect, but it illustrates clearly the results of placing material over an uncontrolled water source without taking adequate precautions.

It is also important to maintain observation on the moisture conditions when, as sometimes occurs, the regrading involves leaving some material in place with a face newly exposed by excavation. In these circumstances the removal of material sometimes exposes a spring line and this could lead to permanently damp patches on slopes or embankments unless action is taken. Where this sort of phenomenon might, even only remotely, be anticipated, allowance should be made within the contingency planning of any contract.

The final general point about drainage relates to contract operation. The smooth and successful operation of contracts depends on maintaining the optimum conditions for working at all possible times. This means keeping the site dry and organizing the operation so that flooding does not result from storms. While it is established practice that the landscape architect or engineer should tell the contractor what to do, but not how to do it, this restricts his control over the operation of a contract. Nevertheless this aspect should be borne in mind in preparing designs. The possible methods of operating particular contracts should be clearly envisaged and any proposals which could only lead to difficulties of this nature in the event of unsatisfactory weather conditions should be replanned if possible.

9 Particular characteristics of wastes from different operations

Most of this chapter has so far been written on the basis of experience of the behaviour of colliery wastes from deep mining. The same pattern is observed in relation to strip mining which forms a major portion of the reclamation problem in the United States. The operations of the National Coal Board Opencast Executive in Britain, in conjunction with the Ministry of Agriculture, remove this type of land from the 'derelict' category in the official sense. Nevertheless the Ministry of Agriculture have long recognized that erosion, scouring of ditches, overloading of drains, and siltation are the basic problems of the short-term reclamation of opencast land. Their solutions to these problems are, like those of other reclaimers, contour ploughing and cutting temporary ditches, and establishing vegetation. They are also much concerned with efforts to recreate proper levels of permeability in the soil which has been consolidated by heavy machinery.

The concentration on colliery wastes can be defended on two grounds: first, that these represent by far the largest proportion of derelict or other land waiting to be reclaimed; and, second, that many of the residues of mineral extraction or areas of land damaged by other operations exhibit the same sorts of problem. Much mineral extraction is associated with wet operations and a high watertable. After extraction a wet pit is left and, except in rare circumstances, it is not reasonable to attempt to alter this situation. Usually the mineral is found on a flat plane or in the valley bottom and it would not be feasible to attempt to drain such an excavation, though of course the alternative of filling is a possibility, provided that no substances that will pollute the ground water are used. There may be cases where a perched watertable is found and in such circumstances the possibility of draining pools and damp areas may be considered. However, such a project would require specialist study and would not be regarded as a part of standard reclamation practice.

Water bodies may form part of the general pattern of drainage of an area providing a capacity for holding storm water in the same way as bunds. It is important that not only should the water body hold water, but that the capacity of water supplies available is adequate to fill any artificially created hollow designed to act as a lake; this sort of feature is sometimes included in grading designs following opencast working, when a void is unavoidably the consequence of the method of working. This is particularly relevant for sand and gravel workings, if they do not occur in areas with a high level of watertable. Most sands and gravels are exceptionally porous and the moisture drains away very quickly to lower layers. These materials, then, may suffer not from inadequate penetration as do colliery shales or clays, but from excessively sharp drainage, with its attendant problems of leaching of essential minerals. The same is true of the micaceous sand residues of china clay operations.

10 Maintenance

Ease of maintenance of a system of drainage on any site is related closely to the design and construction of the system. Clearly a well designed

Figure 37. A cut-off ditch left open to carry away surface water in the development stages.

system, and in particular one which is designed as simply as possible, will be the easier to maintain. If the pipes are laid to levels within which they are self cleansing and yet do not scour, and adequate silt pits are introduced, maintenance will be an easy routine. It is also important that rubble drains are not filled before the major dangers from siltation have passed (Figure 37), and that allowance is made for possible subsidence, or damage by chemical action, particularly sulphates. If these points are noted and their dangers successfully avoided, the problems of maintenance will be minimal. Open ditches must be kept clean, desilted and cleared of debris which can be a particular difficulty near centres of population. The same will be necessary for those lengths of drain intended to be piped and filled as rubble drains after the initial period (Figure 38). The clearance of these will be allowed for in the capital cost of the development. In cases where erosion or damage occurs to the walls or junctions of water courses, some

Michael F. Downing

Figure 38. Contour ditch showing backfilling with open rubble, in this case carried out prematurely and liable to result in silting up of the medium.

special provision may be required to repair erosion, in the form of gabions or polypropylene matting. Particular watch should be kept on open water courses for these vulnerable points (Figure 39), and also where open water courses link up with pipes as these are potential areas of weakness. Of course, there are perfectly satisfactory methods of constructing such junctions recommended by the Ministry of Agriculture. Apart from open water courses which need regular inspection on at least an annual basis, there should be no need for any maintenance on a well designed system other than the removal of a little silt occasionally.

11 Summary

The following points provide a short checklist relating to the design of drainage systems with reclamation of dereliction particularly in mind:

Figure 39. An example of erosion damage on the banks of an open ditch in shale.

- Investigations prior to drainage design should be comprehensive and should include an estimate of the additional watershed area beyond any site to be served by drains or water courses. Standard requirements are set out in BS Code No. 301 : 1971.

- Attention must be paid to the legal requirements for the discharge of surface water as listed in BS Code No. 301 : 1971.

- Observation of hydrological conditions should include actual site conditions, stream flow, areas of standing water, etc, over several seasons.

- Design of new landform should take drainage into account at all times.

- Design of the permanent drainage pattern should be compatible with temporary provision for high initial rates of run-off, but should be as economical as possible unless some dual use justifies the higher cost.

- Temporary drainage measures should be designed to be inexpensive and easily dispensed with, to avoid interference with permanent uses.

- Attention must be paid to the quality of water leaving the site and entering watercourses or sewers.

- Sufficient means must be provided for controlling silt in the early years of establishment.

- Materials for drain construction must be carefully selected, bearing in mind the damaging effects of chemicals contained in waste. Materials must be selected to be resistant to such damage.

- A significant contribution to drainage as well as to the improvement of the soil for plant growth may be the re-creation of permeability by opening up with rooting tynes.

- Adequate arrangements must be made for regular inspection of drains and minor maintenance on an annual basis.

6 Soils of reclamation

G. P. Doubleday and M. A. Jones

1 Nature of soil materials on derelict land

Man has operated in a remarkable variety of environments and has used a great diversity of materials when creating derelict land.

The materials now left on the land surface for subsequent reclamation can roughly be divided into the three groups of 'chemically inert', 'chemically toxic' and 'chemically fertile'. Slate, china clay, sand and gravel and much quarry waste are examples of the 'inert' group. Chemically toxic materials would include heavy metal ore wastes (zinc, lead, tin, etc), much colliery shale and many industrial residues. Very few materials left at the surface of derelict sites are fertile; some will become vegetated in time but the only real examples of this group are in the opencast mining of Britain and West Germany. By deliberate planning, either the original soils are replaced, or other more fertile strata in the overburden are placed at the final surface prior to cultivation.

1.1 Chemically inert materials

Slate is formed from a muddy sediment which has been subject to great pressures and high temperatures. Such has been the metamorphosis that the individual sedimentary particles have been fused together forming a rock which disintegrates only with great difficulty. As the material tends to stay in large particles any chemical reactions are slow.

China clay waste is composed mainly of quartz and mica which has been separated from the more valuable kaolin originally formed by the hydrothermal weathering of granite. The quartz is in small crystalline fragments measuring up to 30–40 mm (1.2–1.6 in) diameter whereas the mica is in flakes usually not exceeding 2–3 mm (0.08–0.12 in) in diameter. These materials tend to be separately dumped, the quartz in high tips and the mica in lagoons. Whereas these materials supply useful quantities of some plant nutrients such as potassium, calcium, and magnesium, other essential nutrients such as nitrogen, phosphate and some micro-nutrients are available in such small quantities that plant life takes many years to establish naturally.

Sand and gravel deposits are usually derived from the action of rivers, the sea or lakes, or from past glaciation. The dominant mineral is usually silica, which is virtually inert and supplies plants with nothing. Sand deposits sometimes contain hydrated iron and aluminium oxides; while these are virtually insoluble they have the capacity to fix phosphate in a form unavailable to plants. The presence of these leads to a problem for any plants attempting to establish on such materials.

Quarry waste ranges from granite and basalt to limestone and clay. Although some wastes will become colonized naturally over several decades, quarry waste is usually unable to provide plants with the complete

Views expressed here are the authors' personal opinions and do not necessarily coincide with the views of Durham County Council.

suite of nutrients needed at a level to sustain anything but sparse growth. When freshly deposited, the material is often in relatively large particles, and only after weathering is the material able to support any vegetation.

1.2 Chemically toxic wastes

Ores of heavy metals such as zinc, lead, tin and copper have been mined for at least two thousand years, but until recently techniques for separation of the ore from other rocks moved during the mining operation have been inefficient. As a result many waste spoil dumps associated with these mines and quarries have high concentrations of these toxic heavy metals and remain hostile to plant life. Examples can be found in Britain in the tin mining area of Cornwall, in mid- and north Wales where lead and zinc were mined, and at the copper mines of Parys Mountain in Anglesey.

Colliery spoil is a naturally variable material which, once exposed to weathering, undergoes rapid and fundamental alterations which give rise to a further dimension of variation.

The commercially valuable coals and the rocks associated with them were formed during the latter part of the Carboniferous Age 220–280 million years ago. At that time much of Northern England was submerged below the sea although the water was probably not more than fifteen or twenty metres deep. The nearest large land mass lay to the north-east of England and from it a massive river poured sediments onto a delta, the front of which advanced in a south-westerly direction. Seawater well in front of the delta would have been clear and rich in calcareous diatoms which sedimented out later to form a stratum of Carboniferous limestone. As the delta front advanced, muddy sediments covered over the calcareous deposit and as the thickness of these sediments increased a point was reached when they broke even with the surface of the sea. The strong water currents on the delta would have allowed deposition only of the heavy sediments such as fine sand, coarse sand and gravel. The upper layers of the muddy sediments in a delta therefore contained a greater proportion of sand particles than the sediments in the leading edge of the delta which were formed more selectively from fine-grained clay and silt.

Distributaries fanning out across the delta tended to weave an ever-changing pattern. Sand and mud banks were breached in places and redeposited. Behind the most seaward mud banks brackish lagoons formed and in the shallow stagnant water lush vegetation grew rapidly, died and fell back into the water which tended to preserve it from total decay and mineralization. As these organic deposits built up they became the raw material from which time and pressure formed coal.

Figure 40* shows a longitudinal section through a delta illustrating the sequence of materials deposited. The complete sequence in this 'Yoredale' cyclothem is limestone, shale, sandstone and coal. During the Carboniferous period either the sea rose or the land sank in relation to sea level, so that what was a coastal swamp became covered by the sea and the process of sedimentation began again. Sometimes the whole sequence was repeated, at other times submergence was less thorough and the Millstone Grit Cyclothem evolved (shale-sandstone-coal). In the 220 million years since the end of the Carboniferous period further rocks have been formed over the Coal Measure materials and the weight of this overburden for such a long time has led to changes in the nature of the original sediments.

During coal mining not only is coal brought to the surface, but also shale, lesser quantities of sandstone and occasionally limestone. Coal spoil dumps are composed therefore predominantly of shale, with lesser quantities of sandstone and sometimes a little argillaceous limestone.

The muddy sediments which later became colliery shale were themselves originally derived from soils or from other fine-textured materials and

*Figure 40 is reproduced by courtesy of Dr G. A. L. Johnson and acknowledgements are given to the publishers of his article (1961) in which the figure originally appeared, Geologisch Bureau voor het Mijngebied; to the publishers, Oliver and Boyd Ltd; and editors Dr Murchison and Professor Westoll of the book Coal and Coal Bearing Strata in which the figure also appeared.

Landscape Reclamation Practice

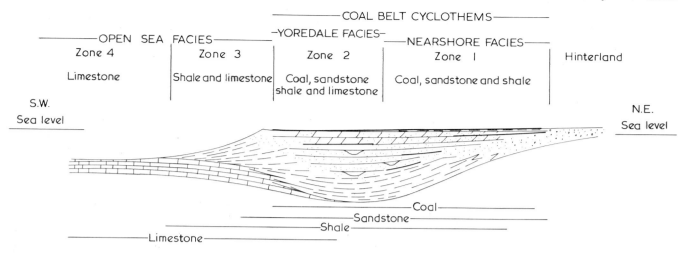

Figure 40. Schematic section through a delta indicating some of the features of variation of sedimentary succession in a single Yoredale cyclothem (after Johnson 1961 and Westoll 1968).

were eroded into the river whose delta formed the Coal Measures. Very possibly the material from which British pit heap soils are now developing were once soils themselves in an area now known as Denmark or Germany. In the interval between being a soil in Carboniferous times and being a soil now there have been many changes.

Some fine-textured sediments are preserved as the original swamp soils on which the vegetation grew. Sometimes these were leached acid soils and are now identified as 'seggers' or 'seatearths'. Some clays were sedimented in brackish water rich in decaying organic debris. There sulphate in the water became bacterially reduced to sulphide and eventually deposited as iron pyrite (FeS_2). The sequence follows several stages: firstly

$$SO_4^{2-} + 2CH_2O \longrightarrow H_2S + 2HCO_3^-.$$

Either the bicarbonate ions were lost from the sediment or precipitated out as carbonates. Hydrogen sulphide is highly reactive and could combine with several minerals; an example would be

$$\text{At pH 6–9} \qquad \underset{\text{goethite}}{2HFeO_2} + 3H_2S \longrightarrow \underset{\text{mackinawite}}{2FeS} + S^\circ + 4H_2O.$$

Further reaction between the products would give

$$FeS + S^\circ \longrightarrow \underset{\text{greigite}}{Fe_3S_4},$$

and

$$Fe_3S_4 + 2S^\circ \longrightarrow \underset{\text{pyrite}}{3FeS_2};$$

while greigite and mackinawite can be identified in recent sediments they are only semi-stable and are not found in colliery shales.

Should there have been insufficient sulphur available to complete the pathway to pyrite, the following kind of reactions would have occurred:

$$\underset{\text{greigite}}{Fe_3S_4} \longrightarrow \underset{\text{mackinawite}}{2FeS} + \underset{\text{pyrite}}{FeS_2}$$

and then

$$\underset{\text{mackinawite}}{2FeS} + CO_3^{2-} \longrightarrow \underset{\text{siderite}}{FeCO_3} + \underset{\text{pyrite}}{FeS_2} + 2e.$$

Siderite is frequently found with colliery shales as clay ironstone nodules and sometimes these have been used as an iron ore.

Iron pyrite was formed as a result of the action of the bacterium *Desulphovibria desulphuricans* and the crystals of pyrite are of appropriate size. Single crystals may be only 2 μm in diameter but are often in framboidal clusters placing the aggregate in the silt or fine sand fractions (see p. 151).

Although much iron pyrite is of biotic origin and was formed concurrently with the muddy sediment, some pyrite was introduced into the shale in veins at a much later stage. Pyrite present as small crystals is capable of rapid oxidation in a moist oxidative atmosphere. Pyrite present in crystals much larger than 15 μm diameter is relatively stable (Caruccio 1973). In colliery shales much of the pyrite has individual crystal size well below 15 μm. When present, the secondary pyrite usually has crystal sizes above 15 μm in diameter.

The ion exchange sites of the clay and organic matter originally present in the soils of Carboniferous times would have adsorbed the cations appropriate to that soil in its original environment. During the journey to the sea and particularly during flocculation and sedimentation in brackish or saline water, the suite of exchangeable cations would have been modified. Interlayer hydroxyaluminium monomers would have polymerized and exchange sites would have become saturated with calcium, magnesium, sodium and potassium at the expense of hydronium ions.

After deposition, the muddy sediment would have been subject to enormous pressures as a greater and greater overburden was formed over it. The result of this was to squeeze out the moisture and leave a stratum of solid mineral material, individual clay particles being pressed together so firmly that the sediment became a hard rock (shale). Shale varies in hardness according to the post-depositional environment. In parts of the Yorkshire Coalfield where the coal is a soft bituminous variety the muddy sediment formed only a mudstone. The shale next to the anthracite coal of South Wales is very hard.

In comparison with the muddy sediments, Coal Measure sand remains little changed since its time of sedimentation. In some situations the sand grains were cemented together with further quantities of silica and now form the extremely hard 'post-stone'.

1.3 Chemically fertile materials

The small size of this group is the reason why most derelict land remains unsightly for many years. Examples of this group are found in the opencast coal mining of Britain and in the lignite mining of West Germany. By law (Opencast Coal Act 1958) the National Coal Board Opencast Executive in Britain must replace both subsoil and top soil during restoration so that re-establishment of a crop cover takes place using a fertile rooting medium.

Similar conditions apply in West Germany although the loess stratum in the overburden is often used as well as the original soils. Loess is a deposit of wind-blown soil formed in periglacial conditions and usually it is very fertile. The occurrence of it in the overburden over the lignite is a happy coincidence frequently exploited to the full.

2 Weathering of materials on reclamation sites

2.1 Chemically inert materials

Geological materials exist in equilibrium with their environment. If that environment is altered the material will alter, the speed and direction of such changes depending upon the type of rock and how far out of equilibrium it is thrown.

A sample of rock which one day was buried at considerable depth in the earth's crust and next day is thrown on a spoil heap on the land surface is subject to a new and totally different environment. No longer is it compressed by the weight of the rock overburden. Previously it was contained at a steady temperature and protected from air and moisture. Now, on the surface it is alternately heated and cooled; it may also undergo wetting and drying cycles, it may be leached or kept continuously wet. It may become the habitat for animals or the substrate for plants. Organic compounds exuded from the roots of plants or washed from their leaves may react with the rock, or weathering products from other rocks may react with it. The possibilities influencing the weathering of newly exposed materials are complex and may lead to quite fundamental alterations.

Most slowly affected are the group of chemically 'inert' materials. Slate, a result of metamorphosis, is a hard rock which weathers slowly. Some weathering is possible especially in dumps of slate waste where the deeper material remains moist. If kept moist for a long period slate may become slightly softened; if subject to both fluctuating moisture content and fluctuating temperatures, some disintegration will follow. Instances are known of slate waste heaps becoming vegetated naturally once weathering has progressed sufficiently (see Figure 41).

Both the minerals found in china clay waste, mica and quartz, are largely resistant to weathering, although there is a tendency for particle-size reduction as a result of physical weathering processes and abrasion between the loosely tipped fragments. Wind blow removes some of the finer particles from the sides of the tips; leaching carries others inside the tip. Chemical weathering is too slow to be of much significance as both mica and quartz are almost non-reactive.

Figure 41. Six-year-old birch growing on slate; near Cologne, West Germany.

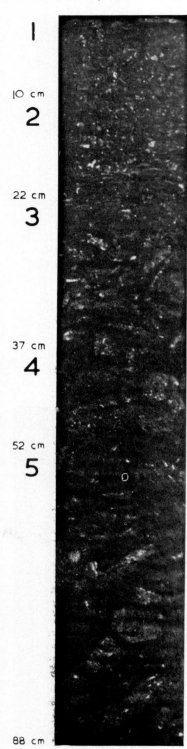

10 cm

2

22 cm

3

37 cm

4

52 cm

5

88 cm

Figure 42. Profile development in a ten-year-old pit heap at the Dean and Chapter site, Co. Durham.

Sands and gravels are similarly non-reactive and little affects them apart from the complex process of podzolization, in which the most conspicuous result is acidification of the surface horizons, which become iron-depleted. Iron pans may then be formed in lower horizons.

Waste from linestone quarries may consist of the calcareous overburden, or rejected rock material. Weathering of the waste may support a succession of calcicole plants quite rapidly. Calcined limestone waste containing high proportions of calcium hydroxide is often too alkaline to support plant life and only after sufficient atmospheric exposure has converted the hydroxide to the carbonate, can colonization begin.

The harder igneous rocks such as granite and basalt weather very slowly although dumps of finely ground material may be found which has weathered to released bases from the feldspar, and in doing so has formed a soil.

2.2 Weathering of chemically toxic wastes

Physical weathering

Weathering of the softer heavy-metal ores can proceed quite rapidly. There is an exponential increase in the exposed surface area of the metal ores which allows more rapid oxidation and hydrolysis to take place. Most heavy metals occur as sulphides; weathering often causes acidification which brings more metal ions into solution.

Colliery shales are subject to a range of weathering processes which affect both the physical and chemical nature of the material and influence every soil-forming characteristic. The pattern of physical disintegration of the shale, and the development of acidity and salinity, are discussed here as major characteristics affected by weathering. The influence of weathering on other aspects of nutrient chemistry is dealt with in section 5.

During deposition of the original muddy sediment, changing conditions in the sedimentary environment sometimes caused clay particles to sediment; at other times either very fine sand grains settled out, or flakes of mica formed as a paper-thin covering over the mud. When all this became pressed into a geological sandwich, the mica flakes (and to a lesser extent the sand grains) formed bands of weakness through the rock. Once exposed to weathering the shale tends to exfoliate into its original separate bands, a process which takes only a few winter weeks to produce obvious results. Examination of the profile in Figure 42 shows this process operating near the junction of horizons 2 and 3.

As the plates of shale become thinner they become brittle and tend to break laterally. Smaller and smaller particles are produced, this being a characteristic easily measured with an appropriate-size sieve. In horizon 1, 71.8% of the total bulk of material passed through a 2 mm screen. Only 17.4% of the total bulk of the material in the deepest horizon passed through the same sieve. The profile was taken from a tip where tipping ceased ten years before sampling. It is reasonable to assume that at the time of tipping, horizon 1 material was similar to the unweathered material seen now only at depth; therefore the increase of less than 2 mm diameter material from 17.4% to 71.8% is a measure of the speed of physical weathering. There are harder shales than the material mined at Dean and Chapter Colliery, Co. Durham, and in these the rate of weathering would be halved. The mudstones of the West Yorkshire coalfield are very soft and would break down 10–15 times more quickly than the Dean and Chapter shale.

Weathering of shale progresses to a point at which the originally sedimented particles separate apart. Mechanical analysis of the resulting 'soil' varies according to the variations in original sediment. One example of a Northumbrian coal shale indicated that the soft coat of weathered material comprised 22% fine sand, 46% silt and 32% clay. This ratio will fluctuate from site to site but the high total of silt and fine sand is probably, and unfortunately, a less variable characteristic of weathered shale soils. Soils with similar mechanical analyses tend to exhibit all the problems of poor drainage, waterlogging, drought, poor crop growth, windblow, etc, associated with poor and unstable soil structures.

Although modern colliery tips usually contain less than 5% coal, older tips contain much more coal as efficient coal separation techniques have been developed only in recent years. Old tips with 15–20% coal are relatively common but in isolated pockets coal may reach 80–90%. Frequently material in those tips was loosely dumped allowing free circulation of air. Once coal is exposed to air it begins to oxidize and generate heat. If this heat is not allowed to dissipate the temperature increases causing the rate of oxidation to increase even further. This cycle is stimulated more and more until one factor, usually oxygen flow, becomes limiting. Flames and smoke may not always be visible, but temperatures exceeding $1000°C$ have been recorded in burning pit heaps. At temperatures over about $550°$ some of the clay minerals melt and fuse together with the result that in burned shale the proportion of silt and clay is rapidly reduced but more conspicuous fusion may lead to boulders of fused spoil of 5–10 m in diameter.

Chemical weathering

Iron pyrite (FeS_2) is usually the most reactive mineral in colliery spoil and its weathering follows a complex path of which acidity, ochre and salinity are the three most obvious end products.

$$FeS_2 + O_2 \longleftarrow FeS + SO_2$$

$$FeSO_4 \qquad H_2SO_4 \longrightarrow S° + H_2O$$
Iron pyrite (label), Elemental sulphur (label)

$$FeSO_4 + H_2S$$

The first products of weathering are ferrous monosulphide and sulphur dioxide, both of which react further. Sulphuric acid is produced by oxidation and hydrolysis of the sulphur dioxide. Ferrous sulphate is formed from the ferrous sulphide and is often found crystallized as a coating of siderotil ($FeSO_4 \cdot 5H_2O$) on the surface of iron pyrite crystals during oxidation. Elemental sulphur formed by the interaction of sulphur dioxide and hydrogen sulphide is most often found on the cool surface of burning pit heaps.

In the presence of sulphuric acid, spoil undergoes other reactions. Calcium and magnesium carbonates dissolve up and form gypsum and Epsom salts respectively. The gypsum is only slightly soluble and is therefore not of great chemical importance, but in quantity it can block up pores and fissures in the soil thus making the material an unsatisfactory rooting medium for plants. Magnesium sulphate is soluble in large quantities and it frequently gives rise to saline solutions which cause stress to the crop cover on pit heap soils (see section 5).

Siderotil ($FeSO_4 \cdot 5H_2O$) and melanterite ($FeSO_4 \cdot 7H_2O$) are only semistable and will undergo further weathering. Ferrous sulphate is at a crossroads and which pathway is then followed depends on whether further reactions are in an environment of increasing acidity or of progressive hydrolysis.

Increasing hydrolysis   *Increasing acidity*

$$Fe_2(SO_4)_3 \cdot 7H_2O$$
melanterite

$$Fe_2(SO_4)_3 \cdot 2Fe(OH)SO_4 \cdot 16H_2O \qquad\qquad Fe_2(SO_4)_3 \cdot H_2SO_4 \cdot 8H_2O$$

$$Fe(OH)SO_4 \cdot Fe(OH)SO_4 \cdot 4H_2O \qquad\qquad Fe(SO_4)_3 \cdot H_2SO_4 \cdot 2H_2O$$

$$Fe_2(OH)_4 \cdot SO_4 \cdot Fe(OH)SO_4 \cdot 2H_2O$$

Acid hydrolysis also affects clay minerals rich in potassium. Some of the potassium, especially that on the exchange surfaces, is removed and becomes carried around in the ambient solution. Some of this potassium combines with the last double sulphate to form a lemon-yellow precipitate —jarosite.

$$Fe_2(OH)_4 \cdot SO_4 \cdot Fe(OH)SO_4 \cdot 2H_2O$$

$$\downarrow K^+$$

$$K^+(Fe_2(OH)_4 \cdot SO_4 \cdot Fe(OH)SO_4 \cdot OH)^-$$

Jarosite can be seen in horizon 3 in Figure 42 but it is only one member of a family of salts. Other members which could be found are natrojarosite, where sodium replaces the potassium ion, and alunite in which the positions normally occupied by ferric iron are occupied instead by aluminium.

Jarosite itself is stable only at pH values between about 1.0 and 3.0. If hydrolysis proceeds to raise the pH or if other minerals affect the system, the jarosite will break down in the last of the steps in the pyrite oxidation pathway.

$$K\,Fe_3(SO_4)_2(OH)_6 \xrightarrow{KOH} 3Fe(OH)_3 + 2K_2SO_4$$
jarosite   amorphous ferric
hydroxide

Amorphous ferric hydroxide is precipitated as a surface coating over other minerals and can be seen in horizon 4 in Figure 42. It is also found in large quantities in drainage ditches on pit-heap reclamation sites and its presence would affect the efficiency of any tile drainage system should one ever be contemplated.

The oxidation of pyrite is only one aspect of the acidification of colliery spoil. The pH of fresh spoil is usually between 7 and 8. Without any contribution from pyrite the pH will slowly fall and would stabilize out at 4.0–4.5 as is the normal situation for highly leached mineral soils containing a clay fraction. The effect of active pyrite in the spoil is to hasten the pH fall and to push it even lower. How low the pH falls depends on factors balancing the acidification process. These are the reserves of carbonate and the buffering capacity of clay minerals in the spoil, and the rate of acid removal by leaching. In a situation where the shale contains much carbonate and little active pyrite, the resulting pH will stay at neutral or above; in a converse situation the pH might fall to 2.0 or even slightly lower. Generally large concentrations of both pyrite and carbonates, especially magnesium carbonates, cause high salinity. Salinity can be generated at any pH value, but at lower values iron and manganese will also be found in solution though as minor components.

2.3 Chemically fertile materials

In opencast working and most reclamation schemes the removal of topsoil and subsoil is involved. The materials are stored in heaps and are subsequently spread. It is commonly found, especially with the heavier soils, that the replaced topsoil is inferior to undisturbed material. This is apparent both as a lower level of chemical fertility and a poorer structural condition. The soils usually have an increased requirement for nitrogenous fertilizers, drainage is slower and, when wet, the surface is more prone to puddling by traffic and livestock. This deterioration has both physical and chemical causes. Mechanical disturbances during earthmoving operations result in shearing and compaction of the soil causing an increase in the water dispersibility of its finer-sized particles (see p. 157). Because of this, the soil clods tend to disintegrate during rainstorms and the fine particles are washed into the voids causing a reduction in porosity and permeability, and leading to the likely development of anaerobic conditions. These effects of mechanical damage to the soil become greater with increasing wetness and can be reduced, though not eliminated, by avoiding the handling of soil with a moisture content greater than its lower plastic limit, and by keeping traffic over it to a minimum. Soils most likely to suffer seem to be those with organic carbon contents of less than about 2% and little or no free calcium carbonate. The chemical changes are mainly due to the development of anaerobic conditions, the most important being denitrification. The activity of micro-organisms in the absence of oxygen results in nitrates being reduced to nitrites and the subsequent loss of these as nitrogen and nitrous oxide. In addition to this, the nitrification process is inhibited so a considerable reduction in available nitrogen results. Ethylene, a substance which inhibits the root growth of many crops, can result from the incomplete oxidation of organic matter under these conditions. Most significant though, organic gums which help to confer stability on soil structure are not produced under anaerobic conditions, and since they need constant replacement their continued absence will add to the soil's physical deterioration. These effects of anaerobiosis will be most marked in the stored soil but may well persist after spreading; careful management and adequate underdrainage are necessary for improvement.

3 Sampling and methods of soil analysis

3.1 Sampling

The validity of soil analysis for advisory purposes depends very much on how accurately a soil sample delivered to the laboratory represents an area of soil in the field. Natural soils vary laterally in the field according to topography, parent material, management, drainage, etc. Vertically the soil is differentiated into horizons, each horizon having its own characteristics and nutrient status.

On reclamation sites soils exhibit even greater variability, first because there is often a more complex distribution of parent materials and secondly because the raw material has been exposed to weathering for varying periods and is at different stages of alteration to reach equilibrium with its new environment. Pit-heap surfaces can vary significantly over distances as small as 100 mm (4 in); sampling must therefore be carried out carefully and any recommendations must take account of soil variability.

Sampling may be carried out before major earthmoving so that information on the nature of parent materials can be used in the design of the scheme. At this stage sampling should be precise spot sampling with the single location of each sample accurately recorded. Each different soil parent material should be examined, if possible by sampling both freshly exposed and weathered material. From this kind of survey it is possible to estimate what kind of material will be exposed for any given earthmoving programme and how that kind of material will weather, once exposed.

A different kind of sampling is appropriate after regrading whether it relates to initial seedbed cultivation or to after-management. The site should be divided up into compartments and ultimately one sample only obtained from each compartment. For soil sampling purposes a site compartment is defined by having in common parent material, previous treatment, and land use. It is helpful if the compartment also has uniform aspect and topography though this is not essential. It is essential for the compartment to be large enough for individual management which generally means a minimum size of about 1 hectare (2.5 acres).

Sampling is carried out by taking cores of uniform diameter from 20–25 locations within the compartment. The locations can be random, which is difficult to guarantee, or in accordance with a strict pattern which covers evenly the whole compartment. It is not necessary to sample any deeper than it is possible to treat so that unless deep cultivations are envisaged sampling to 100 mm (4 in) is generally sufficient.

The design of reclamation schemes should give great importance to distributing soil parent material uniformly within land-use compartments. A future pasture field, for example, should have a uniform surface, not one half of shale and the other half of soil. If such considerations have been made at the design stage, subsequent soil sampling and treatment is simplified. Bulk samples should not usually represent an area greater than 2 hectares (5 acres) but the reclamation scheme may have provided land-use blocks of up to 8 hectares (20 acres). Usually over such a large area there are variations in aspect or topography which provide a good basis for dividing the compartment. It may be shown over a few years that such subdivisions are artificial and that one composite sample adequately represents the whole land-use block.

Methods of soil analysis have proliferated in recent years. Sometimes one method stands out as particularly suitable for one type of soil; at other times the choice of method is rather more personal preference. Where possible, the suite of analytical procedures should remain unchanged as it is then possible to build up the bank of interpretative experience necessary in transforming analytical results to field recommendations.

The Ministry of Agriculture Agricultural Development and Advisory Service (ADAS) offer a useful soil analytical service throughout England and Wales. Although ADAS normally confines its services to agriculture most regional centres are also prepared to assist where possible with the non-agricultural parts of schemes. Soil analytical techniques employed by ADAS are fully described in the MAFF Technical Bulletin 27, *The Analysis of Agricultural Materials* (HMSO, 1973). As these techniques are nationally available they are outlined in the following section with comments on their value in derelict land reclamation.

3.2 *Preparation of samples for analysis*

After slow air drying, the raw field samples should be broken up gently to allow separation of rock material from the finer particles which are then used in soil analysis. It is important not to pulverize solid rock material as it has a quite different nutrient status from the weathered finer fraction which forms the 'soil'. Where soil grinding is by a roller mill, only the light roller should be used and the procedure ended when the weathered aggregates have been broken up and before the raw rock material is ground. All material which passes through a 2 mm screen in the roller mill is collected, thoroughly mixed, and sub-sampled for subsequent analyses.

3.3 Measurement of soil acidity—pH

Method

Using the fraction of the soil passing the 2 mm screen an aqueous 1 : 2.5 V/V soil : water suspension is prepared and the pH of the suspension is measured.

Comments

pH 7.0 is neutral. Most agricultural crops grow satisfactorily at pH 6.5. For permanent pasture, the pH should be within the range of about 5.8–6.8. For woodland, soils should fall within the range 5.0–6.0; where the pH is lower than optimum liming will be necessary.

3.4 Lime requirement

Method

The aqueous suspension obtained for pH measurement is mixed with a buffer solution of pH 7.0. After a given time the pH of the system will be below pH 7.0 by an amount proportional to the quantity of acidity in the soil, therefore proportionally also to its lime requirement.

Comments

According to the specification for this method, contact between soil and the buffer is allowed for only 5 minutes before the pH of the system is measured. Such a short period is inadequate to allow the buffer to react with all the acidity in a very acid soil. As the quantity of 'unaffected' acidity varies from soil to soil it is better to allow the system to come to equilibrium which is obtained after contact of about 5–7 days. During this period the suspension should be protected from evaporation and should be stirred time to time. A method modified specifically for very acid materials is reported by Doubleday (1971a).

3.5 Measurement of salinity

Method

Using a saturated calcium sulphate solution at 20°C a 1 : 2.5 soil : solution suspension is prepared and shaken for 15 minutes. The electrical conductivity is measured on the filtered extract, this being proportional to the concentration of salts dissolved in the extract.

Comments

The 1 : 2.5 suspension is a quick way of obtaining a solution on which conductivity can be measured. The wider the ratio the more dilute any salts will be; therefore it is important for the ratio of liquid phase to solid phase to be known. Nevertheless, set ratios tend to be misleading. It is better to extract the soil solution from a system at field capacity as this is a meaningful and natural parameter for each soil. This method takes rather longer to perform but yields more realistic data (Doubleday, 1971a).

The method used by ADAS expresses results as micro (μ) Ω^{-1}. Other methods use milli (m) mho per cm. Now in use is the unit 'Siemens per metre'. They equate as follows:
$$1 \text{ Siemens/metre (S/m)} = 10 \text{ mmho/cm} = 10\,000\ \mu\Omega^{-1}$$

3.6 Extractable potassium

Method

The soil is shaken for 30 minutes in a 1 : 5 (V/V) soil : 1 M ammonium nitrate suspension; potassium is measured using a flame photometer on the filtered extract. During contact between the ammonium solution and soil, ammonium ions replace a proportion of potassium ions likely to be available to plants. The quantity of potassium thus brought into solution is taken as a measure of potassium availability to plants.

Comments

This method is designed to cope with large numbers of soils on a routine basis and to give reasonably accurate answers. It gives an estimate of the quantity of potassium available over a short period to plants. It does not indicate what level of supply could be sustained. This problem can be overcome by regular sampling and soil analysis to check the level of potassium availability over a period of time.

3.7 Extractable phosphate

Method

The soil is shaken in a 1 : 20 V/V soil : 0.5 M sodium bicarbonate solution for 30 minutes. Phosphate ions thus brought into solution are estimated quantitatively using a spectrophotometric method to estimate the optical density of the molybdate blue complex.

Comments

Plant roots under some circumstances exude bicarbonate ions which are able to desorb phosphate from soil mineral surfaces. Using this analogy, phosphate desorption by bicarbonate is generally accepted as a useful routine method for estimating phosphate availability to plants.

The method does depend on some phosphate being desorbed in order to categorize the soil. Many raw soil parent materials have no available phosphorus and therefore register zero. A guess then has to be made concerning the quantity of phosphate fertilizer to be applied to raise the level of availability to a point suitable for a particular plant cover. In reaching this level some soils need large quantities of phosphate, other soils need one tenth as much or less. This bicarbonate extraction technique gives no information on phosphate requirement. Such information can be obtained by applying a known quantity of fertilizer, allowing it to react with the soil, sampling the soil and retesting it. This is very much a trial-and-error technique needing perhaps two or three years before a satisfactory result is obtained.

Soils which fix considerable levels of phosphate, such as colliery shale soils, should be analysed using an adsorption isotherm technique such as that reported by Doubleday (1971b). From the results obtained by equilibrating different levels of phosphate with the test soil an estimate is made of how much fertilizer should be added to the soil to allow a sufficient quantity of phosphate to remain available to plants.

3.8 General

If soil analyses are carried out by ADAS either the analytical results will be reported to the customer, or else field recommendations will be made. Most regional centres of ADAS are conscious that they do not have sufficient experience yet in derelict land reclamation to convert laboratory analyses into field advice. This is left to the customer with such guidance as is possible. Whether the test is lime requirement or P and K status, the best procedure for the customer is to apply a test quantity of the limestone or fertilizer, allow time for contact and then sample and retest the soil.

4 Reclamation techniques: choice and treatment of surface

In some instances extractive industries have been genuinely unable to provide a surface on the land they have spoiled which is now able to support an adequate plant cover. An example would be a coal field in Wyoming where the overburden covering a 30 m (100 ft) thick seam of coal is the thin dust layer derived from mineralization of the coal below.

Through thoughtlessness, incompetence or avarice only too often certain industries have tipped their spoil without any regard to the value of the environment. Such examples would be found in the Lower Swansea Valley which is scarred with tips resulting from the smelting of lead, tin and zinc. Environmental considerations were minimal until recently with strip coal mining in the USA; deep coal mining in Britain paid little attention to its effect on the environment until forced to by planning law and tragic accidents. A legal technicality places most china clay extraction and waste tipping beyond the control of local authorities and planning conditions. For most of the areas in which the china clay industries operate reinstatement will be entirely dependent on their own volition and good will.

In those industries where there is no long-term plan for reclamation in the original mining operations, reinstatement is made difficult. Elsewhere industries have been encouraged to clear up their mess and have given the matter some thought at the appropriate stage. There is a levy on iron ore extracted in Britain and the amount accruing is used for reclamation. Sand and gravel extraction is often covered with a bond lodged with the planning authority. Opencast coal mining in Britain includes reinstatement as specified in the Opencast Coal Act 1958 and achieves a very high standard of finish (Doubleday 1974). Reinstatement works include the replacement of the original subsoil and top soil with appropriate cultivation. Brown coal mining in West Germany follows a similar pattern with either the original soils, or if better materials are found in the overburden, these are placed at the final surface.

Loosely tipped materials such as quarry waste, heavy metal waste ores and china clay have the advantage of containing an adequate system of voids to allow air and water to circulate and in which roots can grow without constriction. Where the spoil is non-toxic reclamation really holds no problem. There is no technical reason why plants should not grow on china clay dumps. If the tips were formed with slopes which were not subject to savage erosion instead of a form which has the steep slopes at the angle of repose, then natural colonization would cover the spoil in 30–40 years. A little help with seed and fertilizers might reduce the timescale tenfold.

Other materials such as the lead and zinc waste ore tips of North Wales are toxic to plants and therefore require different treatment. Some grasses contain a sufficient genetic variety within a normal population to include a few extreme forms which have much greater tolerance to specific toxicities than the bulk of the population. *Agrostis tenuis* is one example of which zinc- and lead-tolerant strains can be found naturally occurring on the waste ore tips. Treatment with limestone and fertilizer stimulates growth considerably and with a seed multiplication programme there is potential for a reclamation programme. The achievement would be a vegetative cover capable of neither wear and tear nor agricultural usage as it would be poisonous to livestock but at least a formerly bare area would merge into the surrounding landscape.

In cases where soils or soil parent materials are replaced at the end of a mining scheme, the good intention may bring problems. Not only do soils alter and generally deteriorate in dumps but, once respread over the surface, they are found to contain little structure. The overburden covering the brown coal mined near Cologne contains a stratum of loess. This is a fertile material which, being friable and stonefree, is often respread to form the final surface of the restored site. If handled as a dry material it goes down as a compacted layer not easy to cultivate. Restoration now provides for the material to be pumped onto the ground surface as a wet slurry. After the water has drained away a system of voids is left which greatly improves the physical character of the soil.

Deep ripping of the subsoil replaced during opencast restoration is required by law and thorough cultivation of the topsoil also helps to overcome the problems of compaction.

Pit-heap restoration presents the worst problems. Early attempts at reclamation usually involved small pit heaps. Afforestation of the heaps without any earthmoving was quite satisfactory both technically and visually, at least on non-toxic shales. The Town and Country Planning General Development Order of 1948 stated that any tips started after 1 July 1948 should come under planning control. Rather than start new tips, and perhaps because of centralization of coal preparation facilities, the response has been to extend existing tips where possible, and elsewhere to create a small number of enormous spoil dumps.

Afforestation of large tips is difficult for exposure reasons but also covering large tips with trees leaves a unit in the landscape which always resembles a planted-up pit heap; it can never look any different. For a combination of reasons reclamation of large tips almost always now provides for a major regrading operation to provide a basic landform which blends in with the surrounding landscape. The machines normally chosen to undertake bulk earthmoving are rubber-tyred scrapers capable of handling up to 40 m³ (52 yd³) of spoil in each load. Fully laden the machine weighs in excess of 100 tonnes and all this load is transmitted through four wheels to the ground. As layer upon layer of fill is thus compressed, the resulting material is left with very few voids at all. Normal calculations of compaction after regrading suggest that a loss of 15% bulk can be expected but on-site measurements before and after movement of the shale have sometimes indicated a loss in bulk of up to 25%. Voids in the material after regrading probably total about 5–7%. Regraded spoil is usually ripped to about 600 mm (24 in) depth prior to cultivation by equipment strong enough to lift and shatter this surface layer completely. This increases permeability in the top 600 mm but below this depth the material is still almost impermeable. Unfortunately because of the structural instability of shale with its high silt and fine sand content, even the top 600 mm often settles to an equally impermeable condition in a matter of months.

While regrading spoil dumps makes new and attractive landforms possible, it also creates problems which cannot be overcome easily when establishing and managing the plant cover. Nevertheless, regrading does allow selection of the materials in forming the final surface. Sometimes there is sufficient variability of materials on site to allow an earthmoving programme to be devised which will bury the most toxic spoil and place the least difficult material at the final surface. Sometimes this can be achieved without increasing haul routes or bulk handling, but at other times increased costs would be incurred. In such circumstances the increased earthmoving costs should be balanced against reduction in the cost of establishing and maintaining the vegetative cover. Not only will there be a saving in the fertilizer required each year but the better material may still give higher crop yields than a well fertilized 'difficult' shale. Probably there would also be remedial works on the difficult shale to add into the budget and a poorer appearance and perhaps even incurable bare patches on the 'difficult' shale site. The budget can be worked out for a period covered by the initial reclamation contract but it should also be projected where possible for the life of the site as the decision on the distribution of shale types is made once and for all.

Often in reclamation schemes there will be pockets of topsoil and subsoil included within the site boundaries and regrading allows these materials to be used to cover colliery spoil. Where soil is available for covering colliery spoil in a reclamation scheme its distribution should be carefully planned. Of greatest importance is to cover toxic material. Acidic shale should be covered with not less than 250–300 mm (10–12 in) of soil material and very heavy applications of limestone, up to 50 tonnes/ hectare (20 tonnes/ acre), should be applied to the shale surface before covering with the soil material.

If there is no toxic material to cover, the criterion for soil distribution should be on land use. There is evidence to show that planting trees in a pocket of soil placed in the surface of a toxic spoil dump is pointless. Eventually the roots fill up the pocket of soil, and as they will not penetrate into the shale the tree stops growing. There is also evidence (see Figure 43) to indicate that planting trees into a thin (100 mm) covering of soil over non-toxic shale also causes problems. Trees (*Alnus glutinosa*) in the foreground planted directly into colliery spoil are growing vigorously whereas those alder planted into the thin soil cover over the shale have mostly died. Probably the reason is linked with moisture stress, this being greater in the fine-textured soil covering which would not have a continuous capillary system down into the shale. During wet periods moisture would tend not to drain vertically into the shale and during dry times, without a continuous capillary system in the soil profile, plants would not be able to call upon the reserves of moisture held at depth in the tip.

Figure 43. Alder growing well on shale, dieing on soil-covered shale; near Essen, West Germany.

Soil should therefore be placed on grassland areas. Moisture stress is less dangerous as a sward can recover from drought better than young trees. Where grass productivity is important, as with pastures, the sward will need renewing every 7–10 years if not more frequently and recultivation of a soil surface is much easier than for a shale surface. The labour-intensive stone-picking operations required during recultivation of shale, the extra-powerful tractors and robust equipment combine to make pasture renewal expensive. Trials in progress at Newcastle upon Tyne University are examining minimal cultivations but results so far indicate that ground conditions must be perfect for such a technique to be effective.

5 Problems and development of soils on reclaimed land

5.1 Chemically inert soils

Development of soils in largely inert material is a slow process and depends on building up a nutrient cycle which can sustain plant growth. Cycles do not have obvious starting points; therefore the problem is to motivate the system and maintain it so that it perpetuates itself.

Under natural conditions inert materials supply virtually no nutrients to plants; therefore the source of nutrients is the outside environment. Rainfall brings about 4–5 kg nitrogen per hectare (3.6–4.4 lb/acre) per year; other nutrients are brought by windblown dust, animal activity or drainage water. With the meagre levels of nutrients now available a plant succession begins. Nutrients are taken up by plant tissue and held by the organic material after death. Mineralization of the organic debris releases the nutrients slowly which are then assimilated by a new generation of plants. This new generation thus gains nutrients not only from the outside environment but also from decaying organic remains of the first generation of pioneer plants. With this double source of nutrients available the second generation of plants is more vigorous and more diverse than the first generation. So the build-up continues until a climax vegetation is reached which is in stable equilibrium with its environment. This process may take several centuries; it may never be reached if some factor (such as man) continuously alters the environment. Nevertheless, in a period of decades a complete vegetative cover can form by natural colonization of inert materials such as sand or china clay dumps. If the system is primed, complete colonization can be achieved ten to twenty times as quickly.

5.2 Chemically toxic materials: colliery shales

Soil development is the summation of many processes, any one of which may be limiting to the yield of the plant cover. In this section the nutrient chemistry of shale soils and their mineralogical alteration is examined and the development of the soils during the years following the initial reclamation works is outlined.

Potassium status

Doubleday (1972) reported details of alteration and weathering processes on nutrients in shale soils.

Ignition of shale in a dump reduces the weight of spoil by up to 30% without losing any potassium. At the same time the potassium becomes more easily available to plants. Therefore by residual enrichment and also by increased availability burned shales generally supply plants with more potassium than unburned shales.

Samples of an unburned shale were subjected to heat treatment for 18 hours then leached with 0.5 M ammonium acetate in 0.5 M acetic acid

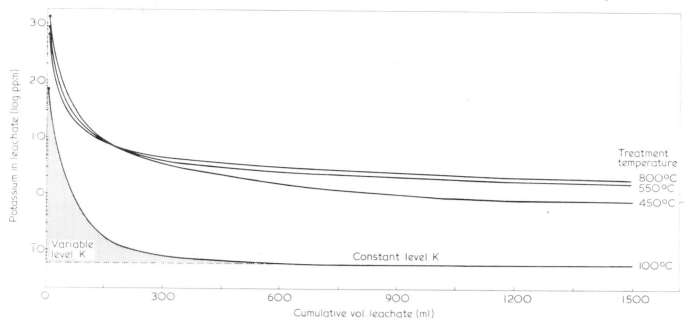

Figure 44. Potassium supply characteristics during leaching of black and red shales.

(Morgan's reagent). The family of curves in Figure 44 show how heat treatment affects the pattern of potassium release. Ignition to 450 C reduces the bulk of the shale and makes any potassium in organic matter available. At about 550 C the kaolinite in shale starts to recrystallize and this process continues up to 800 C. Over this range there is a decrease in 'variable level K' leached out and an increase in 'constant level K' supply: a feature consistent with the recrystallization of kaolinite and the disruption of other clay lattice structures. Variable level K would be leached out of a profile quite rapidly; constant level K is much more important as it is a measure of the long-term K-supplying power of the shale.

Acidification of colliery shale affects its potassium status. As shale becomes more and more acid potassium can be increasingly leached out of the profile. As a result the shale becomes depleted in potassium and may have difficulty in supplying enough of this nutrient to a vigorously growing crop cover. Theoretically this point would be reached with soils at pH values around 4.0; further acidification would result in a shortage of potash. In practice a soil at pH 4.0 is too acid to allow crops to grow vigorously so that liming would be undertaken to raise the pH, or more likely to have prevented such a degree of acidity ever having been reached. Liming very acid unburned shales tends to restore the K-supplying power. Liming of less acid shales and red shales slightly reduces the quantity of exchangeable potassium but this is not usually important as at its lower level it is still high enough to sustain healthy plant growth.

Grass crops on some colliery shales show anomalous responses. In a greenhouse pot trial S24 perennial ryegrass was grown on five red shale soils and five black shale soils. Leaf yield data show that during the initial growth period potassium depressed yields on two soils by up to 63% but on two red shale soils growth was increased slightly. Results of the second harvest showed a general but small increase in growth of the ryegrass. It is difficult to draw conclusions from this trial as complex physico-chemical processes in the soils appear to interfere with crop behaviour (Doubleday 1971a). Nevertheless, potash fertilizers should be used with caution and will not often give large increases in yields; more usually there will be no response and a few times significant depression in yield will be noticed.

Soil analyses by ADAS will place the soils usually within indices 0 to 3. Applications of potash should be given to maintain the availability index at 2 to 3. Very often immediately after regrading, a soil or shale surface

Table 7 P $\times$ K $\times$ 10 shale soils factorial trial. First harvest leaf weights (g dry matter/pot) and potassium/soil type interaction.

Soil	Type	K_0 (g)	K_1 (g)	Potassium response (g)
NMN		0.842	0.313	− 0.527*
NFS/2	Black	0.913	0.712	− 0.142
BNF/2	shales	0.500	0.583	+ 0.083
BBS		0.883	0.585	− 0.298*
RNB		0.743	0.565	− 0.178
SRS		0.612	1.472	− 0.140
BSF/4	Red	0.750	1.097	+ 0.347*
BRU	shales	1.225	1.112	− 0.113
RNF/4		0.675	0.598	− 0.077
BRS		0.988	1.333	+ 0.345*

*Significant at the 5% probability level

will have an index of 3 to 4 or perhaps higher. Little or no potash need be applied at this stage but as the index tends to fall steadily after first exposure of the surface the index must be monitored and applications of potash should be timed to catch the fall within the index range of 2–3.

Where potash levels are high, there may be problems of hypomagnesemia in spring grazing for cattle and sheep. This disease has complex and not fully understood causes but high soil K levels tend to depress uptake of magnesium in the lush spring grass. When cattle start grazing on this type of sward there is a danger of hypomagnesemia which may take as little as 30 minutes from the first symptoms to death in an adult cow. Heavy applications of potash should therefore be avoided during the spring. Potassium given towards the end of the season helps clover to gain winter hardiness and therefore prolongs the duration of this legume. Where a grass sward is grazed, nearly all the potassium taken up in the fodder is returned through the grazing animal and the reserves of potassium in the shale will go some way to making up any deficit. If grass is removed off site for hay or silage, potassium depletion may be significant and heavier applications of a potassic fertilizer will be needed.

Phosphate status

During ignition of colliery shale two processes having opposite effects influence the material's phosphate status. As the temperature of heating is raised to 450°C iron present as FeS_2 is oxidized and in this new form it has a much increased ability to adsorb phosphate. When all the iron is oxidized a peak phosphate requirement is achieved. Heating above 550°C tends to cause the clay fraction to recrystallize and fuse so that the total surface area of a unit weight of shale is decreased. As phosphate adsorption is a surface phenomenon the quantity of phosphate adsorbed and 'fixed' by shale is now greatly reduced (Figure 45).

The intensity of phosphate fixation by a red shale will depend largely on two factors. One factor is the total surface area available for fixation, per unit weight of shale. This is largely determined by the hardness of the shale, intensity of weathering and the temperature at which ignition took place. All three factors vary considerably; ignition temperatures for example can range up to 1000°C. The other main factor is the total quantity of iron in the shale and this can range from zero to 25% or more. The net result of so much variability is that phosphate fixation by shales ranges over wide limits. It is important to have an estimate of what level of phosphate fertilizer will give maximum plant growth as too much phosphate depresses plant yields quite significantly.

Phosphate requirements of shales are also influenced by any acidification

Figure 45. Effect of heat treatment on phosphate sorption by a shale soil. P sorption data adjusted to compensate for weight loss during heat treatment.

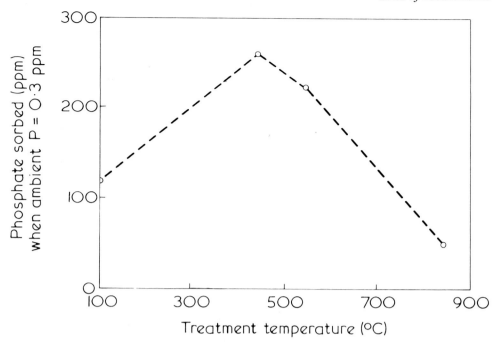

occurring in the system. As iron pyrite weathers it produces acidity as one effect and amorphous ferric hydroxide as another product. Amorphous ferric hydroxide strongly adsorbs phosphate molecules so there is a tenuous link between pH and a shale's phosphate requirement (Figure 46). Unfortunately not all shales can be drawn into one simple relationship, as in some shales a little generation of acidity causes marked falls in pH; in other well buffered shales a great deal of iron pyrite may weather before the pH falls significantly. Whatever the complexities of this relationship a simple law holds: as a shale becomes more acid, its phosphate requirement increases. A point is reached when liming the

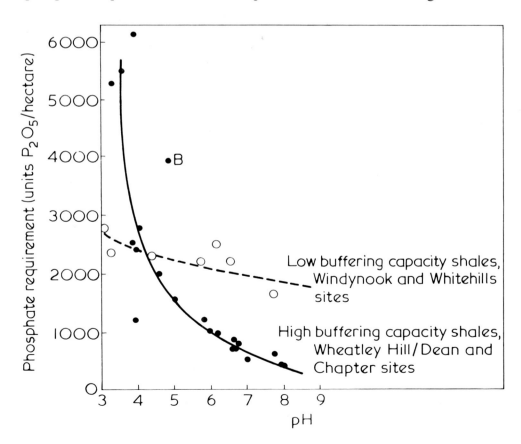

Figure 46. Effect of acidification on the phosphate requirement of black shales.

shale is necessary; unfortunately raising the soil pH does not reduce the soil's ability to fix phosphate. Raising the pH up to 3.0, or higher, precipitates soluble iron as a hydroxide. When iron is in solution as at pH values below 3.0 there would be an ionic interaction between iron and phosphate. In this kind of system the total precipitation of phosphate would cause an even greater phosphate deficit than is caused by the more usual adsorption onto a ferric hydroxide surface layer which happens at pH values above 3.0. Liming very acid shales up to pH 3.0 therefore slightly reduces phosphate requirements but once the pH is above 3.0 the adsorptive surface is formed and further increases in pH have little effect on the shale's phosphate status.

The more shale is broken down by physical weathering the larger is its surface area per unit weight; as phosphate adsorption is a surface phenomenon phosphate requirements are therefore influenced by the degree of weathering experienced by the sample. Figure 47 shows this relationship for samples of colliery shale taken from the Thrislington site in Co. Durham. The percentage of material less than 2 mm in diameter in the bulk sample is a good indication of the extent of physical weathering. Plotted against this index is the phosphate requirement of the less than 2 mm diameter fraction. Clearly there are two systems operating, depending on whether the sample came from depth as bore-hole material or whether the shale had been exposed at the surface for some time prior to sampling. Such a distinction may be expected. Adsorption is largely by iron hydroxide. In buried material the adsorbent would be a ferrous compound but after atmospheric exposure ferric hydroxide would be the more common adsorbing surface and as such it would fix greater amounts of phosphate.

It has often been noticed that shale surfaces immediately after regrading soak up large quantities of phosphate without achieving a stable equilibrium. This process of increasing P demand is to be expected from the data in Figure 47. If, for example, regrading newly exposed shale containing 30% less than 2 mm material, the P requirement would be $30\% \times 494$ units P_2O_5/hectare = 148 units P_2O_5/ha. After atmospheric exposure and adjustment to surface conditions the same material would have a P requirement of $30\% \times 1566 = 494$ units P_2O_5/ha. Should physical weathering increase the 2 mm diameter fraction of the soil to 40% the P requirement would be $40\% \times 2223 = 889$ units P_2O_5/ha.

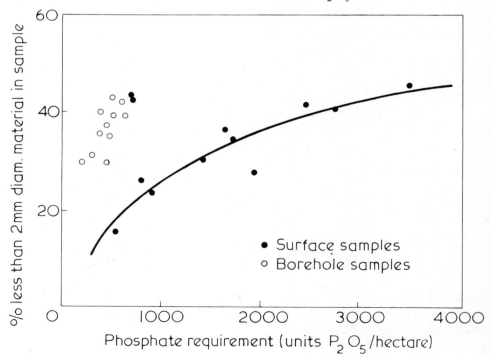

Figure 47. Effect of physical weathering on the phosphate requirement of black shales.

Table 8 P × K × 10 shale soils factorial trial: first harvest leaf dry weight yields (g dry matter/pot). Soil type phosphate response interaction.

Soil	Type	P_0 (g)	P_1 (g)	Phosphate response (g)
NMN		0.205	0.952	0.747
NFS/2	Black	0.203	1.482	1.278
BNF/2	shales	0.162	0.922	0.760
BBS		0.302	1.167	0.865
RNB		0.203	1.105	0.902
SRS		0.780	2.303	1.523
BSF/4	Red	0.332	1.515	1.183
BRU	shales	0.667	1.670	1.003
RNF/4		0.407	0.867	0.460
BRS		0.467	1.855	1.388

Two samples of shale collected as supposedly surface material appear in the cluster of borehole points in the figure. Site records indicated recent regrading in the area from which these two samples were taken. This suggests that adjustment of shale to surface conditions requires a period measured in months rather than days or weeks. This process was not monitored on the Thrislington site as later analyses used the sodium bicarbonate extraction technique for estimating available P rather than adsorption isotherms. On another site monitored during the year following regrading, phosphate requirements of the new surface increased $2\frac{1}{2}$ to $3\frac{1}{2}$ fold. During this period there was no change in pH.

Phosphorus is a component of all biological genetic material; it also plays a role in energy metabolism. Without adequate supplies of phosphate, plant cell division (and therefore growth) is impaired. When phosphate is supplied to plants on P-deficient soils there are considerable responses in growth and vigour. Table 8 shows leaf dry matter weights of S24 ryegrass in response to a seedbed application equivalent to 370 units P_2O_5/hectare. These data were obtained in the same P × K × 10 shale soils factorial greenhouse trials quoted in Table 8. All responses to phosphate were statistically significant at the 5% probability level or higher. Of the ten soils treated the phosphate application was optimal probably only in one case (SRS). In some cases 370 units P_2O_5/hectare represents too little phosphate; with other shales it was too much.

Not only does phosphate influence leaf growth, it also promotes root growth. At the end of the P × K × 10 shale soils trial the root systems were very carefully removed from each pot, washed, dried and weighed. Under trial conditions the phosphate application had increased the root systems three and a half fold, this being a statistically significant response ($P = 0.05$). In Table 9 mean root system weights are quoted as all ten soils behaved similarly, there being no significant differences between their individual responses.

There are several benefits gained by increasing the size and vigour of the root systems. A greater volume of soil is explored by the roots so uptake of other nutrients is increased. Richardson and Greenwood (1967) showed that at 250–300 mm (10–12 in) depth there is adequate available moisture for plants throughout the summer even on the driest parts of

Table 9 Response of S24 ryegrass root systems to 370 units P_2O_5/ha applied to the seedbed.

Phosphate level	Mean root weight (g/pot)
P_0 (Nil)	0.126
P_1 (370 units P_2O_5/ha)	0.401

pit heaps. Applying phosphate to depth in the seedbed would encourage roots to reach this depth and ensure their survival even during dry spells. Increased root systems tend to encourage improved soil structures; therefore the moisture and oxygen flow through the soil more easily and allow the roots to grow even more: a beneficial cycle in fact. Dead organic material, derived from a vigorous root system, also helps to improve soil structure. As well as this it holds plant nutrients in an organic form and releases them slowly, this being an important contribution to a long-term nutrient cycle in the soil. For trees a deeper and more vigorous root system means all those advantages but also a reduced danger of windblow as the trees become mature.

Nitrogen status

Colliery shale can supply small quantities of nitrogen to plants, thus supplementing nitrogen contained in the incident rainfall. Cornwell and Stone (1968) noticed that more nitrogen is available in acid rather than neutral shales and that the net supply is adequate for some tree species such as *Betula populifera*. This may be so but it is also obvious that shale soils are unable to supply productive grassland with anything like the quantity of nitrogen required. Under British conditions a highly productive sward needs about 1250 units N/hectare per season. In a mature brown earth soil mineralization of organic matter would yield up to about 375 units N/hectare and clover in the sward could contribute a similar quantity of nitrogen. Maximum yields would be obtained by the addition of about 500 units N/hectare as a nitrogenous fertilizer. In new shale soils nitrogen resulting from the mineralization of organic material is negligible and there appears to be little transference of N from clover to grass although data are scarce on this point. This means that the seasonal nitrogen deficit on shale soils is about 1250 units N/hectare. This figure does not take into account any differences in efficiency of utilization of nitrogen. Most probably nitrogen uptake by plants is less efficient on shale soils so the requirement for N is even higher than 1250 units/hectare per season. As the shale soil matures and the sward becomes more established both above and below ground, the nitrogen requirement will fall but in the initial years of management it is frequently underrated.

Nitrogen is a component of protein and is therefore fundamentally important to plants. In grass a nitrogen deficiency is indicated by an abnormally pale green colour of the leaves; in acute cases the leaves will be yellow. Growth is stunted and the plant will tend to go to seed earlier than normal.

Plants can take up nitrogen either as the nitrate ion (NO_3^-) or as an ammonium ion (NH_4^+). To maintain electrostatic neutrality if the plant takes up a nitrate ion it must either exude another anion or also take up a cation. The converse situation holds with the uptake of an ammonium ion. Not surprisingly it has been shown that on supplying ammonium nitrogen to a plant the pH falls in the soil immediately round the root, because the root exudes H^+ ions while absorbing NH_4^+ ions. Similarly when supplied with NO_3^- nitrogen the roots exude bicarbonate ions; these have the effect of raising the pH of the soil immediately round the root (Riley and Barber, 1969).

The data quoted in Table 10 were obtained in a greenhouse trial reported by Doubleday (1971b) in which an acid colliery shale soil from the Dean and Chapter Colliery, Co. Durham, was limed to three levels. Two crops and the two nitrogen forms were used in the factorial trial. The results were analysed statistically; *** indicates very highly significant ($P = 0.001$) differences in interface pH according to whether nitrogen was applied as nitrate or ammonium,** indicates highly significant differences ($P = 0.01$).

Raising the pH of a soil containing fixed phosphate has the effect of loosening the bonds on the phosphate; a little P becomes available to

Table 10 Root/soil interface pH values in a shale soil as influenced by the form of nitrogen fertilizer (Doubleday 1974).

Seedbed pH	Lolium perenne		Brassica oleracea	
	$NO_3^- N$	$NH_4^+ N$	$NO_3^- N$	$NH_4^+ N$
7.9	6.8	6.4	6.4	6.2
4.9	5.2***	4.1	5.0**	4.1
4.4	4.8***	3.8	4.5	4.0

the plant. Bicarbonate ions have an ability to exchange positions with fixed phosphate ions so that as the bicarbonate is fixed, phosphate becomes available to plants. Both these systems, elevated pH and introduction of bicarbonate, occur when the plant takes up nitrate anions. Where phosphate supply is the factor limiting plant growth, a supply of $NO_3^- N$ rather than $NH_4^+ N$ will ease the problem.

Yields of ryegrass and rape in the trial quoted were measured and are given in Table 11. The same total amount of nitrogen was applied (165 kg N/hectare); only the form differed as ammonium or nitrate.

In most cases the yields of nitrate-fed plants were significantly higher than the yields of ammonium-fed plants; in no case was the yield significantly lower. The phosphate uptake by the plants was also measured and a similar pattern was established; where there was a significantly higher yield there was also a significantly higher phosphate content of the leaves and also a higher total phosphate uptake. But this was probably the cause not the effect; nitrate nitrogen helped the plant to obtain more phosphate from the soil, therefore the plant grew more vigorously.

Micro-nutrient status

Webb and Atkinson (1965), Thornton *et al.* (1966) and Webb *et al.* (1968) studied the micro-nutrient status of Viséan and Namurian shales with particular relevance to the occurrence of bovine hypocuprosis in cattle-grazing pastures on these shales. Because of the related nature of colliery shales, interest has been shown in the trace-element uptake by grass on reclaimed pit heap sites. Samples of grass/legume swards growing directly on shale at the Roddymoor site in Co. Durham and the West Sleekburn site in Northumberland, have been analysed for cobalt, nickel, molydenum, iron, lead, zinc, tin, vanadium, titanium, chromium, copper, manganese, barium, strontium, aluminium, boron and silicon. Levels of each element were normal for grass fodder; no deficiencies or excesses have yet been identified. The swards were one to three years old at the time of analysis and although compound fertilizer had been applied, there had been no liming.

Doubleday (1971a) reported a greenhouse pot trial with four colliery shale soils where liming had anomalous effects. In one soil only (Figure 48) was a normal phosphate response curve obtained; in the other three soils (an example is shown in Figure 49) liming depressed yields. Such depres-

Table 11 Mean yields (g dry matter/pot) of ryegrass and rape in response to nitrogen given as nitrate or ammonium (Doubleday 1974).

Seedbed pH	Lolium perenne		Brassica oleracea	
	$NO_3^- N$	$NH_4^+ N$	$NO_3^- N$	$NH_4^+ N$
7.9	1.610	1.243	2.480	2.560
4.9	1.407	1.270	2.423	1.970
4.4	1.423	1.113	1.970	1.290

Minimum significant difference 0.255 g ($P = 0.05$).

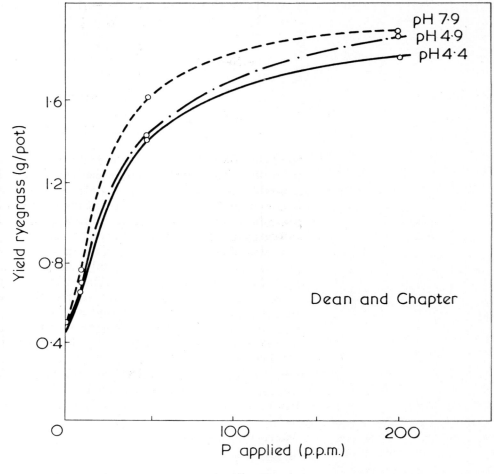

Figure 48. Relationship between ryegrass yield, P applied and seedbed pH.

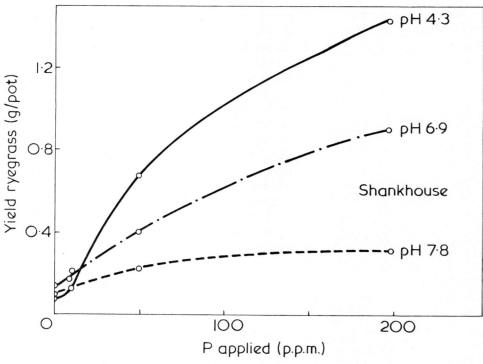

Figure 49. Relationship between ryegrass yield, P applied and seedbed pH.

sions usually occur because of induced micro-nutrient imbalances. Of the following trace elements applied singly as foliar sprays, boron, zinc, copper, manganese and iron, only iron gave a positive response. Boron, zinc, copper and manganese were applied in addition to the iron spray but with no extra effect. The yield increases on the two shale soils tested ranged from 27.4% to 119.4%; both responses were statistically significant at the 5% probability level or higher.

Profile development

Profile development in colliery shale is influenced by several factors. If there is no pyrite present in the shale, weathering will be mostly physical leading to a higher proportion of small particles of shale at the surface while at depth coarse rock fragments will be dominant. If there are both pyrite and carbonate minerals present in roughly balancing quantities, not only will there be physical weathering but amorphous ferric hydroxide will be formed in one horizon and quantities of gypsum will form where the two minerals interact. If iron pyrite predominates, a profile will develop such as the example shown in Figure 42 from the Dean and Chapter Colliery site, Co. Durham. This profile developed before reclamation and several similar profiles have been identified at other pit heap sites. For such development to occur there must be a free movement of air and moisture through the profile; this means the shale must be moderately hard so that spaces between rock fragments are preserved. Profile development like this does not take place after shale has been regraded as there is such limited movement of air and moisture.

Tipping on the Dean and Chapter site was completed ten years before the profile was examined. Chemical weathering did not extend more than 520 mm (20 in) below the surface but at the Maria Colliery site in the County of Tyne and Wear where tipping finished about 1923 weathering had reached a depth of 2.6 metres (8.5 ft).

The Dean and Chapter profile is a useful illustration of the processes of soil development in acid shale.

Using a 2 mm sieve to separate soil particles from rock and stone size particles the extent of physical weathering is shown by the data in Table 12. Physical weathering is caused by alternating cycles of heating and cooling, freezing and thawing and wetting and drying. Such agencies are most intense near the surface; hence there is a crust of weathering quite distinct from less weathered material which does not dry out, seldom freezes and hence cannot complete the cycles. In horizons 1 and 2 the intense acid probably also softens the shale and facilitates breakdown.

When shale breaks down it releases fine sand, silt and clay size fractions as described in section 2.2. While regraded colliery sites do not show such distinctive horizon development as shown in Figure 42, there is a direct breakdown into these particle size fractions so that a soil such as a rock dominant silt loam develops. In such soils, structure tends to be poorly developed and difficult to maintain.

Measurements of salinity down the Dean and Chapter profile are given in Table 13. Salinity was estimated by measuring electrical conductivity of the saturated moisture extract of the less than 2 mm diameter fraction of the sample. Results are quoted as Siemens/metre; at values above about 0.5 S/m a grass legume sward can show damage which is first noticed as a premature onset of drought symptoms. In this soil, salinity

Table 12 Physical weathering in the Dean and Chapter profile.

Horizon depth (mm)	2 mm material (%)
0–100	71.8
100–220	75.3
220–370	15.5
370–520	15.9
520–880 +	17.4

Table 13 Salinity in the Dean and Chapter profile.

Horizon depth (mm)	Electrical conductivity of the saturated moisture extract (S/m)
0–100	0.31
100–220	0.70
220–370	0.46
370–520	0.40
520–880 +	0.34

was caused by calcium sulphate, magnesium sulphate and in the 100–220 mm (4–9 in) depth horizon also by iron and manganese.

Problems of salinity are often associated with newly regraded pit heaps. Cutting into a pit heap can expose shale which is slightly or moderately saline. If these earthworks are completed in the spring, exposure of the new surface is followed by a period during which evaporation of moisture into the atmosphere exceeds rainfall. During the net upward movement of moisture through the shale to the surface, salts are carried to the ground surface and left there when the soil moisture evaporates away. Salt enrichment at the surface can cause severe salinity problems where a spring seeding operation is attempted. Figure 50 shows how salinity levels fluctuated at the surface of the Roddymoor, Co. Durham pit heap reclamation site after regrading. The degree of salinity experienced depended not only on net moisture movement but also aspect and depth of shale and hence volume of saline moisture subject to evaporation.

Immediately after regrading, the distribution of salinity at the surface of the Roddymoor site varied from 4% of the site being non-saline to

Figure 50. Variation of salinity with water movement at Roddymoor, March–November 1968. Net moisture figures based on data supplied by the Meteorological Office and the MAAF (private communications).

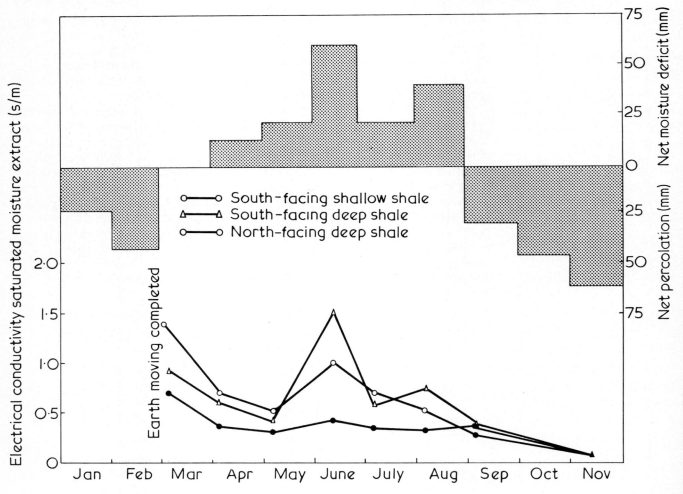

12% of the site being very strongly saline. About 83% of the site was too saline to sow with grass during the spring and early summer. Reference to Figure 50 indicates that in September salinity fell to safe levels and seeding was then undertaken.

Salinity can reduce the percentage germination of a crop to zero although different crops have different tolerances to salinity. Damage to plants is usually by making it more difficult for plants to absorb moisture from the soil. In severe cases moisture is pulled out of plants into the soil; while this is unusual the premature onset of drought symptoms is common. Plants become dehydrated, stop growing, leaves and stems become thin and brittle. To a point these symptoms are reversible, but if they are sufficiently severe and prolonged the plant will die.

It is unusual for salinity to have any direct effect on grazing animals. The sward becomes less nutritious so that weight gains by fattening animals would be minimal. In one instance some evidence points to a direct link between salinity and animal health. During a dry summer spell sheep were allowed to overgraze a pasture sown directly into colliery shale. So close was their grazing that grass was grazed down to the base of the stem and no doubt contact was made at times with the 'soil' surface. During this period of drought the ground surface became enriched in salts brought up to the surface as the soil moisture evaporated away. Scouring was observed in many sheep; at best the sheep did not increase in weight, at worst the scouring was fatal. Pine, a cobalt imbalance and worms were eliminated as possible causes of the trouble. The possibility remains that salts accumulating at the soil surface and round the base of grass plants may have contributed to the problem, as the salts were largely magnesium sulphate—'Epsom salts'.

Measurements of acidity down the ungraded Dean and Chapter profile are given in Table 14.

The lowest pH values are obtained not in the surface horizon but at 100–220 mm (4–9 in) depth. To produce acidity iron pyrite must be supplied with oxygen and moisture. The ground surface frequently dries out, but at depth there is permanent moisture. Weathering of pyrite occurs most rapidly where there is both permanent moisture and greatest access to oxygen. Below 220 mm the pH value rose steadily, and reached 7.4 at 520–880 mm (20–35 in) depth. At 18 m (60 ft) depth in the spoil dump the pH was 7.5. Site records indicated that tipping had ceased at the point of sampling ten years previously; hence the pH value had fallen at the average rate of 0.5 unit per year. On another site in Co. Durham a fall of 2.5 units over two years was observed. Falls in pH values of 3.0 units per year have been recorded in the soft mudstone colliery discard of West Yorkshire (see p. 151).

The rates at which pH values change in colliery shale are unlikely to be uniform. Assuming for simplicity that the rate of acid production from pyrite is uniform irrespective of pH, when a shale is first exposed, any acid present reacts with the carbonate minerals in the shale. During this process the pH value does not fall, but once the reaction has proceeded as far as

Table 14 pH values and lime requirements down the Dean and Chapter profile.

Horizon depth (mm)	pH	Lime requirements (tonnes limestone/ha)	
		2 mm fraction	Total sample
0–100	3.7	6.2	4.5
100–220	2.5	30.0	22.5
220–370	4.4	7.5	1.3
370–520	5.4	1.3	0.3
520–880 +	7.4	0.0	0.0

it can, the pH then falls. Between pH 5.5 and 4.5 some of the clay minerals start to break down and again a considerable quantity of acid is consumed without the pH value changing greatly. Once below this barrier the pH may again fall relatively freely although other geochemical constraints restrict the value falling much below 1.8 as measured in a 1 : 2.5 soil : water suspension.

Not only do pH values fall at irregular rates but the reverse is equally true during liming. Reactions take place within set pH ranges which, until completed, hold the pH steady. At pH 3.0–3.5 iron is precipitated as a hydroxide; at pH 4.0–4.5 aluminium is precipitated as a hydroxy-aluminium monomer which undergoes polymerization at about pH 5.6.

Acidity in a pit heap soil may be caused by weathering of iron pyrite *in situ*. Less commonly, pyrite weathers well inside the dump and acidity is brought to the ground surface by movements of ground water. There may be areas associated with spring lines around the base of the spoil dump where acidity is extreme and virtually incurable. Limestone may be added to neutralize the acidity in the soil at one moment but a fresh supply of acid groundwater will maintain the pH at its original value. In this case drainage must be installed before abortive dressing of limestone causes the soil to set solid with gypsum, this being produced when a calcium limestone is in contact with sulphuric acid. Not only are these problem areas found associated with spring lines but similar phenomena may occur on some south- and west-facing slopes. Excessive evaporation may cause a supply of acid ground water to reach the soil surface and once again acidify a previously limed area.

For grassland, pH values of 6.2 to 6.8 are optimal, and for woodland soils the pH should have values within the range 5.0 to 6.0. These values apply to natural and mature soils. There is some evidence that liming much over 5.5 on some colliery shale soils seriously reduces the yield of grass, at least during the early years of establishment. Over-liming must be avoided on any shale soil and wherever possible no shale with a high potential acidity should be left at the surface of a reclaimed site. After applying 50 tonnes/hectare (20 tonnes/acre) of limestone the material should be covered with soil material to a depth of 300 mm (12 in), or preferably more.

In practice it is almost impossible to achieve and maintain a satisfactory plant cover over colliery spoil which produces large quantities of acid. Any weathered shale which exhibits pH values below 4.0 must be regarded as suspect, and probably better avoided as a surface-covering material.

Phosphate requirements vary largely according to the total adsorbing surface area of the soil and the extent to which this surface area is covered with a skin of aluminium and iron hydroxides. The more weathered chemically and physically the spoil is, the greater the phosphate demand, and this is greatly accentuated by the presence of iron pyrite in the shale. Table 15 gives the phosphate requirements down the Dean and Chapter profile. In the horizon at 100–220 mm (4–9 in) depth there has been the

Table 15 Phosphate requirements, Dean and Chapter profile.

| Horizon depth (mm) | Phosphate requirement (units P_2O_5/ha) | |
	2 mm fraction	Complete sample
0–100	2248	1613
100–220	4408	3394
220–370	5367	832
370–520	3100	494
520–880	646	113

greatest physical breakdown and also the most intense weathering of iron pyrite; here also the shale has the greatest phosphate demand.

On a regraded colliery site, the same principles apply. If the shale becomes acid the phosphate demand will increase very greatly. Liming does not substantially decrease the demand because once the adsorbing surface is formed by acid weathering, liming only stabilizes it. Whether or not the shale becomes acid, it will break down physically and thus cause the P requirement to increase. It is therefore most important to monitor a site carefully in the years following the initial cultivation as the availability of phosphate to plants growing on shale can fall rapidly. Should this be allowed to proceed too far crop yields will fall and a point will be reached where productive species such as *Lolium* will give way to less productive species such as *Agrostis* and *Festuca* which can survive rather better in low-nutrient conditions.

In the Dean and Chapter profile weathering of iron pyrite yielded two minerals whose distribution in the profile is pH-dependent. Jarosite is a lemon yellow powdery mineral which exists when the micro-environment has a pH of 3.0 or below. It was found at 220–370 mm (9–15 in) depth though it may be found at depths of 1 m (3 ft) or more in older profiles. Jarosite probably does not have much effect on the growth of vegetation. It is formed in a process which acts as a 'sink' for labile potassium in the spoil but even so there is probably sufficient K still available to plants to sustain as high a level of growth as the supply of other nutrients allows. Below jarosite in the Dean and Chapter profile there was an accumulation of amorphous ferric hydroxide formed by the decay of jarosite in an environment where the pH was too high. Amorphous ferric hydroxide is important as it fixes large quantities of phosphate; unfortunately at this depth there is little possibility of ameliorating the situation.

5.3 Chemically fertile materials

It is often found that even though the chemical fertility of reclaimed soils may be restored relatively easily, there are still problems in cultivation and in establishing and maintaining vegetation. Such difficulties are frequently associated with poor soil physical conditions, the main factor being the structural state of the soil. Structure is a description of the manner in which the individual particles constituting the soil are aggregated to form 'clods' of varying shape and size. In the absence of structure most soils except those with a high content of coarse sand will become 'massive', the spaces between the larger particles being filled by smaller ones. This results in poor aeration and drainage and offers a physical barrier to root penetration. The root system of a plant needs moisture, oxygen and space to grow in if it is to develop fully. In growing, the roots produce CO_2 which must be removed before it reaches a toxic concentration. This implies that there must be a system of interconnected air-filled channels reaching the surface of the soil in which gaseous diffusion can occur. Such channels, which exist between the soil aggregates, also provide space for the roots to develop. The aggregates themselves contain much smaller spaces which hold water by capillarity and provide most of the water which the plant requires. So an ideal soil structure consists of granular units with a size of about 5 mm (0.2 in) and this is the sort of structure generally found under established grassland.

Figure 51 shows the profile of a typical grassland soil and Figure 52 is a magnified thin section showing its granular structure. In such a soil the roots are able to establish contact with a large volume of soil and can utilize fully the nutrients and moisture which it contains. The relatively large spaces between the structural units are also important because they allow rainfall to enter the soil readily and replenish the finer pores while the excess water can drain away to either the subsoil or land drains. The

Figure 51. Soil profile
developed under permanent
pasture on gault clay near
Wye, Kent (courtesy
G.P. Askew).

stability of the structure when subjected to mechanical stress, especially
when wet, is of considerable importance. Grassland soils seem to possess
the most stable structure and such stability may remain for a few years
after ploughing out, but as the organic matter content inevitably decreases
under arable usage, and its composition changes, the stability will
decrease. The granular structure is gradually broken down and compaction
occurs due to pressing together of the unstable granules and the filling of
larger pores by fine material. The impact of raindrops on the exposed
soil surface can also destroy the structure, washing fine material into the
larger pores to form a surface capping or pan with a low permeability.
This will cause increased surface run-off, reducing the amount of water
reaching the rooting zone with the added possibility of erosion. The
surface pan can cause reduced germination in many crops by physically
hindering seedling emergence. A pan may also form at the base of the
plough layer because of shearing and compaction of wet soil by the plough
sole. This is often a serious problem resulting in impeded drainage and
reduced rooting depth.

   Soils formed from shales on reclaimed sites are often particularly
difficult. The shale quickly weathers physically to yield material with a
high content of fine sand, silt and clay (Doubleday 1972) and virtually
no humified organic matter (see pp. 156–157). In such material the effects

Figure 52. Thin section of a topsoil developed under permanent pasture.

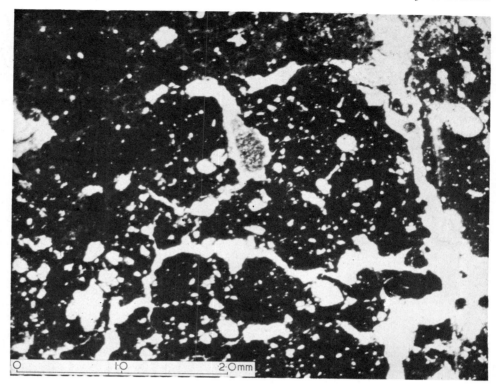

of deep cultivations aimed at loosening the soil quickly disappear and it becomes structureless, compacted and more or less impermeable. Figures 53 and 54 show the profile of a shale soil and a thin section of the topsoil; the contrast with Figures 51 and 52 is very marked. The only practical way of creating a favourable structure in such material is probably by the incorporation of rotting organic material and putting it down to grass with adequate and continuing dressings of fertilizers (see p. 156). Much research is at present being carried out to solve this problem.

6 Cultivation of materials on reclamation sites

Almost every known modern cultivation technique is used in reclamation. The choice of a particular sequence of operations depends on the material involved, constraints imposed by the nature of the site, the end result required, and by finance available (see p. 164).

Reclamation as it is envisaged on the heavy metal ore tips of mid- and north Wales, and on the china clay dumps in Devon and Cornwall, will probably receive a basic 'cosmetic' treatment which contrasts with the thoroughness of the cultivations of regraded pit heaps.

The reclamation of the Welsh ore tips is set within a situation where surrounding land prices are often low; the tips are located in areas of low population to which there are relatively few visitors or tourists. Apart from some damage to immediately surrounding farmland and contamination of certain streams and small rivers which may reduce their value as sources of drinking water, the presence of these tips does not greatly influence the economic wellbeing of the region. Reclamation techniques have to be cheap and cannot involve major regrading or the importation of adequate quantities of soil to cover the toxic spoil. A possible technique in such circumstances would involve the collection of seed of indigenous grasses which have a tolerance to the toxic nature of the spoil. A seed multiplication programme would then be undertaken on site or in circumstances where the seed would not lose its specific tolerance characteristics. Using commercially available seed of the same species as a diluent, the

Figure 53. Profile of a
regraded shale soil showing
complete lack of soil
structure; West Sleekburn,
Northumberland.

tolerant seed would then be broadcast over the area to be reclaimed and
such cultivation techniques as possible used to increase the germination
and survival rates of the grass. Whether applied by hand or machine,
fertilizer would be essential to nurse the sward which, if allowed to
complete its life cycle, would provide a second generation of seed to
thicken up the ground cover.

Hydroseeding seems the most likely technique to be used on china clay
dumps. With some exceptions it does not appear to be the general policy
of the china clay industry to form or mould the spoil heaps it creates to
a landform with slopes gentle enough for vehicles to travel on. While
hydroseeding is a valid technique it has limitations. Only a limited quantity
of soluble fertilizer can be placed in the slurry with the seed prior to
application. Too much fertilizer will kill the seed and the amount of
fertilizer which can safely be included in the hydroseed mixture may not
be sufficient for the soil onto which the slurry will be applied. Hydroseeding is an expensive technique and once applied there is a reluctance on
the part of the user to apply any further quantities of fertilizer even when
these are necessary to keep the vegetation alive (Figure 55).

The one possibility which could ease the situation is the use of slow-
release fertilizers which, releasing a complete suite of plant nutrients,
allow the ground cover to develop a nutrient cycle. As yet no such

Figure 54. Thin section of topsoil developed under grass on reclaimed colliery shale after three years.

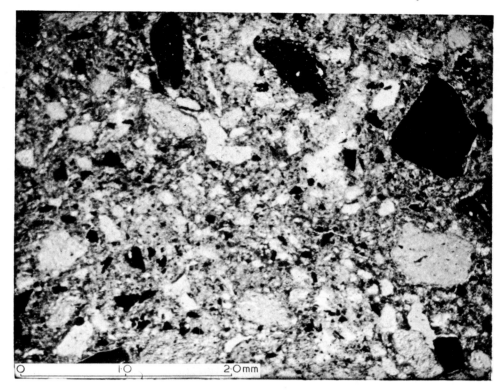

materials are available although the fertilizer industry has made some effort along these lines. Such materials as are available generally have a lifespan of one season or less whereas a fertilizer which releases its nutrients over several seasons is really necessary.

Contracts for the cultivation of British opencast sites are designed and supervised by the Ministry of Agriculture, Fisheries and Food. Usually the work is executed to a very high standard of finish and because of the consistent nature of the work and a steady demand contracts have tended to go to a relatively small group of specialized and highly skilled agricultural contractors.

Figure 55. Hydroseeding on a china clay waste dump showing the effects of neglected management.

Finance is no problem with opencast work for the simple reason that it is not undertaken unless the operation will be profitable, including the cost of reinstatement. Sites are of finite size and usually have a life span of only a few years. Quantities of overburden to be moved and coal to be sold are known in advance, therefore the economics can be calculated with fair accuracy for the relatively short life span of an opencast site. The earthmoving contract is separate from the cultivation contract so that it is finished and when cultivation starts no other works interfere.

Works begin with deep cultivation and stone picking on the subsoil and topsoil in turn, these being replaced by statutory obligation. Further works would be based on the following sequence or one similar.

Plough	If appropriate
Remove stones	
Disc	Three passes or one pass with a triple K and disc twice
Cambridge roll	One pass
Disc	One pass
Remove stones	
Harrow	Two passes
Spread fertilizer	502 kg/ha (4 cwt/acre) or as appropriate
Harrow	One pass
Remove stones	
Harrow	One pass
Cambridge roll	One pass
Sow seed	30.3 kg/ha (27 lb/acre) or as appropriate
Harrow	One pass
Roll	Two passes

Seed is usually supplied by the Ministry of Agriculture who purchase it in bulk.

The specification listed above relates to reinstatement of an opencast site where the surface covering is a heavy glacial till. This is typical of very many opencast sites but if the soil were lighter in texture rather less cultivation might be required. The sequence in full is very adequate to produce a tilth, possibly even too exhaustive. There is sometimes a tendency to overcultivate and in dry conditions to produce a very powdery tilth which the nineteen passes per acre specified roll down to a dense structureless seedbed. Should a heavy rainstorm saturate the site, upon subsequent drying out the ground becomes caked solid and less than ideal for seeds to germinate.

The Opencast Executive relinquish responsibility for the establishment of a sward about five years after the initial cultivations. Usually after three years the ground will have experienced any settlement likely to occur and a land drainage system is then installed. The initial sward is designed as a vigorous short-term ley and is ploughed in when the drainage works are completed. A long ley is then established which is maintained usually for a further six or seven years when an arable use might become possible.

For several reasons the problems of reclaiming colliery spoil dumps are more difficult. There is no profit set aside for reinstatement works; the total cost is borne by rate- and taxpayers and therefore works have to be carried out as cheaply as possible and to be seen so. The material involved can be much more difficult. The soils on opencast sites have already weathered for a minimum of 12 000 years prior to cultivation and are inherently fertile. Shale on pit heap sites is raw geological material and sometimes inherently toxic. The Opencast Executive work on a five years establishment programme for each site including a first- and second-generation sward. In some circumstances in pit-heap reclamation, grants covering up to 100% of the management costs for three years after seeding can be obtained but usually for only one year. Unless it could be shown that the first sward had utterly failed grant would be most unlikely for a second-generation sward.

Pit-heap reclamation starts with more difficult material, and must achieve a successful result cheaply in a shorter time than opencast restoration. Contractually there are difficulties. Cultivation is usually undertaken in subcontracts to the main earthmoving contractor. Frequently the main contractor releases fragmented areas for cultivation and then runs his heavy traffic across them during and after cultivation. Often he has little understanding or sympathy for the problems facing the cultivation subcontractor and his supervision is nominal. While some sites are large, e.g. the 275 ha (680 acre) reclamation site at Ashington, Northumberland, most sites are much smaller and can be tackled by relatively small cultivation contractors. Many 'fly-by-night' cultivation contractors have sought work in pit-heap reclamation with the result that contract rates have sometimes been excessively low. The skilled specialist may be priced out of the market, leaving the employing authority the unenviable task of ensuring the workmanship still meets specification. This is achieved only by constant supervision to prevent the contractor taking short cuts. In the end the contractor in meeting the specification makes a loss and does not seek more work, but there always seems to be another similar outfit ready to take his place.

Where a bare shale surface is to be cultivated most local authorities specify that the first operation shall be rooting to a depth (usually) of 600 mm (24 in) with the tines set at 600 mm intervals. Sometimes a second pass at an angle to the first pass is also specified. The purpose of this operation is to alleviate compaction and to expose any cables or wire and sizeable pieces of metal, wood or stone within the depth which might be attained by future cultivation or drainage works.

Stones or other hard objects exceeding 150 mm (6 in) in any dimension are then removed and buried, usually in a hole dug somewhere on site. Some hard objects such as fused blocks of red shale may be quite large and leave significant holes in the ground surface after removal. It then becomes necessary to lightly grade the surface. Because the equipment required for rooting (see Figure 56) and light grading is more likely to be used by a civil engineering contractor rather than an agricultural contractor, many authorities include these three operations within the main contract. Other authorities see these operations as within the cultivation sequence and begin the cultivation subcontract, or contract, with them.

Ground limestone is usually specified as having a total neutralizing value (TNV) of 50 or higher, and ground to have at least 40% volume passing a 100-mesh screen. Basic slag is specified to have a citric acid soluble phosphate (P_2O_5) content of 11–13%. Both these materials where required should be worked as deeply as possible into the shale surface and therefore some authorities require their application before the rooting. If not applied then they should be applied no later than this point in the sequence.

Further cultivation works vary from local authority to local authority and from consultant to consultant. One technique now in use is to specify a 'pool' of operations from which sequences of operations can be assembled to cope with different land uses and different standards of finish. A typical 'pool' would be:

Figure 56. A le tourneau ripping a compacted 'fill' area after regrading.

Operation

1 Apply ground limestone at a rate not exceeding 10 tonnes/ha (4 tonnes/acre).

2 Apply basic slag at a rate not exceeding 2.5 tonnes/ha (1 tonne/acre).

3 Chisel plough to a depth of not less than 150 mm (6 in); repeat at 30° to the first pass.

4 Disc to a depth of 100 mm (4 in).

5 Rotavate to 100 mm depth or power harrow to 100 mm depth.

6 Remove all stones, bricks, wire, wood or other hard objects exceeding 50 mm (2 in) in any dimension. Cables and wire shall if possible be pulled out. If this is not possible they shall be cut off at least 250 mm (10 in) below ground level.

7 Scrub to leave the ground surface with true and even grades. This operation shall be undertaken only during dry ground conditions.

8 Chain harrow and Cambridge roll until a firm fine tilth is obtained.

9 Spring tine harrow (Triple K or equivalent) and Cambridge roll until a firm fine seedbed is obtained.

10 Spread fertilizer at a rate not exceeding 0.5 tonne/ha (0.2 tonne/acre).

11 Light harrow.

12 Supply and broadcast the seed mixture as specified for the area. The seed shall be applied in two passes, the second at right angles to the first, half the seed being spread in each pass. (If immediately before seeding the tilth of the seedbed has deteriorated further cultivation work must be undertaken.)

13 Cambridge roll.

14 Remove any stones, bricks, wire etc, of greater than 50 mm (2 in) dimension.

Public open space surfaces and agricultural surfaces must have a high standard of finish. The surface must be smooth to allow close cutting or grazing and must be free of any rough or sharp objects likely to cause injury. The sward must be dense and, for pasture, capable of high productivity. The operations required on shale would be: 1 (?), 2,3,6,7,8,10,11,12, 13,14. Shale soils must not be worked under wet conditions; the result would be loss of any tilth and the necessity to start again. Very dry conditions do not interfere with cultivations and there is no reason to delay seeding providing a period of damp weather can be expected in the near future. Considerably more damage is caused by a dry period following germination rather than a dry period during and after seeding. A tilth at this stage would be like that shown in Figure 57.

For aesthetic reasons and for surface stabilization most authorities prefer to establish a sward on future woodland areas. Trials in several areas have shown that grass does compete with newly planted trees to the extent that the survival rate of the trees is significantly depressed. Some local authorities screef or forestry plough to provide a strip of bare ground into which the trees are planted. Usually in combination with screefing the ground is rooted. In either case there is considerable disturbance of the ground surface. The requirements of an area to be tree planted are therefore that the sward should be non-competitive and in

Figure 57. A seed bed on colliery discard ready for sowing a pasture sward.

view of later disturbance the surface finish need not be to a high standard. For a woodland area on shale the cultivation sequence should be: 1(?), 2,3,8,10,11,12,13. The expensive item of stone picking is omitted, though objects exceeding 150 mm (6 in) in diameter will have been removed previously by the main contractor. Undoubtedly the surface will be rougher (Figure 58), but in this circumstance it is not important. Grass can be cut to 100 mm (4 in) height instead of 50 mm (2 in) as usually required on public open space or pasture areas.

The cultivation of soils on reclamation sites requires different techniques. Unlike shale surfaces soil cannot be worked successfully during very dry conditions; however, it is possible to cultivate soils under much wetter conditions than shale. To some extent it is possible to switch work from shale to soil or *vice versa* depending on ground conditions.

Soils spread on reclamation sites usually have a history of poor original condition followed by storage in a heap prior to respreading. By the time the material is spread on site its physical condition is very poor and whether it was a topsoil or subsoil it is better regarded as a subsoil and treated accordingly. Topsoil may recover its condition more quickly than subsoil, and one further important difference is that topsoil will contain a burden of weed seeds which will germinate during or after cultivation and must be controlled by subsequent management.

Cultivation of soil material especially when too dry produces a very coarse tilth composed of sub-angular blocky peds. These become smaller and harder until they are undamaged by discs. A roller presses them down firmly and harrows only stir them around again. During these works a tilth is produced in which a continuous covering of clods about the size and hardness of golf balls overlies a compressed layer of dust. If this is seeded the seed is lost in the coarse voids and drops to 20–30 mm (0.8–1.2 in) below the surface level. During any subsequent wet period the surface clods coalesce forming a thick covering over the seed. Species such as *Phleum pratense* and *Agrostis tenuis* hardly germinate and the clovers suffer badly as well. The techniques for cultivating shale, while suitable for shale, tend to produce just this result on soils; therefore a different sequence is suggested, in which it is assumed that a high-quality

Figure 58. A seed bed during preparation on colliery discard prior to seeding for a woodland ground cover.

finish for a pasture or public open space after-use is required: 1(?), 2,3,4,6,7,9,10,11,12,13,14. A technique is needed which does not produce the extremes of clods and dust, lifts damp and friable material from depth up to the surface and which keeps an even distribution of different-size aggregates (Figure 59). For this reason a Triple K or equivalent harrow is used but depending on conditions a rotavator or power harrow is also highly effective but more expensive. Discs are pointless on shale; their value is to cut through friable material. Clods of shale fall apart with a gentle tap but the stones in a shale surface can cause severe damage to such expensive equipment. Their use on soil surfaces is best confined to following chisel ploughing when the ground is moist. With the discs set at an angle soil is thrown up into ridges with troughs between. This undulating surface is not acceptable on public open space areas and is better avoided on pasture areas also. Discing should precede scrubbing and never follow it.

Whether with shale or soil surfaces chisel ploughing to depth is the key operation without which no tilth can be obtained. The aim should be as well structured and coarse a tilth as possible below the surface but a firm fine seedbed on top in which to sow the seed.

Seed and fertilizer can be broadcast separately or drilled together. Most contractors prefer to broadcast those materials as drilling equipment can be punished badly by the tough conditions on reclamation sites. Drilled seed is confined to rows with bare strips between, which take a season or two to fill up. Seed rates need not exceed 40 kg/ha (16 kg/acre), and on woodland areas where a thin sward is acceptable rates down to 25 kg/ha (10 kg/acre) are quite adequate. The seed mixture depends on the after-use (see pp. 161, 163). Pastures based on perennial ryegrass–timothy–white clover are ideal. Current trends in agriculture favour the mid-season and late-heading ryegrasses. Timothy should be the S48 type and both the S100 and wild white clovers are desirable.

Swards for amenity or public open space should be based on a highly tillering type of ryegrass, e.g. S23, but *Agrostis tenuis* (common bent) and *Festuca rubra rubra* (creeping red fescue) should also be included. The small-leafed legumes such as wild white clover and bird's foot trefoil

Figure 59. A seed bed produced on subsoil prior to seeding for a pasture sward.

(Lotus corniculatus) help to make the sward self-sustaining. Crested dog's tail *(Cynosurus cristatus)*, which is a very hard-wearing grass, can also be added where frequent cutting is envisaged.

Woodland areas where trees are planted after screefing or forestry ploughing should be sown with a mixture based on *Agrostis tenuis* and *Festuca rubra rubra* together with wild white clover and bird's foot trefoil to add both visual interest and nitrogen. Where forestry transplants are planted directly into the sward, non-creeping varieties of grasses and legumes should be sown. The fescue should be Chewing's fescue and S100 should be used instead of wild white clover.

Grassland is highly sensitive to management. Poor management gives a poor sward; good management is essential to improve or to preserve a sward in a healthy and productive condition. The rules of good husbandry must be applied in full to grassland on reclamation sites. Furthermore, the better the sward the more efficiently the soil develops below; hence good grassland management is doubly important.

7 Soil fauna populations

M. L. Luff and B. R. Hutson

1 Introduction

Although the most obvious features of any reclaimed industrial site are the topography and vegetation, these in their turn are dependent on other, less obvious, considerations and factors. The vegetation will be influenced by the soil structure and chemistry, which are determined partly by the activities of the animals living in the soil.

Animals which live in the soil range in size from microscopic single-celled organisms, through the familiar earthworms, to mammals such as moles. In numbers some can occur in tens of thousands beneath a single square metre of soil surface. The existence of many is largely unknown to all but specialists in zoology or soil biology, yet they are essential to soil development and plant growth, as well as serving as an indicator of soil conditions.

The value of soil animals has been studied mainly in ordinary soils, rather than in reclaimed land. In this chapter, therefore, an outline of this work is given first (section 1.1). This is followed (section 1.2) by an introduction to the major types or groups of soil animal, and the role that each of these plays in the soil. A brief survey of methods of sampling soil animals in order to assess their abundance is given in section 2. These are applicable to soils generally, but sections 3 and 4 contain more specialized and detailed reviews of the resistance of soil animals to the peculiar environmental conditions of some reclamation sites, and of work on the development of the fauna on such sites. This information has previously been scattered throughout research journals and theses, and is not readily available for comparisons to be made, and conclusions to be drawn. Section 5 considers the special importance of animals as litter decomposers on reclamation sites. In the final section (6), the conclusions from the more specialized sections are brought together in a simplified form; the importance of the soil fauna populations is stressed, and recommendations are made as to how the fauna should be encouraged during reclamation and subsequent management of derelict land.

1.1 The value of soil animals

There are three main benefits resulting from the soil fauna. First, they assist in the breakdown of litter and recycling of plant nutrients. Secondly, they are important in the mixing and aeration of the soil. Thirdly, they can be used as indicators of soil conditions. Each of these will be considered in a little more detail.

The natural supply of organic material to the soil is plant litter. This is the dead or dying parts of plants which have previously grown on the soil. Within the soil the litter, if it is to be of value, must be decomposed further into constituents which can be re-utilized. Such constituents comprise the bulk of the humus in the soil. The nutrients in the litter are

then available again for further plant growth: without such litter decomposition, and recycling of nutrients, soil fertility and plant growth depend
entirely on artificially added components such as fertilizers.

For reclaimed soil to be at least partially self-supporting in organic
material, therefore, litter decomposition must be encouraged as much as
possible. The process of decomposition is summarized by Satchell (1974).
It starts with the action of bacteria and fungi on the ageing material of
the living plant, and continues with the action of similar micro-organisms
within the soil. The soil fauna assists by feeding on the decomposing litter
within the soil. This has two important results. First, there is further
direct assimilation and chemical breakdown of the litter. The proportion
of litter assimilated by animals is not certain, but is probably not less than
10–20% of the litter input on developed soils. The second result of feeding
by soil animals is possibly more important: their influence on the rate
and extent of the microbial and fungal decomposition processes. Many
litter-feeding animals, when feeding, break up or comminute the plant
material into small fragments. This greatly increases the surface area
exposed to microbial attack. It has also been claimed (Macfadyen 1963)
that the soil fauna enhances microbial activity by: transmission of spores;
enrichment of the soil with excreta which support a rich microbial flora;
browsing on ageing colonies of micro-organisms, which stimulates their
growth. Soil animals therefore assist both directly and indirectly in the
decomposition of plant litter.

The second useful role of soil animals is in the mixing and aeration
of the soil. In the absence of such mixing, litter remains on the surface.
There are wide fluctuations in both temperature and moisture within the
surface litter, making the environment within it frequently unsuitable for
the decomposer organisms. The larger soil animals are particularly
important in mixing and aeration of the soil. In mull humus types, for
example, the upper soil horizons are derived largely from earthworm
casts, and the plant detritus is mixed intimately with the mineral soil as a
result of the same animals' activity. A further benefit from such mixing
is that the increased water-holding capacity of the soil, and decreased
evaporation from the buried detritus, result in a stable high humidity,
which is essential to microbial activity (Satchell 1974).

The third benefit to be derived from the soil fauna is a more artificial
one. It results not from some activity carried out by the soil animals, but
from the possibility that they may be used as an artificial measure of the
state of the soil. As the soil is their home they are in intimate contact
with it, dependent on physical and chemical conditions therein, and
might be expected to react at once to any changes in such conditions.
The resulting changes may be in both the numbers or types of animals
present. As is shown in section 1.2, there are many major groups of soil
animal, and each of these may contain hundreds or even thousands of
species which can occur in any particular locality. Exact classification of
the soil fauna is therefore the task of experts. Simple analyses, considering
the ratio of, for example, earthworms to arthropods, often in terms of
weight (or biomass) rather than numbers, can however be used as a ready
measure of the suitability of the soil for the fauna. Dunger (1968) has
prepared such a system for studying the colonization of lignite spoil
heaps in East Germany, and his conclusions are outlined in section 6.
On a smaller scale, Davis (1963) concluded that the soil arthropods of
reclaimed mineral soil were a better indicator of local (within site) soil
conditions than was the macro-vegetation, which was relatively uniform
over each site. The next section gives an outline of the types of soil
animals, with some indication of the roles that each plays in the soil.

1.2 Types of soil animals

Almost all the major groups of terrestrial animals occur occasionally in the
soil, but there are certain types which are to be found regularly in nearly

all soils, often in very large numbers. These make up the bulk of the soil fauna, and are considered in more detail in this section. General accounts of soil zoology are given by Burges and Raw (1967) and Wallwork (1970) among others. The fauna can be classified into taxonomic divisions, or by other factors such as body size, permanence of their soil existence, and types of behaviour such as feeding or locomotion.

The division by size is useful in that it mirrors, to some extent, the grouping of animals into taxa. The categories used here were defined by van der Drift (1951).

Microfauna, body size less than 200 μm. These comprise mainly the single-celled animals, or Protozoa, although the smallest Nematoda and Acari are also included.

Mesofauna, body size 200 μm–2 mm. This section includes the so-called microarthropods, of which there are two important taxa, the Collembola (springtails) and Acari (mites) (Figure 60). Also common are the Nematoda (threadworms).

Macrofauna, body size 2–20 mm (Figure 61). In this group are contained

Figure 60. Soil micro-arthropods on decomposing leaf litter: Collembola (C), Acari (A).

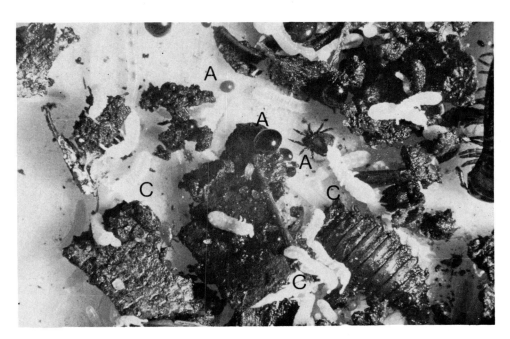

Figure 61. Soil macrofauna: dipterous larvae (D), Enchytraeidae (E), Mollusca (M). The smaller white animals are Collembola.

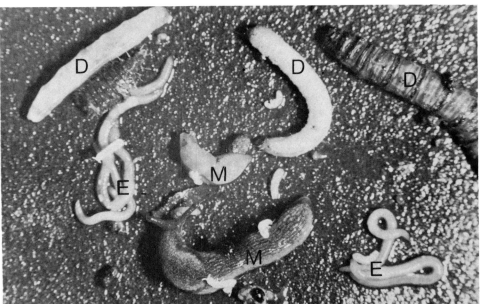

the smaller of the two types of oligochaete worms, namely the Enchytrae-idae (potworms). Most of the soil-inhabiting insects are of similar size, as well as the Diplopoda (millipedes) and Isopoda (woodlice); these together are sometimes termed the macroarthropods. The smaller Mollusca (slugs and snails) are also included in this size division.

Megafauna, body size greater than 20 mm. The most important and numerous animals in this section are the larger oligochaetes, or Lumbricidae (earthworms). The larger Mollusca, especially slugs, and the small soil-inhabiting mammals are also included.

Generally the smallest animals tend to occur at the highest densities, whereas the largest are least numerous. More than 10^6 protozoan individuals may be found in a single gram of soil, but they are thought to act mainly as predators on bacterial populations, and not to play a direct role in organic breakdown. Despite this, Stout (1974) states that the catalytic effect of Protozoa on microbial metabolism can be very great: the close association between Protozoa and other micro-organisms makes it very difficult to assess the relative roles of the two, and Stout concludes that it is more realistic to consider their joint role in the ecosystem, which is therefore largely one of litter decomposition.

Among the mesofauna the Nematoda may occur at densities of up to $20 \times 10^6/m^2$ in grassland soils (Nielsen 1967); they are commonest in lush grassland soils and much scarcer in poor soils. Plant feeding is probably the dominant habit, but many are bacterivores or fungivores. Their role in the decomposer cycle is generally considered to be of little significance, but requires further investigation.

The microarthropods include many species of diverse habits. The Collembola are minute insect-like arthropods, with six walking legs, and frequently with a complex jumping organ at the apex of the abdomen. They may occur at densities of up to $200 \times 10^3/m^2$. Culture experiments have shown that Collembola feed on a wide range of organic material, including fungal hyphae, spores, bacteria, decaying plants, algae, faeces, exuviae, carrion and living prey. Hale (1967) summarizes their feeding habits: many feed indiscriminately on whatever medium they inhabit, so that gut contents do not give a valid idea of what is utilized as food. They will often feed on fresh plant leaves, but prefer those which have been attacked by micro-organisms, and are starting to decay. Ashraf (1969) made direct observations of leaf feeding by Collembola. Although fresh litter may not be the preferred diet, and may not even be assimilated if eaten, it certainly forms a significant part of the gut contents of many Collembola, which therefore serve to break the litter up into smaller fragments.

Acari are the second group of microarthropods which are present in very large numbers in many soils; the density of a single family, the Oribatidae, can be as high as $130 \times 10^3/m^2$. They resemble minute spiders, with eight walking legs, and a body comprising two main sections, which are sometimes fused into a hard carapace. Most soil-inhabiting mites belong to one of four orders, the Cryptostigmata, Mesostigmata, Prostigmata and Astigmata. These differ in their feeding habits (summariz-ed, as far as these are known, in Wallwork 1970), and consequently in their roles in the soil community.

Cryptostigmata are generally believed to feed on fungi and bacteria, and may control the growth of these organisms. They will consume decomposing plant material in laboratory cultures, so that although their contribution to primary breakdown is probably of little importance, they may still be an important part of the decomposer food chain in some soils. Mesostigmata, especially the larger species, are mainly predatory, feeding on Collembola, Nematoda, Enchytraeidae and other mesofauna, but some, such as many Uropodinae, are fungal feeders. The Prostigmata also include some predators, but there is little information on the feeding habits of the smaller and more abundant species. These have been observed to feed on fungal threads or spores, or to suck organic substances being liquefied by bacteria and fungi. The Astigmata are closely associated with anaerobic processes of putrefaction and feed mainly on liquids or plant detritus in an advanced state of decomposition. There is thus little evidence of mites feeding directly on undecomposed plant litter, but many may contribute to the later stages of breakdown of plant material, as well as being important in the soil faunal community.

Harding and Stuttard (1974) summarize the overall role of micro-arthropods in litter decomposition. Direct chemical changes are virtually restricted to mesophyll tissue, leaving the leaf skeleton intact, but there is some evidence for the presence of cellulolytic enzymes, and Harding and Stuttard conclude that 'their role as primary decomposers may be greater than was previously believed'. The physical effects of feeding by microarthropods, however, are obvious; litter is comminuted by the mouthparts into fragments ranging in size from a few microns to more than 100 μm, which leave the body as faeces. The importance to litter break-down seems to depend on the site and soil type; in mull sites where there is a high density of earthworms and millipedes they are relatively unimportant (Edwards and Heath 1963), but their influence is greatest in pioneer soils, and in mor and certain moder sites (Harding and Stuttard 1974). Mor soils are characterized by poorer conditions of drainage and aeration and lower pH. Decomposition occurs more slowly and less completely, and the organic material accumulates in a narrow surface zone (Wallwork 1970). Moder soils exhibit the same phenomenon, but to a lesser degree. It will be shown later (see section 6) that reclaimed industrial land comes into such a category.

Macroarthropods are found at lower densities than the Collembola and mites, although their larger size to some extent compensates for this. Edwards (1974) has attempted to assess the relative importance of macroarthropod taxa in litter decomposition. The most important group is probably the Diplopoda, which are especially common in calcareous woodland, and are generally important to litter breakdown in temperate woodlands. Insects, especially the larvae of Diptera (flies) and Coleoptera (beetles), may also sometimes be of importance.

The oligochaete worms are represented by two families: the Enchytraeidae or potworms resemble small, pale-coloured versions of the larger, better known Lumbricidae. Enchytraeidae are usually most numerous in permanently damp soils with high organic content, where their densities may exceed $200 \times 10^3/m^2$. Lumbricidae are commonest in mull soils, at densities of up to $500/m^2$; when present they are of much greater importance than Enchytraeidae in litter burial, breakdown, and formation of the soil profile. Lofty (1974) has outlined six stages in the importance of all oligochaetes to litter breakdown:

- the removal of leaf and other litter material from the soil surface (*Lumbricus terrestris* (L.) can remove up to 90% of the annual deciduous leaf fall on mull soils);

- litter burial by casting on top of the litter;

- fragmentation of litter, greatly increasing the surface area on which other decomposers may feed;

- incorporation of fragmented and decomposed plant material throughout the soil horizons within which they live;

- reduction of the carbon: nitrogen ratio in the plant organic matter towards the level at which the nitrogen can be directly assimilated by plants;

- multiplication in the gut of the soil microflora, so that the faeces are much richer than the surrounding soil in micro-organisms, many of which are involved in final humification of plant material.

2 Methods of sampling

Study of the soil fauna involves either separating or extracting animals from the soil *in situ*, or taking samples of soil which can then be treated or processed to remove the fauna from them. Some animals can also be assessed by their movement on the surface of the soil. Comprehensive reviews of the main methods of obtaining population estimates of soil animals are given by Southwood (1966) and Phillipson (1971); only a brief outline of the most widely used techniques will be given here. Whichever methods are used, it is important to take samples over a period of at least six months, as most soil organisms undergo marked seasonal fluctuations in numbers.

2.1 Sampling

The total number of samples taken, and the size of each sample, depend on the degree of precision required, and on the distribution and density of the organism under study. Generally the larger the animal, the bigger the volume of sample required, and the sparser the population, the greater the number of samples. Thus cores of 5 cm (2 in) diameter are frequently used for the mesofauna, whereas for the large macrofauna 25 cm (10 in) square blocks are sometimes needed. The number of samples should be enough to reduce the coefficient of variation for each set of samples to an acceptable level, usually less than 50%. The amount of variation will also be affected by the extraction method used, and this should be chosen to give the lowest possible ratio of standard error to the mean number of animals per sample. For fairly numerous animals, 15–20 samples are generally sufficient from each site on each sampling occasion.

Samples should ideally be taken randomly from over the whole site. If a site consists of several rather distinct sections which differ in some obvious characteristic such as slope, or vegetation cover, random sampling may result in most samples coming from one section on a first occasion, but from a different section on the next sampling date. This will lead to differences between dates resulting in part from the different siting of samples on each date. To avoid this, a stratified random sampling scheme should be used instead. This consists of treating the different sections (termed 'strata') of the site separately, and taking a certain number of random samples from each section on each sampling date. The fauna extracted from all sections is then bulked or pooled to give an estimate of the fauna of the entire site which is not biased towards any one section of that site. A further problem is that randomization of sampling positions is difficult. Simply walking around a site taking samples 'at random' will almost inevitably lead to an unconscious bias, often towards evenness, or away from the margins of the site. True randomization requires random coordinates within the site to be selected by some means such as from random number tables, and the samples to be taken after measuring out these coordinates on the site itself. This is a lengthy and time-consuming procedure, and Milne (1959) has considered the alternative of non-random sampling. He advocates taking samples in a regular grid pattern throughout each sampling site (or section of a site). This scheme, termed centric systematic sampling, is quicker to carry out, and gives results indistinguishable from random sampling. The scale of the sampling grid will depend simply on the size of the site or section of site, and the number of samples to be taken from it.

Taking each sample consists simply of inserting an auger or other tool, depending on the size of sample, into the soil, and removing the soil into a bag or other container for transport to a building where the fauna can be extracted. Actually searching the soil for animals *in situ* is slow and usually inefficient, although some animals such as earthworms can be extracted from the soil *in situ* without first digging it up (see section 2.2).

2.2 Extraction

There are many methods of extracting animals from soil samples, but these are basically of two types, mechanical and behavioural. Mechanical methods rely on physical differences, e.g. in size or density, between animals and the surrounding soil; they include wet and dry sieving, flotation and elutriation. The commonest method involves washing soil and animals through a graded series of sieves with a jet of water; the retained material is then mixed with a dense liquid such as saturated magnesium sulphate solution, in which organic material floats but soil particles sink (Figure 62). The floating animal and plant constituents can then be separated either manually, or by mixing with benzene or similar hydrocarbons. Mechanical methods have the theoretical advantage that they extract both mobile and sedentary stages of the soil fauna, and are not dependent on the behaviour of the animal or condition of the substrate. Also, the samples may be stored frozen for long periods before extraction. Disadvantages are that much time must be spent on each sample, and the efficiency depends on the skill and experience of the operator; some animals may be damaged, and errors arise from extraction of animals which were dead at the time of sampling.

Behavioural or dynamic methods depend on active participation by the animals, which are made to move out of the soil in response to a repellant stimulus, such as heat, moisture or a chemical. Commonest are variations of the basic 'Tullgren' funnel in which the sample is placed on a mesh

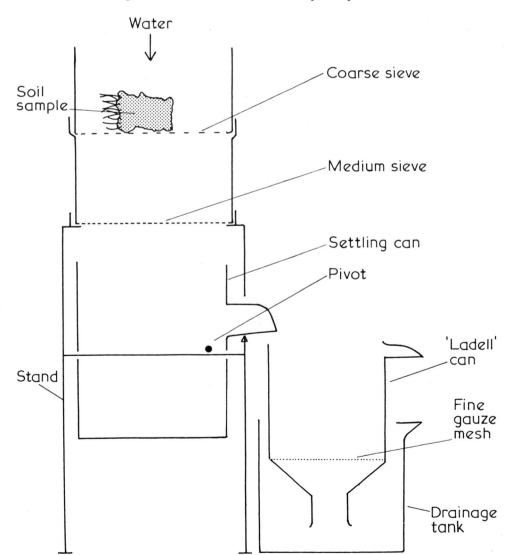

Figure 62. Soil washing apparatus for mechanical extraction of soil animals. After sieving the 'ladell' can is filled from below with magnesium sulphate solution, and agitated. Animal and plant material floats to the top, and is poured off for examination (from Southwood 1966).

floor, and heated (often by a light bulb) from above. Animals are driven down by the gradual heating and drying out of the soil, and eventually fall through the mesh into a collecting funnel leading to some sort of container (Figure 63). Once set up, samples may be left unattended and large numbers of samples may be treated simultaneously in batteries of extractors. The method is useful for soils with a high organic matter content, but less efficient for soils with a high clay content. Only mobile stages are extracted, and efficiency is also influenced by condition of the animals, climate before sampling and water content of the soil.

Behavioural extraction without the prior taking of samples is widely used for estimating earthworm densities (Satchell 1967); either potassium permanganate or formaldehyde solutions are poured onto the soil to expel the worms. Edwards and Fletcher (1971) compared mechanical and behavioural methods of extraction for terrestrial arthropods. They concluded that no single extraction method or size of sample was best for all groups of animals, and that it may be necessary to use several methods and sample sizes. Where a single method is to be used for most of the estimations, they stress that its efficiency for each group of animals in that particular site should be investigated before it is used intensively. The best general method was considered to be a Tullgren funnel with steep gradients of temperature and moisture through the sample.

Once extracted, the animals must be counted, usually after sorting and identifying them to the required degree of precision. Identification to species of all the fauna is very time-consuming and each taxon may need to be examined by a specialist in that particular group of animals. For many purposes, classification into the main taxa outlined in section 1.2 is quite sufficient. The relative number of whole groups such as microarthropods or oligochaetes can then be compared from site to site,

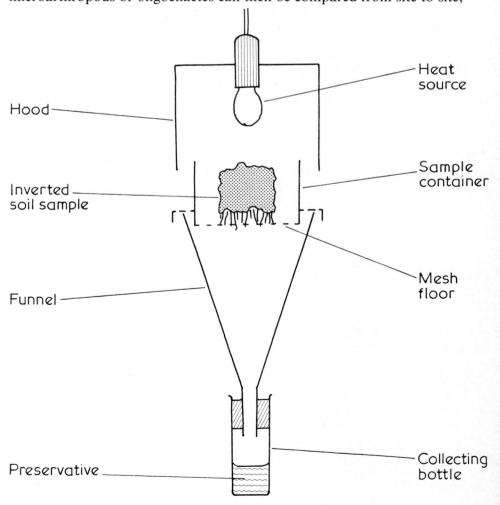

Figure 63. Basic Tullgren funnel for behavioural extraction of soil animals.

or changes monitored over a period of time. It is usual for the numbers of animals found in each sample to be transformed to logarithms before any statistical analysis is carried out. This stabilizes the variance, which otherwise tends to be correlated with the mean per sample because of the aggregated spatial distribution of most soil animals. Furthermore, animal population growth is basically exponential rather than linear, so that when studying population density over a period of time, conversion to logarithms shows up such increase as a straight line relationship (e.g. Figure 64).

As an alternative to counting, the weight or biomass of animals present can be used as a measure of their abundance, and potential importance. Biomass is measured by drying the animals to remove all moisture, and then weighing them. Separate estimates of biomass can, of course, be made for each taxonomic group being studied, and comparisons then made on a basis of biomass instead of numbers of individuals.

2.3 Pitfall trapping

Relative population estimates of soil surface animals may be obtained by pitfall traps. These are containers, such as glass jars, or plastic cups or troughs, set into the soil with their mouth level with the soil surface. Animals moving over the surface fall into the traps, and are unable to escape. A surface baffle may be used to increase the effective collecting area of the trap, and preservatives can be added to keep the catch in an identifiable condition, although the chemicals used may themselves have an attractant or repellant effect. Although cheap to install, and requiring little labour, pitfall traps suffer from the difficulty of relating numbers caught to population size. The catch is determined both by the numbers of animals present and by their mobility or activity; the traps' efficiency is also influenced by the species of animal, surrounding vegetation, and the construction and materials of the trap itself. The method cannot therefore be used for quantitative estimates of the fauna of any area, but is useful for comparing abundance/activity in different areas, and has been used, for example, for monitoring the ingress of insects and spiders into reclaimed polders (Meijer 1974).

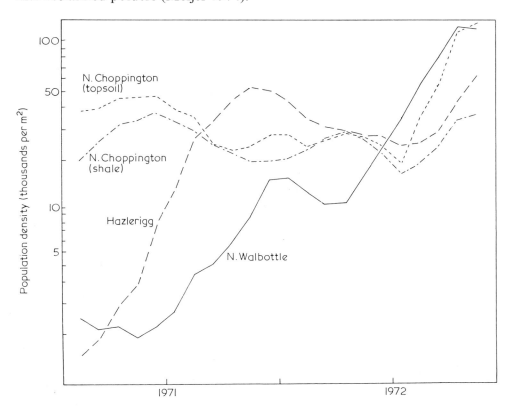

Figure 64. Colonization of four reclaimed pit heaps in Northumberland by Acari (mites).

3 Environmental factors

The environment within reclaimed waste may be initially unsuitable for both plant and animal life. In this section some of the factors responsible for this are discussed, and their importance to soil animals, where known, is outlined. The exact conditions prevailing will of course depend on the type of substrate being reclaimed; the environment in reclaimed coal pit heaps will differ in important respects from that in land newly reclaimed from the sea, especially in moisture content and salinity. Knowledge gained from reclaimed pit heaps will, however, illustrate most points (see Richardson *et al.* 1971).

The factors which render reclaimed soil so inimical are both physical and chemical. The physical process of soil formation is outlined in Chapter 6, but some details are especially relevant to the soil fauna by virtue of their influence on the moisture and temperature characteristics of the resultant soil.

3.1 Moisture

Freshly tipped hard shale has a wide range of particle sizes and often even after 50 years, only half the spoil breaks down into sufficiently small particles for incorporation into soil aggregates which retain moisture. Large shale stones weather along fine bedding planes and splinter into a fine plate form: this is aided on regraded sites by mechanical movement of the shale. In a few years the surface consists of soft stony material with a fine sand, silt and clay fraction which often results in restricted percolation, especially after compaction by earthmoving equipment. This can lead to waterlogging and subsequent erosion in wet conditions, as well as to extreme drought conditions during dry weather. Davis (1963) found that the mean water content of unreclaimed mineral soil was only two thirds that of similar soil after reclamation and about one third that of old pasture. At Roddymoor, Co. Durham, the summer moisture content of a reclaimed pitheap soil was 15% compared to 30–40% in normal agricultural soil (Hutson 1972). As moisture status is probably the main limiting factor for soil invertebrates, drought may have serious effects on the fauna.

The Protozoa and Nematoda, as well as other minor taxa, are essentially aquatic, and depend on a film of free water for maintenance of normal activity. Protozoa, however, can survive desiccation by encystment (Stout and Heal 1967); Nematoda become dehydrated at pF values above about 3.0, which occur even in normal sandy soils during the summer, but again many can probably survive drying out in a state called anabiosis, in which they are almost totally desiccated, and not dependent on moisture (Nielsen 1967).

Microarthropods are especially sensitive to the moisture status of the soil; the distribution of Collembola in particular is governed mainly by humidity, and these animals may be used as indicators of soil moisture conditions (Hale 1967). Among the mites, many Cryptostigmata require nearly saturated humidities, and are restricted to the soil environment. The predatory Pro- and Mesostigmata, however, are generally less dependent on high humidity, and range more actively through the soil and more exposed habitats (Wallwork 1967). Unlike the animals dependent on free water, microarthropods cannot resist extreme desiccation and must maintain their moisture content in drought conditions by moving deeper into the soil. On many reclamation sites this is not possible because of the impenetrable layers caused by the dense nature of the shale soil, so that summer drought is potentially lethal. Flooding is probably less damaging: most Collembola, for example, have a hydrofuge cuticle consisting of many small tubercles which retain an air film around the body and enable respiration to take place by gaseous exchange with the surrounding water.

Larger arthropods are less dependent on a saturated atmosphere within the soil, but again most cannot withstand extreme drying out; many are prevented by their size from moving deep into soil crevices, and must therefore move horizontally to avoid drought.

Enchytraeid worms are also affected by drought (O'Connor 1967). In permanently moist habitats their numbers are regulated by the effects of temperature on reproductive activity, but drought reduces numbers severely. Although active worms are killed, cocoons containing eggs or embryos can survive, and allow population increase when moisture is available again. Earthworms are heavily dependent on water, but are much more able to withstand desiccation. They can lose up to 70–75% of their body water content and survive drought in a quiescent state (Roots 1956). Some, such as *L. terrestris* are, however, prone to mortality after heavy rain, when they leave their flooded burrows, owing to lack of oxygen, and are liable to be killed by ultra-violet light.

3.2 Temperature

In the initial stages of reclamation and soil formation, temperature conditions may also be unsuitable for soil animals. Lack of vegetation and litter leads to direct insolation raising the surface temperature by day, and allows maximum heat loss at night. These fluctuations are accentuated by the dark colour of materials such as black shale. In drought conditions heat is not conducted into the deeper layers of the soil, causing even more violent temperature fluctuations at or near the surface. Thus temperatures as high as 57°C have been recorded on south-facing slopes of reclaimed pit heaps (Richardson 1958). Heat may also rise from below from burning shale.

Most active soil animals cannot survive temperatures above about 30°C, although Protozoa can withstand hotter conditions when encysted (Stout and Heal 1967). Mites, especially Cryptostigmata, have distinct temperature preferences, and show regular vertical migrations during the 24 hour cycle which help to maintain them at this temperature (Wallwork 1970). Hutson (1974) kept the collembolan *Folsomia candida* (Willem) at temperatures from 0 to 30°C. No reproduction occurred at 0 or 30°C; the highest fecundity was at 15°C, and the slope of the rate of development/temperature curve was greatest at 18°C. This corresponds approximately to the mean summer air temperature in north-east England where *F. candida* is found in reclaimed pit heaps. The species is thus adapted to the highest ambient temperatures which it is likely to experience over any long period, and must rely on behaviour to escape extremes near the surface.

Species of Enchytraeidae have been shown by Reynoldson (1943) to have a similar temperature optimum of about 18°C, and the influence of temperature on their reproductive rate has already been mentioned. Earthworms, in contrast, often have rather lower optimum temperatures for activity, reflecting their nocturnal habits. *L. terrestris* can, however, survive in a quiescent state at temperatures up to 28°C.

For all soil animals the direct effects of high temperatures may be less important than the resultant increase in their rate of water loss by evaporation. This is proportional to the saturation deficit of the soil atmosphere, as stressed by Wallwork (1970), which varies with temperature even though the relative humidity may remain constant. Hot and dry summer conditions in newly reclaimed soil therefore constitute a doubly severe hazard to the soil fauna which colonizes the site. Even if not killed outright, many species will only survive in an inactive state, contributing nothing to the soil ecosystem at this time.

3.3 Chemical factors

The commonest chemical factors which may make reclaimed soil unsuitable for animals are pH and salinity. On shale soils, pH values from 1.8 to

8.5 have been recorded, with extreme acidities caused by the weathering of iron pyrites. Although the most abundant fauna is generally found in neutral and weakly alkaline soils, this is at least in part due not so much to hydrogen ion concentration as to calcium deficiency, leading to poor aeration and a heavy texture in more acid soils. Shale soils however often have a high calcium content whether the pH is high or low, so this may be less important on such sites. In the absence of these secondary effects of acidity many animals can live in soils with surprisingly low pHs.

Most widespread soil Protozoa probably have a range of tolerance from about pH 3.5 to about pH 9.7 (Stout and Heal 1967). Cryptostigmatid mites are common in peat bogs as acid as pH 3 (Kühnelt 1961). At the other extreme, Ashraf (1969) showed that the collembolan *Onychiurus bhatti* Yosii laid few or no eggs in conditions more alkaline than pH 7.5 although it could survive up to pH 8.5. It is important to realize, however, that the extremes of any factor which limit reproduction may be more important than those actually causing death. Hutson (1974) kept four species of the dominant Collembola found on reclaimed pit heaps at seven pHs ranging from 2.5 to 7.6. The maximum egg production of three species occurred at pH 5.2 with few or no eggs laid at the extremes, 2.5 and 7.6; only one species, *Proisotoma minuta* (Tullberg), showed greatest fecundity at pH 7.2. The pH of the pit heap soils examined ranged from 5.3 to 7.8, so that the common Collembola of shale soil seem well adapted to these values.

Among the oligochaetes, there is a rather distinct division of species according to soil pH. Enchytraeidae are commonly found in mor-type soils with a high organic content and low pH, whereas Lumbricidae are typically inhabitants of more neutral mull-type soils. Wallwork (1970) states that provided variations in soil moisture content are not a limiting factor, the general distribution of lumbricids is governed mainly by the pH conditions of the soil. Many species, such as *L. terrestris*, show a sharp avoiding reaction to pH values below about 4.0, and even the most 'acid tolerant' species are restricted to a pH range between 5.0 and 3.8 (Satchell 1967). A further requirement of earthworms is calcium, which plays an important part in their metabolism; they may therefore be absent from soils with a suitably high pH because of calcium deficiency. Hutson (1972) kept earthworms in soils from a reclaimed pit heap at Roddymoor. In moist soils, with pH values from 5.5 to 7.1, the worms survived, but in one particular soil of pH 2.3 they reacted violently and were all dead on the surface within 15 minutes. They lived, however, in soil from another part of the same field. Local conditions may therefore be unsuitable for soil fauna without the site as a whole being impaired.

Saline conditions can occur due to the presence of magnesium and iron sulphates, and can rise to very high levels (2.5 S/m) on reclaimed shale soils during dry periods. Where land is reclaimed from the sea, this will also be highly saline initially. Colonization will then be by littoral or estuarine fauna well adapted to high salinity (Meijer 1974). On saline sites distant from the coast, the colonizing fauna will be those available species which are able to tolerate the salinity level. Hutson (1974) measured fecundity and longevity of the collembolan *F. candida* at salinities from 0 to 3.2 S/m (0 to 2 g NaCl/100 cm³ H_2O). Increasing salinity above conductivity 0.8 S/m adversely affected time until oviposition, duration of egg laying, proportion of eggs hatching and adult survival time. Data from the inhabitants of reclaimed soil are lacking, but it would seem likely that anything above a moderate salinity level may seriously limit the soil fauna. It is not known whether the same conclusion applies when salinity is caused by other salts such as $MgSO_4$.

The effects on the fauna of other likely chemical contaminants of reclaimed soil, such as heavy metals, are little known, although such pollutants have been shown to limit microbial activity (Gadgil 1964).

Inorganic lead was found by Williamson and Evans (1973) to have no direct toxic effects on the soil fauna, when added in the form of lead salts. Soil samples taken by the same authors from overgrown lead mine spoil heaps showed that the Acari actually became more abundant with increasing lead level, even up to the maximum level found of 19 000 ppm. Invertebrates in the soil of roadside verges, where lead levels are also abnormally high, were also apparently unaffected. Maurer (1974) found, however, that the surface-active fauna (ground beetles and spiders) of meadows near busy roads was reduced. This was associated with an increase in their body lead content, but no causal relationship was established.

4 The fauna

From the preceding section it would seem that reclaimed soil is potentially suitable for colonization by various animals, provided that moisture conditions are not dry for too much of the year, and that extremes of acidity or salinity are not widespread. Actual surveys of the fauna of reclaimed land are very few, and data are largely restricted to the arthropods, especially microarthropods. Street and Goodman (1967) examined microbial activity in tip materials by burying cellophane strips; amoeboid Protozoa were found after primary colonization by microflora (fungi and bacteria). When sewage sludge or domestic refuse was added to the material, colonization was faster, and mites became an important factor in the breakdown of the cellophane. Walsh (1910) listed the Coleoptera of some old pit heaps in Co. Durham. These were surface-living species however, and not representative of the true soil fauna.

Although not directly comparable with colonization of soils formed from sterile materials, some idea of the animals potentially available to invade reclaimed land can be gained from the fauna re-colonizing artificially sterilized soils. Baweja (1939) found that in the first month after steam sterilization myriapods and Arachnida (spiders and mites) predominated, but after this an increasing proportion (up to 70%) of the recolonizing fauna were Collembola. Populations took about six months to reach the level of a control population, and then continued to increase to a density two to three times that of the control. Almost identical results were reported by Buahin and Edwards (1964) in a similar experiment, although chemical sterilization was used rather than steam. Collembola again predominated, and increased to previously unattained numbers. It was suggested that colonization by Collembola took place by wind transportation, as they were caught in traps up to 1 m about the soil (see p. 142).

The first survey of soil fauna of reclaimed industrial land was probably that by Davis (1963), who compared the microarthropods of three sites at Corby, Northants. One of these was a levelled ironstone quarry, the second an area which had been opencast quarried and then reclaimed and sown with grass, and the third an old pasture which had not been quarried. Samples were taken in 1958–1959, ten years after levelling, and four years after sowing of the reclaimed area. Initial colonization of the soil was therefore complete, but there was an overall increase in total numbers over the three sites, probably reflecting their relative suitability for the fauna. The densities were only moderate; details are given in Table 16 for comparison with other industrial sites. Davis also recorded various other larger arthropods from these sites, with a combined density of about one quarter of that of Collembola.

In East Germany a thorough study was made by Dunger (1968, 1969a) of the fauna in and on the surface of reclaimed dumps resulting from opencast mining for brown coal or lignite. Two types of dump were studied: the first consisted largely of Pleistocene-Tertiary mixed materials,

M. L. Luff and B. R. Hutson

Table 16 Densities (thousands/m^2) of Collembola and Acari on reclaimed land and adjacent pasture.

Site and author	Total Collembola	Total Acari	Percentage of Acari in each Order			
			Cryptostigmata	Mesostigmata	Prostigmata	Astigmata
Corby, Northants (Davis 1963)						
Levelled ironstone quarry	6.8	7.7	23.0	51.4	18.9	6.7
Reclaimed ironstone workings	7.1	11.9	46.5	40.4	7.0	7.0
Old pasture	11.1	14.1	47.4	20.7	3.7	28.2
Reclaimed lignite opencast sites (Dunger 1968)						
One year after reclamation	4.2	18.1*	—	—	—	—
Three years after reclamation	62.1	67.1*	—	—	—	—
Seven years after reclamation	39.0	22.6*	—	—	—	—
Ten years after reclamation	13.9	12.6*	—	—	—	—
Roddymoor, Co. Durham (Hutson 1972)						
Reclaimed pitheap shale	1.1	0.4	—	—	—	—
Reclaimed pitheap, with topsoil	1.6	0.6	—	—	—	—
Adjacent pasture	1.1	0.5	—	—	—	—
Adjacent scrub	0.7	3.6	—	—	—	—
Lead mine spoilheaps (Williamson and Evans 1973)	28.4	22.5	—	—	—	—
Reclaimed pitheaps, Northumberland, 1972 mean (Hutson 1974)						
N. Walbottle	2.9	55.3	0	0.8	73.0	26.2
Hazlerigg	53.6	37.8	0.8	1.6	87.0	10.6
N. Choppington, shale	28.5	26.7	0.4	2.6	81.6	15.4
N. Choppington, with topsoil	11.2	58.8	0.3	1.2	70.1	28.4

*only Cryptostigmata were listed.

with few mineral acids, the second of tertiary sandy loams with a high mineral acid content. Sites were studied from one to fifteen years after reclamation and afforestation with mainly deciduous trees.

In the less acid deciduous sites the soil fauna developed quickly, initially consisting largely of microarthropods, especially Collembola and Cryptostigmata (Table 16), and dipterous larvae. Enchytraeidae were also found at this stage. After the fifth year, earthworms began to occur, and the numbers of both species and individuals increased until by the tenth year they were the dominant soil animals. The development of the soil fauna was much more restricted on the more acid tertiary sites, where earthworms were limited to the edges of the site even after 15 years, and Collembola were the most numerous animals. The study was concerned in particular

Landscape Reclamation Practice

with the importance of the fauna in litter decomposition, which is dealt with in section 5.

The surface fauna colonizing similar afforested dumps near Cologne was studied by Neumann (1971). Unreclaimed spoil banks and recently reclaimed and planted heaps had a pioneer association of very many species and individuals of ground beetles (Carabidae), which gradually, over a 10–15 year period, changed to a typical less diverse woodland fauna. Other arthropods, such as millipedes and woodlice, however, did not show a pioneer fauna, but simply increased gradually as the woodland developed.

Williamson and Evans (1973) found high densities of both Collembola and Acari in the overgrown spoil heaps of disused lead mines (Table 16) in Co. Durham. The major groups of soil-inhabiting insects were also present, together with low numbers of oligochaetes.

Hutson (1972) carried out a preliminary study of the soil and surface fauna of a reclaimed coal pitheap at Roddymoor, Co. Durham. Sampling started almost a year after the area was sown, so the initial stages of colonization were missed, and was restricted to the summer, when micro-arthropod numbers are usually lowest because of drought and high temperatures. Mechanical disturbance reduces the numbers of animals in any agricultural soil, but comparison of the reclaimed land with un-disturbed pasture showed similar densities (Table 16), indicating that rapid colonization of the site had taken place, obviating the effects of earth-moving only 17 months earlier. Pitfall traps showed that there was normal surface activity of animals all over the site. The high catch on shale areas may have been caused by the increased activity of a smaller number of animals than on unreclaimed pasture, because the less dense vegetation permitted easier movement. Most of the surface-active animals were either general scavengers, or predators. Within the soil, insects, especially Coleoptera and Diptera, were found as well as microarthropods. Both enchytraeid and lumbricid worms were absent from the main samples, but earthworms were later found near the edge of the site nearly two years after completion of earthmoving. They were in fields where mown grass had been left to lie on the soil surface, which supports Hutson's (1972) experimental conclusion that a layer of grass cuttings is both of nutritional value to the worms, and reduces evaporation from the soil, rendering it more suitable for colonization (see also section 5).

In a subsequent thesis, Hutson (1974) gives the results of an intensive survey of the microarthropod soil fauna of four reclaimed pitheaps in Northumberland during 1971–1972. As these results have not yet been published, the main findings will be summarized here. The sites involved were at North Walbottle, Hazlerigg, and North Choppington, listed in increasing order of time since reclamation. The established site, N. Choppington, was divided into two areas, one with a topsoil of firesand, the other with exposed shale, which were sampled separately. Monthly soil sampling began in January 1971, respectively five months before, three months after and 18 months after earthmoving was completed on each site. At that time vegetation was well established on N. Choppington, with a grass/clover mixture on the topsoil-covered area, as well as forestry transplants on the shale portions. The remaining sites consisted of exposed shale; plant cover had developed by late spring 1971 on Hazlerigg, and by summer 1971 on N. Walbottle. N. Choppington topsoil area and N. Walbottle were then grazed, but the remaining areas developed a very dense sward in 1972. On all sites salinity was low (conductivity not more than 0.2 S/m), and pH near neutral except towards the end of 1972, when more acid conditions were developing on N. Walbottle and N. Chopping-ton (topsoil area). Regular fertilizer applications were made on all sites to supply essential nutrients for plant growth. Twenty samples were taken per month from each site until December 1972, and the fauna extracted in Tullgren funnels.

The densities of mites (Figure 64) on the recently reclaimed sites were low initially, but rose rapidly. By the end of the survey very high numbers were recorded ($115.7 \times 10^3/m^2$ on N. Walbottle). On the more established site at N. Choppington the mean mite density was already in the range $10-50 \times 10^3/m^2$, but considerable seasonal fluctuations occurred. The mite populations on all sites were dominated by Prostigmata ($>70\%$), especially families of smaller, non-predatory species, such as Tarsonemidae. These were also found commonly on the reclaimed ironstone sites studied by Davis (1963). Loots and Ryke (1967) found that Prostigmata were more abundant in soils with low rather than high organic matter content, which is supported by their abundance in these recently reclaimed soils.

The most abundant mites in most soils are Cryptostigmata, especially in forest mor, but this group was almost absent from these reclaimed sites. Many prefer wetter soils, and they frequently require a saturated humidity. In cultivated soils, where continued mixing of the mineral and topsoil layers results in an unstable environment and a poorly structured profile, the population may be sparse, since these mites prefer the environment provided by undisturbed organic layers lying on the surface of mineral soil. The mean density of Cryptostigmata from the Northumberland reclamation sites was very low ($< 1\%$ of total Acari). As the recently disturbed soil is clearly a very unstable environment, particularly in relation to moisture content and surface litter, this confirms the requirements of these mites. Luxton (1967) suggested that pH may be an important regulating factor for many Cryptostigmata, possibly by influence on their food supply. Although pH was not extreme on these sites, the acidity of shale typically increases with weathering, and this may contribute to the unsuitability of the soil for this group.

The Mesostigmata were also scarce in comparison with more established soils, and the lack of these active predatory species may account in part for the rapid colonization by the non-predatory mites and Collembola. The bulk of the mites other than Prostigmata were Astigmata, which were not originally regarded as a soil-inhabiting group. They have recently been found, however, in heathland, arable soils and upland pasture, but are generally scarce, and their role in the soil community has been little studied. They tend to be associated with drier conditions, and have been reported from desert areas (Wallwork 1967). This may help to explain their comprising up to 28% of the mites on the reclaimed sites; similar densities have only been recorded previously from old pasture (Salt *et al.* 1948; Davis 1963).

Thus the mite fauna reached very high densities, but differed markedly from that of established soils. Prostigmata and Astigmata were successful first, whereas the remaining orders had not really become established by the end of the survey. This sequence is remarkably similar to that colonizing soil in the Antarctic (Janetschek 1970) and may be characteristic of that in newly formed soil. Colonization was dependent on vegetation; before reclamation had started on N. Walbottle there was a patchy distribution of plants which had invaded the undisturbed heap naturally. Where plants were present the mite density was about $15.0 \times 10^3/m^2$, whereas under the bare shale it was only $1.2 \times 10^3/m^2$. After reclamation the presence of a form of topsoil also favoured mite populations, which at N. Choppington were always more numerous in the area covered with firesand. Seasonal changes in mite density, most marked on the established site, were almost entirely due to fluctuations in numbers of the dominant Prostigmata. There was a tendency for their density to decline in summer/autumn, and to rise in winter/spring. It is generally accepted that such fluctuations are caused by climatic conditions, and drought would seem to be the limiting factor on these sites. In August 1971, for example, there was much rain, humidity was high, and numbers did not decline until the autumn; in 1972, however, there was less rainfall in July and August, humidity was low, and at this time numbers fell on both N. Choppington and Hazlerigg. The special features of reclaimed soil which may render drought especially severe have already been discussed (see section 3).

*Figure 65. Colonization of
four reclaimed pit heaps
in Northumberland by
Collembola (springtails).*

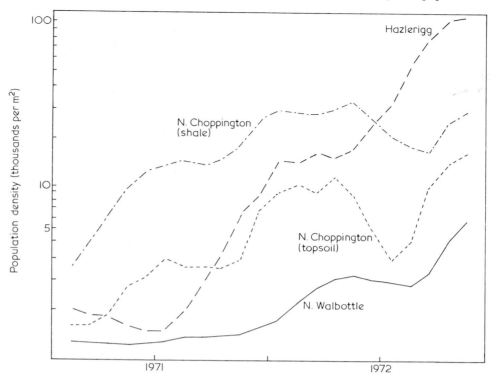

The rate of colonization of these sites by Collembola (Figure 65), although rapid, was generally slower than by mites, except by a single species, *Isotoma notabilis* Schäffer, on Hazlerigg. On N. Choppington the densities at the beginning of the survey were comparable with those on Roddymoor at a similar stage after reclamation. By the end of the survey numbers had risen on all sites, and lay within the range (5–50 × 10³/m²) found in normal soils; the density of 152 × 10³/m² on Hazlerigg is extremely high for Collembola. Investigation of the age structure of the collembolan populations showed that many had at least two generations a year. This, together with the absence of large predatory mesostigmatid mites, may have been responsible for the rapid population growth.

The first species found on the recently reclaimed sites were those, such as *Entomobrya albocincta* (Templeton), which are especially adapted to dry conditions. These were superseded in 1972 by a more typical soil fauna, usually dominated by either *I. notabilis* or *Tullbergia krausbeueri* (Börner). Most of the biomass was made up of *I. notabilis* or the related *I. viridis* Bourlet. Davis (1963) also found *T. krausbeueri* commonly in reclaimed ironstone soil; *I. notabilis* occurred as well, but was not as numerous. Towards the end of the Northumberland survey, some sites became more acid, and there was an increase in the numbers of *Willemia anophthalma* (Börner), a relatively uncommon species which is normally restricted to acid peat soils. Seasonal fluctuations were especially noticeable on N. Choppington, with a drop in numbers each late summer/autumn. As with the mites, drought was probably the cause of these variations. In contrast to the mites, however, the numbers in the topsoiled area of N. Choppington were persistently lower than in the shale area. This may have been a result of the sandy soil used; several authors (e.g. Ashraf 1969) have shown that soil-inhabiting Collembola lay few eggs in sandy soils.

Other invertebrates occurred irregularly, usually in low numbers. The commonest insects were dipterous larvae, with a peak density of 4.9 × 10³/m² in one month on the topsoil area of N. Choppington. They were, however, highly aggregated, and their mean density on this site over the two years was only 1.2 × 10³/m². They were less numerous initially on the other sites, but began to be found regularly about six months after reclamation, reaching locally high densities on all sites by the end of 1972. Being much larger than the microarthropods they probably contributed more to the total weight or biomass of the fauna. The remaining arthropod soil fauna comprised Coleoptera, Thysanura (bristle tails), Araneida (spiders), Isopoda, Pauropoda and Symphyla, in decreasing order of numbers.

Enchytraeidae were found occasionally in very low numbers on the top-soil section of N. Choppington, and also appeared, 18 months after reclamation, on Hazlerigg. Earthworms were not found at all during the two years of intensive sampling, although two specimens were obtained from the edge of the N. Choppington site (one in the soil, the other on the surface) early in 1971. The small sample size used was not suited to efficient earthworm sampling, but it would seem that although worms may be present near the edges of reclaimed pit heaps from about two years after reclamation, their numbers do not build up rapidly on the bulk of the reclaimed area.

The contrast between the rapid build up of selected microarthropod populations in reclaimed or sterilized soil, and the slow colonization by most larger invertebrates, may reflect their varied means of access to the site. Colonization by microarthropods, especially mites, occurs at a far greater rate than would be expected from active migration (i.e. walking) alone. The non-feeding deutonymphs of some Astigmata have a complex sucker, and are known to be carried in great numbers by dung-inhabiting flies and beetles. Both fly and beetle larvae were found in the sites sampled by Hutson (1974), indicating that adult insects had flown on to the site and laid their eggs; dung from stock grazing the sward would attract these insects, and thus also aid the immigration of their mite passengers.

Wind is probably the most important aid to dispersal. Although neither mites nor Collembola can actually fly, both have been found at considerable altitudes, simply being blown by air currents. Recently reclaimed land usually presents a smooth, open aspect, across which winds can blow largely unimpeded, carrying microarthropods, as well as smaller fauna such as protozoan cysts, on to the new soil. On the open, flat areas of polders in the Netherlands, even large surface-moving beetles are blown on to the reclaimed soil, unable to maintain their grip on the vegetation-free surface (Meijer 1974).

Normal immigration by larger invertebrates must be by walking or flying. Dunger (1968), Neumann (1971) and Hutson (1972) all caught large numbers of surface-active species, especially ground beetles, on recently reclaimed sites, where the lack of vegetation allowed easy movement. The less active animals can only colonize newly reclaimed soil more slowly: thus earthworms usually spread at less than 10 m/year even in suitable soils.

5 Litter breakdown on pit heaps

Available knowledge on the biology of those animals colonizing reclaimed land suggests that the high densities of microarthropods may render them of considerable value in the physical breakdown of organic material such as dead plant remains. Two methods have been used to obtain some proof of this. The first, a more direct method, involves burying rot-proof mesh (usually nylon) bags containing litter in the soil of reclaimed sites. Meshes of different hole sizes can be used to exclude animals above any desired size, and thus, for example, to compare the role of micro- and macroarthropods in litter breakdown. After a given period of time the bags are lifted, and the amount of litter left is measured.

Such a method was used by Edwards and Heath (1963) to assess the relative roles of micro-, meso- and macrofauna in litter decomposition, but the technique has been criticized by Satchell (1974) and others. It is fair to say that leaf disappearance does not mean that complete decomposition has occurred, merely that the tissue has been broken up into smaller fragments which have fallen away from the leaf skeleton. But as already stressed, such comminution of plant tissue may well be one of the most beneficial functions of the soil fauna, permitting increased microbial activity. Other drawbacks to the technique are that containing litter in bags results in an artificial environment, and that some litter, such as widely used oak leaves which are rich in tannins, is slow to decompose anyway. Both these factors weigh against leaf loss; if breakdown takes place in such bags, more suitable unconfined litter, such as grass mowings, is likely to be fragmented even faster. Evidence of confined oak leaf disappearance therefore augurs well for the removal of natural litter.

The alternative is to use the methods of energetics and production studies. Details are given by Southwood (1966) and Phillipson (1971); basically these methods use the dynamics of energy flow as a measure of processes taking place in the system under study. In the context of litter breakdown, the energy available from litter is measured; the amount then consumed by litter-feeding animals is estimated by combining the resulting biomass of such animals (converted to energy units) with energy lost by respiration of the same animals.

Hutson (1974) used the leaf-bag method on the reclaimed pit heaps referred to in section 4. Nylon bags containing 75 × 25 mm pieces of oak (*Quercus robur* L.) leaves were buried in the soil on each site. Bags of three mesh sizes were used: 3.5 mm (coarse) allowing the ingress of large invertebrates such as earthworms and molluscs, as well as both macro- and microarthropods; 0.5 mm (medium) permitting entry of microarthropods and the smaller macroarthropods such as some dipterous larvae; and 0.02 mm (fine) excluding all except the microfauna. Three leaf pieces were placed in each bag, and a total of 135 bags buried in July 1972, both in the reclaimed soil, and in the soil of uncultivated pasture as a control site. After eight months, when degradation in coarse mesh bags on this control site was almost complete, all the bags were lifted, and the area of each leaf which had disappeared was estimated photometrically.

Results showed in fact that breakdown occurred on all sites (Figure 66), but at a slower rate overall than on the pasture control site. On the control site the loss rate from coarse meshed bags was much greater than from medium mesh, showing that the larger invertebrates (e.g. earthworms) were removing a significant amount of litter. In the reclaimed soils, however, there was no overall significant difference between the loss rates from coarse- and medium-meshed bags, because, apart from the larger dipterous larvae, such macrofauna were almost entirely absent. The rate of leaf disappearance from each reclamation site was more or less proportional

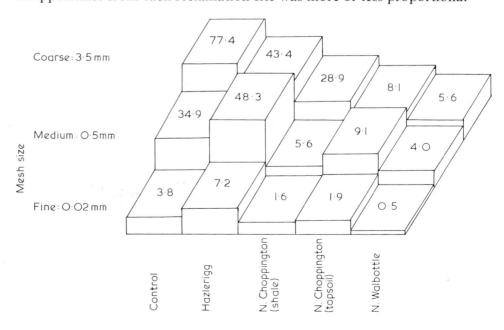

Figure 66. *Rates of breakdown of confined oak leaves in bags of three mesh sizes, buried in reclaimed pitheaps and in a control pasture soil. Numbers on each column are the percentages of leaf material lost after eight months.*

Table 17 Consumption (kcal/m²/yr) of litter-feeding soil animals in reclaimed brown coal dumps (from Dunger 1969b).

| | Years after reclamation | | | |
	1	3	7	10
Microarthropods	20	160	75	40
Enchytraeidae	5	13	31	18
Macroarthropods	1	80	70	20
Lumbricidae	1	2	300	900
Percentage of total litter consumed	0.6	4.6	27.3	76.3

to the relative numbers of Collembola on each site. Thus Hazlerigg, with very high collembolan densities by December 1972 (Figure 65) had the highest loss (45%), whereas there was only some 5% loss from N. Walbottle, which had the highest mite densities (Figure 64), but the lowest numbers of Collembola. Dipterous larvae (mainly Chironomidae) were found feeding on the leaf tissue in some coarse- and medium-meshed bags, but on the Hazlerigg site in particular many Collembola were found on the disintegrating leaves in the absence of fly larvae. It was therefore concluded that Collembola, and to some extent larvae of Diptera, were responsible for physical breakdown of litter on these sites, mites having little or no influence.

Both direct (litter bag) and indirect (energetics) methods were used by Dunger (1968, 1969b) to assess changes in the rate of litter breakdown by various soil animals on East German reclaimed brown coal opencast workings. This study covered a longer period than that of Hutson, with measurements on sites from one to ten years after reclamation. In the initial stages (up to three years) after reclamation microarthropods consumed the most litter (Table 17), although less than 5% of the available litter was actually decomposed. By the seven-year stage lumbricids were established, and were the most important litter decomposers. Total litter breakdown rose to 27%, and this coincided with a change from moder to mull conditions in the soil. Enchytraeids, although only responsible for a relatively small amount of litter decomposition, were at their peak at this time. By the ten-year stage earthworms were the sole important decomposers, removing 70% of the litter fall. There was thus a change after about seven years from moder-like humus formation, with limited litter breakdown by arthropods, to mull conditions with extensive litter removal by earthworms. The sites studied by Hutson would seem to be in the first stage of this succession, but with less litter input because they were grass-covered and trees, if present, were still very small.

6 Conclusions for management

Although detailed studies of the soil fauna of reclaimed derelict land are limited to those described previously in this chapter, some general conclusions can be drawn as follows.

- Reclaimed industrial land can support a large and varied soil fauna within a year of reclamation.

- This fauna may differ markedly from that of 'normal' soil of fields or woodland.

- In the first five years or so after reclamation, arthropods (especially Collembola), mites and fly larvae are usually the dominant soil animals.

- Earthworms only become established after seven or more years on suitable sites. On acid sites they remain absent.

In section 1.1, the three benefits derived from the soil fauna were outlined: litter breakdown; soil aeration and amelioration; and as indicators of soil conditions. How far can each of these be justified on reclamation sites?

The results discussed in section 5 show that the soil fauna makes a significant contribution to litter breakdown. In the first stages of development of the fauna litter is eaten by microarthropods, especially Collembola, and by dipterous larvae. In wooded sites Cryptostigmatid mites and Enchytraeidae may also be important, and moder-like humus conditions develop, with a layer of undecomposed litter lying on the surface of the acid soil. In grassland sites the amount of litter available is less, so that a higher proportion can be assimilated or broken down by the limited fauna, and such conditions do not develop to the same extent. After about seven years earthworms may become numerous, in which case the rate of litter removal is greatly increased as the worms become the dominant soil animals.

The advent of earthworms demonstrates the second benefit of a soil fauna, namely amelioration of the soil. By greatly increasing the rate of litter removal, and by burying much of the undecomposed litter, the soil structure is improved, with greater water-holding capacity, and a change from moder to mull-like soil. Whether or not worms can colonize the site would seem to depend on at least three factors: acidity, moisture, and food. Some interest has been expressed in the artificial addition of earthworms to reclaimed land, in the hope that they will encourage the formation of a more 'natural' soil profile, and improve aeration and drainage, rather than for their use in the recycling of litter. In Dutch polders, worms became established both naturally and by artificial introduction. The common *L. terrestris* was not suited to the reclaimed soil, and *Allolobophora* species were successfully introduced, together with *L. rubellus* Hoffm. which colonized the polders naturally (van Rhee 1969). Dispersal rates of introduced worms were slow, however: only 4–6 m/yr. In land recently reclaimed by irrigation in Australia a mat of dead vegetation accumulated in the absence of earthworms, and it was found that ten years or more were needed for natural establishment of worms. Artificially introduced worms could survive in loamy soils, but did not become established in clay (Barley and Kleinig 1964).

It is naive to expect that simply spreading earthworms on reclaimed industrial land such as coal pit heaps will magically restore the soil to normal. The species used must be carefully selected to suit the site conditions, especially pH. The commonest earthworm, *L. terrestris*, is relatively abnormal in that it makes deep burrows, whereas many other species only tunnel near the soil surface. This will limit the depth of litter burial, but could be an advantage if soil conditions, such as stratified hard shale, prevent deep burrowing. Liming may be needed to enable worms to survive acid conditions, but even so their rate of spread is limited to about 12 m/yr (Stockdill and Cossens 1966). If worms are to survive they must have food, generally in the form of surface litter and dead plant roots, and adequate moisture. In newly reclaimed industrial soils the lack of an established litter layer is probably the chief factor acting against earthworm colonization or artificial addition. Thus Dunger (1969a) showed that *Allolobophora caliginosa* (Sav.) could successfully be introduced into reclaimed tertiary brown coal dumps after mulching the soil surface with leaf litter compost to provide food, and to stabilize fluctuations in moisture content. The soil was, however, too acid for *L. rubellus* or *Dendrobaena octaedra* (Sav.), two further species which were known to colonize the dumps at a later stage in their soil development. As a general conclusion, therefore, earthworms can be introduced to ameliorate the soil, but the species must be selected to suit soil conditions, and some form of food and moisture must also be provided.

The use of the soil fauna as an indicator of soil conditions is possible within rather wide limits. As yet too few sites have been studied for detailed conclusions to be drawn from any one survey, but some general stages of development of the soil fauna can be distinguished. These will reflect changes in the soil conditions, and therefore can be used as indicators of such changes. The following provisional classification is based on that prepared by Dunger (1968), and may serve as a guide to the stage that any particular soil has reached.

- Pioneer stage: extreme conditions of temperature and moisture, without humus formation, resulting in a limited fauna, mainly of micro-arthropods, whose density is less than $10 \times 10^3/m^2$.

- Colonization stage: fairly extreme conditions, but with some organic litter becoming incorporated into the soil. Faunal biomass mainly of microarthropods, especially Collembola, with densities in excess of $50 \times 10^3/m^2$, mites, which may be mainly Cryptostigmata or Prostigmata, and dipterous larvae. Animal respiration about 20 kcal/m². Decomposition mainly by microarthropods.

- Intermediate stage: only slightly extreme conditions, with moder (woodland) or mull (grassland) conditions. Faunal biomass of Collembola, macroarthropods, Enchytraeidae and some earthworms. Annual respiration abut 50 kcal/m². Decomposition mainly by larger arthropods and earthworms.

- Advanced stage: stable conditions, with (usually) mull conditions. Faunal biomass largely of earthworms, which incorporate most litter into the soil. Annual respiration about 80 kcal/m².

Non-acid soils reach these stages in about 1, 3, 7 and 10 years respectively, whereas more acid sites may not progress past a depleted third stage, with earthworms still very scarce or absent. Within any one site, samples of the soil fauna of any particular area may give indications of variations in local soil conditions, if the fauna is studied in detail, and major taxa identified to species. This is time-consuming, however, and the identifications can often only be carried out by specialists. Some general opinions may be valid nonetheless. Thus a microarthropod density of less than $10 \times 10^3/m^2$, other than in dry summer conditions, or within six months of reclamation, would indicate that soil conditions are unsuitable. The presence of earthworms on any reclamation site, other than at the boundary of the site, would suggest that the soil is developing well, and has enough organic matter incorporated to support the worms.

Management of reclaimed industrial land should clearly aim to encourage the soil fauna. Such encouragement will help to develop the soil, and will aid plant growth with a minimum of additional fertilizers. This can be done in the following ways:

- In the initial stages after reclamation, the physical conditions in the soil should be stabilized as much as possible. Extremes of drought and high temperatures should be minimized by establishing a close vegetation cover as soon as possible, and by leaving natural mulches such as grass mowings or leaf litter to lie on the soil surface.

- If topsoil is added, a sandy soil dries out too readily for many soil animals, and a loam is more suitable.

- Mechanical cultivation of the soil should be kept to a minimum; it has a disturbing effect on the soil fauna, bringing many microarthropods to the surface where they die of desiccation.

- Extreme acidity should be countered by liming, so as to bring the soil pH above 5·5.

- The organic content of the soil should be supplemented wherever possible, e.g. by manuring or adding slurry. These materials both enable the soil fauna to become established, acting as a source of food for the animals, and subsequently provide organic compounds and minerals for plant growth.

● If the site is not markedly acid, earthworms such as *A. caliginosa* can be introduced in a mulch of compost or manure.

More research is still needed on reclaimed sites, if management is to optimize both the soil fauna, and the contribution that the fauna makes to the development of each site. Areas needing further study are:

● the subsequent development of the soil fauna community on long-established and reclaimed sites (Dunger (1968) stresses that the process of soil formation is still continuing after 12 years on brown coal dumps);

● the effects of management, especially the addition of fertilizers and other chemicals, on this development;

● the relevance of the fauna to soil improvement on a wide range of types of reclaimed land;

● the dispersal mechanisms of soil animals which enable them to colonize reclaimed land.

Understanding of these topics should lead to the encouragement of a soil fauna best suited to the long-term aim of any particular reclamation project.

8 High-performance plant species in reclamation

J. A. Richardson

1 Introduction

In the past, man has often been profligate in his use of the countryside and until recently there was very little attempt to clean up the mess left behind after mineral extraction and industrial activity. Now there is a move towards the reclamation of damaged land; it has taken a long time to gather momentum but steady progress is being made in those countries where the pressure on land use is the greatest, e.g. in parts of the USA, Britain and Germany. Suitable regulations for safeguarding the countryside are now commonly written into the operating conditions laid down by governments, and this is happening not only in densely populated areas but also in those with comparatively small numbers, such as Australia, Africa, New Guinea.

A first step towards upgrading land damaged, for example, by spoil heaps, is to shape the waste dumps into new contours that either harmonize with the surroundings or form attractive new landscapes (see Chapter 4). Where the climate is suitable for plant growth the next step is to cover the ground with appropriate vegetation. Whatever the nature of the waste material, be it coal shale, limestone, pulverized fuel ash (PFA), sand from china clay and gold mining, ironstone and sulphur waste or copper and tin tailings, the medium must be accepted not so much as a soil but as a parent material. In the course of either weathering or regrading or both, it may have been broken down into particles that correspond in size to sand, silt and clay; and it may have been supplied with some organic material. The proportion of these materials is described by soil texture. Soil structure refers to the type and extent of the grouping of these components into aggregates (or crumbs). A soil with a good structure has an active microbial population, about 50% solids, 20% air and 30% water at field capacity. There is a network of large and small pores that allow for drainage and water retention, gaseous exchange and for the extension and development of roots. The structures give the soil stability in flood and drought, and, because they have elastic properties, they can recover from mechanical compaction. All of these properties have to be developed in the parent material by the interaction of the growing plants, the climate and any additives such as organic and inorganic manures given in husbandry.

When the parent material possesses the characteristics described above to a greater or lesser extent it may be described as fertile, and Thomas *et al.* (1973) have summarized the soil conditions for healthy growth of plant organs, e.g. seeds and roots containing adequate food reserves. These conditions are as follows: available water must be present and the hydrion concentration and the balance of inorganic salts in the external medium must be suitable; the temperature must be within the proper range; the oxygen level must be sufficient to inhibit anaerobic respiration; narcotic conditions (e.g. too high concentration of carbon dioxide) must not exist; light must be supplied to some plant organs before growth will begin; and there must be no severe mechanical impedance to enlarging organs.

The first question to be answered is to what extent does the waste material meet the requirements of a seed bed. The second is what, if any, treatments are needed before it can support a cover of vegetation. The now familiar physical, chemical and biological properties of waste heaps most likely to influence plant growth have been described elsewhere (e.g. Whyte and Sisam 1949; Richardson 1956; Goodman and Bray 1975) and they are listed here for convenience:

- Slope and aspect
- Wind effects
- Surface temperatures
- Water stress
- Stability of surface
- Nutrient status
- Spontaneous combustion
- Erosion
- Compaction
- Toxic substances
- Soil-forming mineral particles and organic matter
- Soil micro-organisms

The quality of the land which in time develops on the reclaimed sites depends on the parent material, the reclamation techniques, the climate, the additives and the cultivations. So far as broad agricultural use is concerned it is likely that most of the land will always be economically marginal; but the most profitable use may lie in pasture, meadow, forests and game reserves. In Britain, for example, there are about 18.4×10^6 hectares (45.9×10^6 acres) of arable grassland and rough grazing, and 1.9×10^6 hectares (4.8×10^6 acres) under forest (private, state-owned and scrub); and all of the spoil heaps in Britain together only come to about 20 000 ha (50 000 acres) or about one thousandth of the total. So even if all this was reclaimed the contribution to agriculture would be small. Accordingly, it has been argued that money invested in schemes to return sites to agricultural use will never show a reasonable return, and it has been urged that money spent in bringing about improvements in existing farmland would be a much better investment. But this argument ignores the increased efficiency of the small farms to which the reclaimed acres are leased, and the dramatic improvement tidy farmland makes in the urban environment when it replaces derelict land. Although it is well known that reclamation for recreation and amenity purposes will provide no revenue, it is now accepted that there is an immeasurable return in terms of the upgraded environment.

2 Some factors affecting plant growth

As the preceding remarks and the sections which follow will show, all reclamation work should be based on the results of careful analyses of as many of these factors as possible and for this purpose fairly comprehensive research laboratory facilities are required. Some factors affecting plant growth may require little measurement or monitoring but others may require close attention. Consider for example one aspect of soil fertility:

nutrient status. One aim of chemical analysis of the medium is to distinguish between the total quantity of a particular nutrient present and that fraction of it that is actually available for absorption by plants. From this information fertilizer recommendations can be made in order that adequate and timely supplies of essential elements can be added to the medium without waste of money or time.

But it must be emphasized that soil analysis has limitations, and it does not give the full answer to fertilizer requirements. Its methods are based on small samples and averages, and it does not account for variations from place to place on a site. The measured maximum availability of an element under one particular set of conditions, say, of water, air, organic matter, concentration of minor essential elements, etc may be very different under other conditions. What the grower of crops on derelict land (whether grass, herbs, shrubs or trees) has to know is the approximate nutrient content above which any selected crop is unlikely to be retarded, even if very adverse circumstances occur; and this information is most likely to be obtained by the combined results of soil analysis, pot experiments and trials on the actual reclaimed site or a comparable one.

2.1 Soil reaction (acidity and alkalinity)

Soil particles, particularly the mineral and organic fraction, possess negatively charged absorptive surfaces, and various positively charged ions (cations), e.g. calcium, potassium, hydrogen, are held by them. In soils there is a constant cation exchange taking place between the solid phase (soil particles) and the liquid phase (soil solution). Some soils, e.g. loams, have large cation exchange capacities because of the large negative charges developed on the clay and the humus fractions whereas sandy soils, which lack clay and humus, have small capacity. In moist conditions leaching of water through the soil tends to remove calcium, potassium and other cations and they are replaced by the hydrogen ions of the percolating water. Hydrogen-charged soil particles impart acidity to the medium. In contrast a soil with particles fully charged with mineral cations is said to be saturated and it imparts an alkaline reaction to the surrounding soil solution.

Soil reaction plays a considerable part in influencing the distribution and growth of plants in consequence of the concentration of hydrogen ions in the soil solution. This has both a direct and an indirect effect. The direct effect is by modifying the permeability of cell membranes and affecting the metabolism, and indirectly the soil reaction modifies the availability of inorganic materials. For example, acidity may bring iron and aluminium into solution and these ions could be toxic to plants, or it may precipitate all the available phosphorus and effectively remove all the calcium. The hydrogen ion concentration, $[H^+]$, is indicated by the pH scale on which the pH of an aqueous solution is defined as the negative logarithm of the hydrogen ion concentration. For example, neutrality is expressed by $pH = -\log[10^{-7}] = 7$; and when $[H^+] = 10^{-4}$, the $pH = 4$. Soil conditions favourable for plant growth are achieved by a balance between the hydrogen ions and the mineral cations bound by colloid particles. Many plants show an optimum range of only one pH unit under controlled conditions with only pH varied, but, under natural conditions, where many other factors operate, the pH zone spreads wider. Most higher plants can grow in soil somewhere between pH 5 and 7, and often in a wider range extending over 2 or 3 units on one or both sides of the pH 5 to 7 range. Soil pH gives valuable indications in any given climatic locality of what is needed to improve fertility (comparison of pH values for different climates is of little practical use). It is a guide to the effect of chemical fertilizers, which may even as neutral salts strongly acidify the soil by leaching out calcium as soluble salts. Of course, in practice the pH of the layer of soil solution actually in contact with the roots of plants under natural conditions is rarely determined. What is generally called soil pH is the value given by suspensions of soil samples in water in the proportion of 1 : 2.

The highest acidity found in natural soils is about pH 4.0, although greater acidity is found in some soils and in some parent materials due to the presence of strong mineral acids (see below). In many countries pasture grasslands are in the range pH 5 to 7, arable land pH 6 to 7 with an upper limit about pH 7.4. For *Trifolium pratense* (red clover) growing in moist areas the optimum pH value is said to be 8.3 to 8.7; in less moist places the range falls to pH 6.4 to 6.8 and red clover declines rapidly at less than pH 5.5.

Acidity in soil can be corrected by the addition of liming materials. Calcium is of course an essential plant nutrient, and it also improves texture in clay soils. It is the most important cation in the soil and it determines the soil's reaction. There are methods available for calculating how much lime is required to increase the pH to any required value (Doubleday 1971 a, b). Satisfying a known lime requirement may be a complex procedure; it is one which requires a careful study of all the conditions of each case and a continual check of both pH value and crop performance. It has to be remembered that soils may have the same pH but have different lime requirements because of the different amounts of colloidal material (clay and humus) present. For some parent materials sufficient lime can be given in a single dressing whereas for others lime must be given in small frequent dressings. Formerly lime was added as burnt limestone (or quicklime, CaO) or as slaked lime ($Ca(OH)_2$) because these materials are easily powdered. Now it is more common to use ground limestone rock. The finer it is crushed the quicker it acts to reduce soil acidity. Limestone coarser than 2 mm is regarded as an inefficient liming material, and a useful sample should contain a range of particle sizes between 2.0 and 0.1 mm in order to give both an initial rapid action and a fairly long residual one. It should be borne in mind that in the early stages of soil formation in acid parent material under suitable vegetation cover there will be considerable losses of calcium in the drainage water, and additional dressings of ground limestone will probably be required.

Over-liming can occur even where there is careful monitoring of the site; it leads to nutrient deficiency, especially with trace elements, and to poor performance in the planted species. Furthermore, heavy surface dressings of lime can react with the spoil material to form an impermeable cap which also reduces yield. The possible over-liming is a hazard that has to be accepted because in reclamation work a poor crop of grass must be better than no grass at all.

Iron pyrites (FeS_2) is a constituent of coal measure shales (see p. 87), and of copper, gold and other metallic wastes. When pyrites comes into contact with air and moisture, oxidation takes place and sulphuric acid is released into the soil solution lowering the pH to values of 2 or less; at this level of acidity growth of higher plants cannot take place (see pp. 91, 92). In the north of England, Richardson (1957) found the total sulphur content of some colliery shales was as high as 12% dry weight and most of the sulphur was present as FeS_2. In some shales the acid and acid-forming substances are quickly removed from the surface layers by weathering and leaching, but in others there may be slow release of acid for many years and at levels which prevent plant growth.

The amount of acidity and its duration depend on such factors as the amount of FeS_2 present, the rate of disintegration of the parent material, particle size and the mean annual rainfall and temperature. The waste from coal and gold mining is frequently only barely acid or is even alkaline in reaction when it is freshly tipped; it turns strongly acid after a few years (see p. 111) and may remain so for more than 60 years so that no natural colonists or planted vegetation can grow on untreated surfaces. Clearly, one cannot base a tree- and grass-planting schedule on laboratory tests carried out on freshly exposed materials, and this tendency to slow persistent acid production underlines the need for careful investigations using pot and field trials. The lime requirement for parent material of this type, calculated from results of normal methods of agricultural chemistry, will be inadequate in the long term. Several courses are available; one can either bury the acid-forming material beneath inert waste, or give massive amounts of ground limestone initially and work it well into the parent material where it can act as a neutralizing agent over a long period, e.g. 25.1 tonnes/ha (10 tonnes/acre). For an account of large-scale amendment trials on acid spoil see Chadwick (1973).

Where the evaporation from the surface in dry weather is high, it seems that the acidity, which has moved downwards from the surface in moist conditions, can be quickly reversed and the pH in the surface layers decreases. In certain gold mine reclamation, the downward movement of acid was continued by using a fine water spray on surfaces which were covered with an organic mulch to prevent evaporation. In this way leaching was continued until the acidity reached a depth from which it could not return to the surface in any known combination of local weather conditions.

Excessive alkalinity (pH = 9–12) in some waste heaps may be corrected by the addition of acid materials such as sulphuric acid, elemental sulphur, calcium sulphate (e.g. 12.6 tonnes/ha; 5 tons/acre), aluminium sulphate (17.6 tonnes/ha; 7 tons/acre). However, while improving the soil reaction, this treatment may result in the formation of an impervious cap to the surface which inhibits root growth. Pulverized fuel ash (PFA) is a highly alkaline waste material which reacts in this way to added lime; and in addition its soil solution possesses excessive osmotic pressure due to a high concentration of soluble salts and also toxic amounts of borate ions. Hodgson and Townsend (1973) have reported that prolonged weathering followed by surface additions of acid colliery shales and peat has proved a suitable amelioration for PFA. Once plants have become established in compacted alkaline material their roots open up cracks in the surface layers and the carbon dioxide given off in respiration further reduces the pH value of the medium. Alkaline-tolerant legumes and grasses may be sown to produce a dense crop which is then ploughed in as a green manure. This not only produces CO_2 in the soil as it decomposes, but it slowly releases essential nutrients such as phosphorus and manganese which are not usually available in alkaline soils.

2.2 Nutrients and soil fertility

The nitrogen, phosphorus and potassium and other essential elements needed by growing plants are supplied from chemical and organic sources. Where the soil parent material is deficient additions have to be made to raise the level of plant nutrients in the soil to one which satisfies the requirements of the selected crop. From the results of a soil analysis the correct amount of additive can be found. Almost uniformly, whether it is coal shale, PFA, limestone waste, china clay waste, copper, gold or iron mine waste, the soil parent material is deficient in phosphorus and nitrogen, low in potassium and often deficient in other elements such as calcium and molybdenum. Where an arable field may have 15–75 ppm nitrogen, the spoil may have a trace to 4 ppm; for phosphorus 9–15 ppm compared with 0.5–2.0 ppm and for potassium 50–100 and 5–15 ppm. A first aim in reclamation is to correct the ion deficiencies rapidly and to take steps to stabilize the net mineral content at a satisfactory level (see pp. 100–106). A balance has to be found between adding too much fertilizer which would be wasteful and too little which could lead to crop failure.

Chemical fertilizers are the chief means of raising the fertility of regraded land because they stimulate plants to produce large root and shoot systems. This provides organic matter which remains in the parent material and contributes to the initiation of a soil structure. For an account of the response of pit heap plants to added fertilizer see Gemmell (1973). Added nitrogen and phosphorus by stimulating root growth help the planted vegetation to overcome the adverse structural conditions which exist at first in raw spoil material. It also follows that as a result of the accelerated growth, larger amounts of other elements, e.g. calcium, magnesium and the trace elements, will be extracted by the plants, and deficiency levels could be reached more rapidly than in arable soils unless adequate replacements are made.

The essential elements for growth added to the soil as chemical fertilizer, manure or by the action of micro-organisms may be lost from the surface layers either by the drainage water leaching out soluble components, or by removal when the crop is harvested.

Nitrogen (N) is taken up by the plant as water-soluble ions of either ammonium or nitrate. Some of the nitrogen associated with organic matter in the soil is mineralized annually to the ammonium ion. This decomposition is a very complex biochemical process carried out by micro-organisms. A portion of the ammonium ions are oxidized to nitrate, a process of two stages each of them brought about by special bacterial groups. Nitrate nitrogen is not held bound to the soil particles and therefore any which is not taken up by living plants may be rapidly leached into the drains or lost by microbial denitrification in the gaseous form. The same applies to nitrate from chemical fertilizers. That which is not taken up by growing plants is lost. On arable land there may be 50% loss of available nitrate and on grassland 25% when applications of 200 kg N/ha/yr (178 lb N/acre/yr) are made.

Potassium (K) behaves differently in the soil; one fraction becomes incorporated on the complex associations of clay particles, some becomes electrostatically attracted to negatively charged clay colloids and the remainder is available for uptake. Potassium is fairly well retained in the soil, the portion not taken up by the plant remaining in the soil. With applications of 125 kg/ha/yr (111 lb/acre/yr) only 2% losses occurred.

Phosphorus (P) is applied in conventional fertilizers as the orthophosphate which is precipitated as either calcium or iron or aluminium phosphate depending on the nature of the soil. Phosphate is made available to plant roots by very slow release from these insoluble compounds or by decomposition from dead or decaying organic matter. If the amount of phosphate added to the soil exceeds that which can be precipitated, as in a light sandy soil, some of it would be lost in the drainage. Generally in good soil the losses are very small.

In a well structured soil the losses of potassium and phosphorus seem to be very small. In a developing soil they will probably vary from slight to considerable. So far as nitrogen is concerned, losses are high on all soils.

The rise in the cost of inorganic fertilizer nitrogen in recent years has renewed interest in nitrogen fixed by leguminous plants. Symbiotic nitrogen fixation is not confined to leguminous plants, although they are the only important nitrogen-fixing crop plants. Nitrogen fixation is also carried out by fungi (Actinomycetes), not bacteria, living in root nodules on *Alnus* spp., *Hippophae rhamnoides*, *Robinia pseudoacacia*. There is also non-symbiotic fixation of nitrogen by the free-living groups of organisms e.g. *Clostridium*, *Azotobacter* and blue-green algae which seem to be most active in wet soils containing appreciable amounts of decomposable material low in nitrogen e.g. cellulose, hay, straw. It is also possible that in young developing soils nitrogen content is built up by organisms other than those now recognized as nitrogen fixers. Present evidence favours the view that non-symbiotic nitrogen fixers are not of significant importance in temperate arable soils. A grassland kept free from leguminous plants may gain from 16 to 34 kg nitrogen/ha/yr (15 to 30 lb nitrogen/acre/yr) while a good clover or lucerne mixture will annually add 112 to 224 kg (100 to 200 lb).

In one of the famous Rothamsted experiments some land was cropped with barley for five consecutive years without any nitrogenous manure added. Then in the sixth and seventh years one half of the land was, as usual, sown with barley but the other half with a clover mixture. Analysis of the crops gathered in the seventh year showed that the barley crop removed 42 kg nitrogen/ha (37 lb/acre) from the soil and the clover crop 169 kg/ha (151 lb/acre). In the eighth and final year barley was grown on both plots with the following results. The nitrogen removed by the control crop was 18 kg (39 lb) and by the 'barley-following-clover' 31 kg (69 lb). Thus the clover not only provided a highly nutritious crop, but left sufficient nitrogen in the soil to enhance the barley by 34 kg nitrogen/ha (30 lb/acre); and this after the previous clover crop had removed 52 kg (114 lb) more nitrogen than the first barley crop.

During the 1960s, when inorganic fertilizer was relatively cheap, reliance on legume nitrogen tended to decrease in many situations. However, at present, and especially in the low-input–low-output systems which might apply to some reclaimed land, legume clover nitrogen has an important role to play in grassland production. On restored land in Europe a clover or lucerne crop can contribute around 125 kg/ha nitrogen (100 units nitrogen/acre) and, as the soil develops, up to 200 units may be expected under the British climate. This could represent a cash saving of £50/ha (£20/acre). It is interesting to recall that in New Zealand under the most favourable soil and climatic conditions additions of around 625 kg nitrogen/ha (500 units nitrogen/acre) have been reported.

Clover is dependent on a number of factors for vigorous growth. It is intolerant to acid conditions and the amount of nitrogen fixed below $pH = 5$ is negligible. Some nodules may form at $pH = 4$ but no nitrogen fixation takes place below $pH = 5$. Lupins fix nitrogen in more acid soils than clover and clover in soils too acid for lucerne. By means of judicious liming the pH must be raised to between pH 5.5 and 5.8 using carefully calculated amounts of ground limestone. Thereafter dressings of say 1250 kg/ha (10 cwt/acre) every three years might be all that is required. But persistent acidity (see p. 152 for details) will require special measures. Phosphorus is essential for growth and nitrogen fixation by clovers. If the level is low nodules may form but they remain small and white. However, at suitable phosphorus levels the nodules turn pink in colour and begin fixing atmospheric nitrogen. Such levels have been attained by adding basic slag or mineral phosphate (25.1 tonnes/ha; 10 tons/acre). Thereafter 630 kg/ha (5 cwt/acre) basic slag every three years could suffice to maintain the sward. The methods of husbandry will affect the rate of application. Clover growth is also stimulated by calcium and potassium and suitable compound fertilizers containing these elements may be applied at sowing time. Water-soluble phosphates are preferred because the alternative, North African mineral phosphate, lowers the pH more. However, the latter is about half the price and may be chosen if pH can be kept above 5.5.

Research has shown that to produce efficient nitrogen-fixing clover plants with large pink nodules, the trace elements molybdenum, boron, manganese and copper must be present. Some of these are provided by the basic slag (or other fertilizers), others are already present in the spoil or may be added to the alkaline material used in the production of pelleted seeds. Molybdenum (Mo) is essential for the actual nitrogen-fixing process; the plants may grow well and form nodules in soils very low in Mo but unless the amount of Mo reaches 10–25 ppm for lucerne and 4–8 ppm for clover no nitrogen is fixed.

So far as temperature is concerned it seems that active clover growth begins at 8°C and nitrogen fixation at 10–11°C; it is important therefore that conditions favouring rapid warming of the soil be created. A wet mineral soil is slow to warm up in spring, it has low oxygen concentration and root growth is depressed. In contrast a well structured loam with high organic content, microbial activity, and good aeration and drainage will reach suitable growing temperatures earlier.

Legumes are the main group of plants that symbiotically fix the free nitrogen in the soil air and the bacterial symbionts are members of the genus *Rhizobium*. The *Rhizobium* component of clover nodules, for example, shows some specificity and for successful nodulation to occur it is also necessary to have substantial innoculation of the bacteria. This is likely to be most important in parent soil material where there is practically no bacterial population. One method is to treat the seed with a culture of the proven *Rhizobium* before sowing and to ensure that the method of sowing does not cause destruction or removal of the bacteria; alternatively the culture may be sprayed on to the land after sowing. Often the first innoculation in this way has little effect because it supplies a very small number of bacteria compared with the population of normal soil. A more satisfactory method is to spread lightly with topsoil from a field in which the clover has been recently grown and harrow in 1000 kg/ha (8 cwt/acre) just before seeding. Growth of the bacteria is encouraged by good cultivation.

Under conditions where the legume crop produces insufficient nitrogen to stimulate growth of herbage, for example in the first two years on a reclaimed site, the only way to add appreciably to the fertility of the soil and the crop yield may be through the use of chemical (inorganic) fertilizers. This is well illustrated by one of the famous experiments carried out in Broadbalk Field, Rothamsted, where wheat had been continuously grown for over 100 years. On plots receiving no additives the yield fell over the years as the soil became more impoverished of nutrients, from about 1500 to 750 kg/ha (from 12 to 6 cwt/acre). This still considerable yield (about average for wheat by world standards) is attributed to the soil nitrogen-fixing bacteria. The plots given farmyard manure yielded 5000 kg/ha (20 cwt/acre), and those with complete chemical fertilizer, 10% more. There have been plenty of field trials carried out in many countries which clearly demonstrate that there is an almost linear gain in yields in response to increasing rates of nitrogen application until optimum levels are reached.

It is not possible to do a simple calculation to find the increase in yield from adding different amounts of fertilizer. Soil types are so variable; there are many levels of fertility and there are other factors to be considered such as climate, method of husbandry, pests etc. Nevertheless, with the aid of soil analysis, greenhouse experiments and field trials on spoil heap material, it is possible to devise manurial programmes which will support sufficient vegetation for the intended use.

Only by experience can a balance be found between high rates of application that will certainly ensure a 'successful' sward at great cost and low rates that might jeopardize the whole scheme. Where the raw parent material contains adequate amounts of potassium increasing use is being made of fertilizers containing only nitrogen and phosphorus. It appears that a mixed fertilizer of, say, ammonium nitrate and triple superphosphate of lime is less effective in producing balanced release of nitrogen and phosphorus than one in which these elements are present in the same compound. Examples are urea ammonium phosphate (30–30–0) and ammonium polyphosphate (15–61–0). There is much more use made in many countries of a compound fertilizer (containing NPK) than of 'straight' fertilizers containing only one essential element. Now that costs and availability have become important considerations there may be a return to 'straight' fertilizers such as nitrate of soda and ground rock phosphate. Also arising from higher costs, it is possible that grass-breeding programmes could at last be directed towards looking for superior growth at low fertilizer level.

2.3 Organic matter

Fertility is by no means a wholly chemical question, dependent on the amount of mineral ions the soil parent material contains. In many instances it is the physical properties, which regulate the supply of water and air to plant roots and to micro-organisms, that are far more important in producing a fertile soil than the quantity of nutrient elements it contains. For example, light sandy land, although containing satisfactory levels of NPK, is often made so dry by natural drainage that only in wet seasons will there be enough water retained for the growth of plants. Again, heavy clay soils may show adequate NPK, but the texture is so close that movement of water and air is retarded and they carry poor crops. On most of the sub-standard land currently being reclaimed it is impossible to effect much lasting improvement by the use of compound chemical fertilizers only.

A fertile soil is one that is rich in the dead and decaying remains of previous vegetation and has been so acted upon by water and the soil fauna and flora to possess a stable structure. The incorporation of organic material into both light sandy soils and heavy clays improves the texture, until they develop a water-holding capacity and air spaces just suitable for the needs of growing plants. Waste heap materials frequently resemble over-worked arable soils which have lost the power of cohering, and they may either fall into dust or set rock-hard when dry. Like worn-out farmland, spoil heap material can be made fertile by the addition of organic material. This may be done by the process of green manuring in which a leguminous crop is turned back into the soil parent material to improve the tilth and at the same time supply nitrogen. Species of *Trifolium* (clover), *Lupinus* (lupin), *Vicia* (vetch), *Medicago* (lucerne or alfalfa) and *Melilotus* (sweet clover) have been widely used and the seeds are sown on land lightly dressed, before seeding, with topsoil (see p. 155) and NPK fertilizer (1004 kg/ha; 8 cwt/acre) to promote vigorous growth. The green crop is ploughed in and the land is resown with legumes once decomposition of the first crop has started. Green manures are particularly effective in mild climates and on saline soils because they reduce evaporation from, and hence salt in, the surface soil. It has been claimed that ploughing-in a green crop is a more efficient way of improving soil tilth than ploughing-in farmyard manure.

Fresh organic matter in which decomposition has not proceeded very far is coarse and retains its cellular structure. In clayey material it improves aeration and drainage and it supports populations of soil-forming animals (earthworms, millipedes etc.) and of soil micro-organisms. Some of the latter produce polysaccharide gums that bind mineral particles together to form the aggregates which give stable structure to light sandy soils.

Partially or completely decomposed organic matter is known as humus. It is black colloidal material which is a source of nitrogen compounds available to plants, and it increases the soil's power of retaining moisture. On light soils humus binds the mineral particles into crumbs. Like clay, humus gives cohesion and structure to a soil. It has the advantage over clay of not 'setting hard' or drying. In a well aerated soil, humus is constantly undergoing oxidation and a high rate of loss is inevitable. Whereas regular applications of organic matter have to be made to maintain the structure and fertility of arable soils, on undisturbed grassland, such as could form on raw parent material, this is achieved from dead roots and shoots of plants.

It is easy to demonstrate the high proportion of water-stable crumbs in a soil from an old pasture and the very low proportion in soil parent material. Unfortunately not all raw materials respond favourably to all of the available bulky organic manures (sewage sludge, farmyard manure, slurries, broiler litter, green manures). Even after large additions of some of these manures when the organic content is high the desired structure and stability remain low. This is an important area of reclamation technique that would repay close investigation. Nevertheless, it can be stated that there is overwhelming evidence to support the view that organic matter makes an important contribution to soil structure and fertility in young soils formed from spoil material; high organic matter leads to rapid vegetative cover.

2.4 Compaction of the surface

Severe compaction may be caused in some waste materials (e.g. PFA, limestone, anhydrite, colliery shale) under certain climatic conditions or arising from the methods employed during regrading operations. For those pit-heap shales which break down in weathering to produce a high proportion of clay rather than a porous mixture of coarse and fine particles, a point is reached when permeability of the surface is so low that puddling occurs and an impervious cap seals the surface. This often happens (Richardson 1975) where there is no vegetation to improve soil texture and in one experiment the infiltration capacity was only 0.01 cm/min (or about a twentieth that of grass sward), and the run-off was rapid and nearly 95% of all the rainfall. A sealed surface not only means a high rate of erosion, but also less gaseous exchange. This in turn limits root development of any plants that are present and leads to little or no penetration by germinating seedlings.

In the process of regrading spoil the surface is covered many times by tracked and wheeled machines. Although the former may weigh up to 30 800 kg (68 000 lb) they produce a very small ground contact pressure, about 0.26 kg/cm² (3.8 lb/in²), because of their broad tracks. Carefully used in suitable weather these vehicles are not likely to impart dangerous properties to the reshaped heaps. However, wheeled tractor-scrapers because of their smaller ground-contact areas have correspondingly high ground contact pressures, e.g. 4.8 kg/cm² (70 lb/in²), which greatly exceed those of crawler tractors. Wheeled tractor-scrapers driven enthusiastically over a reclamation site will produce compaction throughout the whole volume of the renewed land, which makes the preparation of a seed bed for grasses lengthy and for trees an almost impossible task.

In north-east England certain places on regraded spoil heaps gave the same penetrometer reading as on a nearby metalled road. At other sites a power-driven borer could not penetrate and the tractor was lifted clear of the surface. To open up the ground for tree-planting resort had to be made to a chisel plough (or parallogram ripper) and this did not auger well for the growth and development of a vigorous root system in this sort of material. This was borne out later by the high failure rate which occurred. Recent experiments carried out in Newcastle and elsewhere (see Richardson 1975) amply demonstrate that apart from the effects of restricted water and air, the dense material places mechanical limitations on the downward growth of roots necessary to avoid surface drought. Even in only slightly compacted soil the seminal root length may be reduced to a third and this is strong evidence in support of placing the final 2 m (7 ft) of material by light broad-tracked machines.

The sowing dates (see p. 160) will depend on the nature of the material, the moisture content, and the temperature at the surface. Known hot dry periods should be avoided and in Britain May, June, and July are not favoured. In March the soil is probably too cold and too wet but April could be suitable on light land. Caution is needed on clayey material;

even if the top 5 cm (2 in) is dry, lower down at 20 cm (8 in) may still be so wet that the poorly structured material puddles into a slurry under pressure of the cultivating machines. A well structured granular soil possesses resilience, i.e. at a given moisture content it will deform slightly under pressure and then return to its original state on release. But the unstructured parent material does not have the elastic and plastic properties to endure or resist strain and is therefore easily deformed.

A reclaimed site rarely dries out uniformly and some parts may be workable when others are still too wet. This may call for the completion of part of the site before the rest is started. This adds to the expense of the job and adds force to the argument in favour of a blanket of topsoil on most sites (see Doubleday 1973; Bradshaw *et al.* 1973).

On a farm which has, say, ten fields, all with slightly different soil conditions, the farmer can choose the right time to carry out the five or six operations each field needs to prepare a good seed bed. In contrast, on reclaimed sites the contractor will generally be tempted to get on with the work irrespective of the state of the ground and the compaction that may result. In Britain, the advantage of sowing a seeds mixture in August is that the ground temperature is still high and the moisture low enough for the land to be worked regularly. The aim is to promote quick germination followed by rapid root growth. In this way losses due to detached roots caused by frost heaving of the soil can be minimized. A further protection against loss of roothold is to make firm the layer immediately below the seeds.

2.5 Available moisture

A period of prolonged drought following a sowing could make it impossible for the grasses and legumes to establish themselves.

The analysis of water loss from soils and heat conduction in soils in the field is complex because the surface is exposed to seasonal, daily and even hourly changes of radiation and soil water content. In general, periods of high soil temperature coincide with periods of low moisture content. Under these conditions, water loss from plants may exceed supply and a negative water balance results.

The creation of water deficits in plants may be due not so much to failure of supply but to an insufficiently rapid supply, and they may be brought about by the accelerated transpiration, e.g. by the opening of stomatal apertures, the drying of air, or the rising of the wind; or by a reduction in the rate of absorption by roots.

Turgor pressures will be reduced in the cells of plant members which are incurring water deficits, and there will be danger of wilting. Prolonged wilting leads to death of the crop.

The conduction of heat downwards in soil leads to water loss, and wilting of the crop is reduced by the presence in it of organic matter (shaley material has a higher specific heat than organic matter). Similarly, a layer of organic material (a mulch) or a plant cover at the surface reduces the maximum temperatures a few millimetres beneath the surface. It seems that even a thin layer of vegetation so reduces the effect of high temperatures that roots of seedlings and rhizomes of established plants would not be subjected to temperatures higher than about 30°C (Richardson *et al.* 1971). Furthermore, after rain the vegetation protects the layers beneath it from evaporation losses and this also produces conditions that favour the growth of plants. In an experiment with the grass *Agrostis tenuis* it was found that whereas the bare shale control had maximum temperatures of 55°C at the surface and 36°C at 7.6 cm (3 in), the temperatures at corresponding positions under the grass were 26°C and 19°C.

All this argues in favour of some organic additive to the parent material of spoil heaps and the rapid establishment of a plant cover with close bottom. In this way soil water will be conserved and soil temperatures reduced at the rooting level. Where spring-sown grasses on a pit heap had wilted and died back in August one conclusion might be that the high summer temperatures acting directly on the shoot and root tissues at ground level had caused desiccation and subsequent death. Alternatively, it could be argued that the high temperatures caused loss of soil water and at so high a rate that the soil surface layers became depleted to the extent that the rate of absorption of water by the plant's roots fell below that of transpiration causing loss of turgor and death. It should be stated here in connection with this alternative view that those species that possess the ability to develop a long tap root reaching down to cooler levels where the moisture content is higher are the ones which survive.

Records of soil moisture were kept for three colliery sites in Co. Durham (Richardson 1956). No plants survived on these spoil heaps, but when samples of spoil were removed to the experimental garden and kept at moisture content approximately half-way between field capacity (FC) and permanent wilting point (PWP), plants grew readily. The data given in Table 18 were from one site and were closely comparable with those for the other two stations.

From the appropriate pF curves and the results of field tests it was found that the PWP for this soil was 5.6%. It will be seen from Table 18 that for quite long periods, e.g. the four weeks from 13 July to 3 August, the moisture content of the top 7.6 cm (3 in) of the soil was in the region of PWP. At greater depths, however, there was always some water available for growth.

These observations underline the importance of the rate of elongation of the roots of seedlings with respect to the progressive drying out from the soil surface downwards. Only so long as the extremities of the elonga-ting root systems keep ahead of the downward extension of the dry zone will the plants be able to extract the water they require to maintain turgor. From Table 18 it appears that even in dry weather the moisture contents at depths of 15.2 cm (6 in) rarely fall below PWP.

In some experiments to examine further the effects of temperature and moisture content on survival of seedlings of the grasses *Agrostis tenuis* and *Dactylis glomerata*, sowings were made at the equivalent of 50 kg/ha (45 lb/acre) in deep trays of fine shale where the moisture content was kept at just below the field capacity (FC). After 5 weeks of growth and for 10 days duration the soil surface temperatures were raised to 47°C for 6 h daily. These were normal temperatures for black pit heaps in summer. In parallel experiments temperatures of 57°C were given for 4 h

Table 18 A record of soil moisture content near the surface of a colliery spoil heap.

| Date | Moisture content (% dry wt) at various depths | | |
	7.6 cm (3 in)	15.2 cm (6 in)	22.9 cm (9 in)
1 June	9.4	8.3	7.8
8 June	7.6	7.0	7.1
16 June	5.9	7.2	6.6
22 June	6.0	7.3	8.6
29 June	5.8	7.2	8.4
6 July	6.8	6.6	7.6
13 July	4.1	6.0	7.0
20 July	5.2	6.0	7.1
27 July	3.9	5.7	6.8
3 August	3.9	5.6	7.0

Table 19 Survival of 5-week- and 20-week-old grass seedlings at two different soil moisture contents when the soil surface temperature was 47°C.

Species	Soil water content	% survival
Agrostis tenuis (5-week-old)	5%	33%
	12%	100%
Agrostis tenuis (20-week-old)	5%	87%
	17%	100%

daily. Some trays were still at about FC (12% moisture) while in others the surface layer had been allowed to fall to PWP (5% moisture) (Table 19).

Similar results were obtained with *Dactylis glomerata*. When the treatment was 57°C for 4 h for the 5-week-old plants there was about 10% survival at the low and 85% at the high moisture content. However the 20-week-old plants were much more resistant and there was 68% survival at low moisture and 100% at high.

These results can be related to events taking place in the field. For August-sown seeds, provided they germinate within a few weeks and the young plants survive the winter frosts, their ages will be in the region of 24 weeks when they are subjected to the hot dry conditions of summer. As the table shows these plants are able to survive. In contrast the seedlings of a March or April sowing will be about 6 weeks old when drought conditions may have to be faced. The results show that many plants that are 6 weeks old could survive the summer provided the moisture content of the soil remained near to FC (12%). If drying out occurs due to the absence of rainfall, or to the absence of organic matter to structure the soil and conserve water, so that the moisture content falls to PWP (5%), the percentage of surviving plants would be small. On the other hand many of the plants that are 24 weeks old at the beginning of the summer could survive even when the soil moisture content at the surface falls to below PWP.

3 Grassland

By basing his judgement on considerations of parent material, local climate, the existing landscape and the interests of the agricultural community and amenity groups, the owner of reclaimed land can generally select from a number of possible future uses. Examples are pastureland, amenity grassland, woodland, conservation areas and nature reserves, and for each one of them there could be differences in the final cultivations and in the species planted.

Pastureland may be utilized in several ways, and if the intention is known before reclamation is completed the seeds mixtures and treatments may be adjusted to give the appropriate vegetation. First, the land may be let to a neighbouring farmer on a grazing licence (e.g. for 7 months per year for 5 years), then later the reclaimed fields can be placed on an agricultural tenancy. Where a farmer has lost land because of mining or other activity it will generally be enthusiastically incorporated into the farm. Clearly, a long lease on attractive terms will give encouragement to the tenant to direct all his expertise and much time to the considerable task of converting derelict ground into near-arable land. Secondly, the land may be leased to livestock dealers for carefully controlled short-term grazing during the growing season, the owner retaining responsibility for the management, including drainage, manurial treatment and any grass cutting to remove withered tops required to give a good appearance to the land in autumn and winter. Thirdly, the pasture could be let for hay or silage making, providing the dangers of metal, rubber and plastic litter near urban areas are fully understood.

3.1 Selection of species

So far as possible the pasture grasses selected for reclamation purposes should be high bulk yielding, persistent, leafy and able to spread vegetatively. They should be able to resist trampling by stock and hard grazing and be able to compete successfully with unwanted grasses and weeds. They should have high nutritional value, be palatable to stock, and hardy. For certain purposes the capacity to remain green in winter and show early growth in spring are desirable characters. Because it is unlikely that all these requirements are found in one species a seeds mixture is used (see section 3.2). Furthermore it has to be remembered that the grasses, e.g. *Lolium* species, which possess most of these qualities on good land may quickly lose them and even die back on poor soils; while a grass that is useful in a hilly pasture on poor soil, e.g. *Agrostis tenuis*, is regarded as an inferior species on lower, potentially more fertile land.

In the UK and other mild, humid, temperate areas in Europe and the USA the most important grass in the best permanent pastures is *Lolium perenne* (perennial ryegrass). It starts well from seed and it produces bulk in the first year. Where balanced fertilizers are available it gives good-quality herbage throughout the growing season but on poor, light land it may be badly affected by extremes of soil temperatures and moisture. It grows well in conjunction with clover. *Phleum pratense* (timothy) is a very palatable and winter hardy grass which grows satisfactorily on heavy, moist land. It is slow to establish; in the seedling stage it is not competitive against other species and this allows it and clover to flourish together. *Festuca pratensis* (meadow fescue) is also non-aggressive and slow to establish, but it is adapted to a wide range of soils and gives good summer growth when some grasses are dormant. *Dactylis glomerata* (cocksfoot or orchard grass) is a versatile grass which is deep-rooting and drought-resistant even in light soils. It is encouraged by lenient grazing or cutting. *Festuca elatior* (tall fescue) is much hardier than *F. pratensis* and it produces greater bulk of herbage which will prove less palatable than other species. *Avena elatior* (tall oat), which should not be confused with the bulbous oat (*Arrhenatherum elatius*), is also a relatively unpalatable grass, but it produces great bulk and is hardy and persistent. In some situations it is said to be comparable to *Dactylis*. *Poa trivalis* (rough-stalked meadow grass) is extremely palatable and when fertilizers are given freely it forms a large amount of foliage and spreads rapidly by stolons to form a compact sward. However, it is shallow-rooted and its rate of growth is drastically reduced at low moisture content and it fails completely in prolonged drought on light land. *Poa pratensis* (smooth-stalked meadow grass or Kentucky blue grass) is more deeply rooted, and, because of its underground rhizomes, it survives well on open-textured light soils that are alkaline rather than acid. It is slower to establish than *P. trivalis* and produces less bulk. *P. compressa* (Canadian blue grass) is a sturdy plant and ideal for impoverished soils. *Festuca ovina* (sheep's fescue), *F. rubra* (red fescue) and *F. ovina tenuifolia* (fine-leaved fescue) are all persistent and, although they do not produce much bulk, they are invaluable on poor thin soils. *Agrostis tenuis*, like the fine-leaved fescues, can produce a sward on shallow soils. It is tolerant of dry conditions and low fertility, and it has a wide range of pH tolerance. *Holcus lanatus* (Yorkshire fog) and *H. mollis* (creeping soft grass) are able to tolerate acid conditions and, although they are regarded as weeds on good land, they make a useful contribution to upland and mountain grazings.

In tropic and subtropic areas of the USA and Africa with 10 to 30 cm (25 to 75 in) rain per year there are several outstanding grasses for reclamation work. These are *Cynodon dactylon* (bermuda grass), *C. plectostachyus* and *Eragrostis lehmanniana* (lehman love grass), *E. curvula* (weeping love grass), *Bouteloua* spp. (gramagrass), and *Bromus inermis* (smooth brome grass). They are deep-rooted, adaptable to drought and said to produce rapid soil cover on a variety of waste materials. *Festuca arundinacea* (tall fescue), *Phalaris tuberosa* (hardy canary grass), and *Paspalum nototum* (bahia) have also been used successfully on spoil heaps.

Legumes are grown to aid the soil-forming processes, to add nitrogen to the soil, and provide a bulky palatable component to the sward. In mild moist climates, legumes such as *Trifolium repens* (wild white clover) and *Lotus corniculatus* (birdsfoot trefoil) are always associated with successful *Festuca–Agrostis* swards making up to 10% of the ground cover. The legumes greatly improve fertility by accumulating nitrogen and, where manuring is not practised, they are largely responsible for maintaining the pasture. In richer pastures, clovers used are *Trifolium pratense* (red clover) and *T. hybridum* (alsike clover). In general the legumes improve the palatability of the herbage, have high nutritive value, increase the yield and improve soil fertility. In Britain *T. pratense* accounts for about 45%, *T. repens* 35%, and *T. hybridum* 11% of all herbage legumes. The remainder consists of *Medicago sativa* (lucerne), *Medicago lupulina* (trefoil), and *Onobrychis vicifolia* (sainfoin). For reclamation work in warmer climates *Lespedeza sericea* and *Coronillia varia* (crown vetch) have been used successfully in grass mixtures and alone. They both tolerate acidity in a wide range of soils. *Melilotus alba* (white sweet clover) and *M. officinalis* (yellow sweet clover) are also useful because the deep tap root penetrates into the waste material and because it thrives under wide climatic conditions; unfortunately it does not tolerate acid soil conditions. Under the best conditions it seems that *Coronillia varia* is the most outstanding legume for stabilizing spoil and initiating soil-forming processes.

Legumes can be aggressive if favoured by added phosphate fertilizer and close grazing; and this could lead to them dominating the sward and perhaps excluding the grasses. For a number of agricultural reasons this must be avoided and by controlling seed rate and management the ratio of grass to clover in the sward is kept to about 3 to 1.

3.2 Seeds mixtures

There may be circumstances when the regraded land can be given a cover of topsoil of substantial thickness (e.g. 0.5 m, 20 in) and then it could be planted down to rotational grassland. Generally, however, the grassland will be developed from spoil that is only slightly modified; for many years it will be permanent grassland and as such it will not enter into any system of arable rotation. The seeds mixture for sowing must be very carefully designed to suit the parent spoil material, the climate and the agricultural use of the land. This could range from dairying, sheep and beef production, mixed livestock farming to forage conservation and cover for game and wildlife. Mixtures of grasses and legumes are sown for two main reasons. First, over a number of years, with changes in weather and on soils of varying properties, exposure and aspect, a mixed sward should be able to produce a more certain crop over the whole of the growing season than a single species. Secondly, the leguminous plants are included because they build fertility in the soil and add bulk and palatability to the herbage.

It must be clearly understood that the grassland produced from the selected mixture will not become a static association of species. On the contrary, there exists from the beginning a strong tendency towards the replacement of sown species by less suitable types and by weeds which move into the sward by the usual seed dispersal mechanisms. The ultimate composition of the sward and indeed the survival of any sort of sward is determined by the soil, climate, and husbandry. Unless highly persistent strains of pedigree indigenous seeds have been sown and the herbage maintained in good condition by suitable manuring and careful management, it may bear little relation to the original mixture after only a few years. For example, if grazing is too intense and for too long a period without time for the sward to recover or if manurial treatment is omitted, parts of the sward will die back and leave bare patches which will be colonized by inferior grasses and weeds from the countryside. Booy (1975) has reported on a seeds mixture composed of ryegrass, cocksfoot, meadow fescue, timothy, and mixed clovers sown on ameliorated Magnesian Limestone spoil at 45 kg/ha (40 lb/acre) in 1965. After six years without attention the ryegrass, the meadow fescue and the alsike clover had all died out, and in the *Dactylis*-dominated sward there were no fewer than 44 invading species.

There are many species of grass and legume available on the world's commercial market and also from a few specialized plant materials centres such as those in the USA (see p. 170). Lists of recommended species and varieties, and mixtures of varieties, are readily available from government agencies. Seeds mixtures are prepared using knowledge of the properties of the varieties both alone and in association and how they react to a range of chemical and physical factors in the environment. The mixtures should satisfy all the requirements of good pasture species listed above (p. 161) and the relative proportions of each component seed are calculated to give a compact high-yielding sward. It was once common to sow twelve or more species to make sure that sufficient of them would survive on difficult ground or in a bad season to establish a closed sward. The custom now, especially on good land, is to sow only a few adaptable and productive species. The most important species in permanent pasture is *Trifolium repens* (white clover) which by fixing nitrogen improves fertility and increases the nutritional value and yield of the pasture.

For a durable sward which allows wide versatility of use, the form of Cockle Park Mixture given below could be used. Reliance is placed on a high white clover content to improve fertility. Silage or hay may be taken as well as providing grazing for part of the year.

Variety	Species	Rate (kg/ha)	(lb/acre)
S23	Perennial ryegrass	4.5	4
S24	Perennial ryegrass	4.5	4
'Endura'	Perennial ryegrass	4.5	4
S37	Cocksfoot	4.5	4
S26	Cocksfoot	4.5	4
S48	Timothy	4.5	4
S51	Timothy	2.2	2
S100	White clover	1.7	1.5
S184	White clover	0.6	0.5
		31.5	28

Other mixtures suitable for more specialized uses are listed overleaf.

Rate of seeding will vary with the circumstances. Where a considerable layer of topsoil has been spread over the raw parent material it should be possible to obtain a very fine tilth for sowing in warm weather. Under these conditions of rapid germination and high rate of establishment, a small amount of seed may be employed (e.g. 31.5 kg/ha; 28 lb/acre). But on poor land with a coarse seed bed, or where it is difficult to work the parent material to a fine tilth, heavier seeding up to three or four times this rate may be necessary. Only experience with a particular type of

A mixture of high-tillering varieties of grass and clover to be used for sheep and beef production:

Variety	Species	Rate (kg/ha)	(lb/acre)
'Melle'	Perennial ryegrass	6.7	6
S23	Perennial ryegrass	11.2	10
S48	Timothy	4.5	4
S184	White clover	0.6	0.5
S100	White clover	1.7	1.5
		24.7	22

For silage or hay on suitable land the following may be used:

Variety	Species	Rates (kg/ha)	(lb/acre)
S215	Meadow fescue	13.5	12
S352	Timothy	6.7	6
S100	White clover	2.2	2
		22.4	20

spoil in a given area will enable one to decide on the most suitable seed rate for the climatic conditions of an average year. Once a seed mixture has been found to suit some local conditions of substrate and climate it is advisable to retain the proportion of the constituent species although the sowing rate of the mixture can be varied.

Cultivations and fertilizers (see pp. 115–123) for the preparation of the seed bed will vary from site to site. If the parent material is acid and it can be treated with lime, fertilizer and a light dressing of topsoil to raise the pH to 5.5 or 6 and the NPK to 35, 12 and 30 ppm, a Cockle Park type mixture after two or three years would produce a grass/clover crop yielding 5 tonnes/ha (2 tons/acre) dry matter per year. Based on a reasonable utilization of the crop the site could sustain 200 cow-days. The practice should be to graze at fairly high intensity, e.g. 5 beasts/ha (2 beasts/acre) ('mob grazing'), for a short time with adequate rest periods in between. This form of management in the early years of a reclaimed site will help to prevent selective grazing of the sward, and if stock are kept off the land in wet weather, the grassland should develop good root and shoot properties that will make it permanent and requiring only low maintenance. Continuous grazing should be strictly avoided. A light mowing at the end of the year, when grazing is finished, would be all that is necessary to remove the debris and leave the grass green throughout the winter. In some areas grazing with sheep would be both feasible and desirable, but in urban areas owing to trespass, dog damage and theft it cannot be justified unless shepherding can be arranged.

Low-maintenance grassland is that which has a place on poor ground in the farming system or which is used for amenity, woodland, wildlife reserves and similar purposes. Some clues to appropriate species to sow may be obtained from examining as many places as possible where spoil heaps of comparable material have been colonized naturally by plants from the surrounding countryside. When nearly 250 pit heap areas in north-east England were examined (Richardson *et al.* 1971) it was found that the percentage occurrence on them of certain grasses was as follows:

Agrostis tenuis	82%
Arrhenatherum elatius	44%
Dactylis glomerata	64%

Deschampsia flexuosa	48%
Festuca spp.	10%
Holcus lanatus	34%

All of these species are permanent members of grassland on the shallow impoverished soils associated with heaths and moorlands. There were few legumes present, and *Lathyrus pratensis, Lotus corniculatus, Trifolium pratense, T. repens, Vicia cracca* together only occurred on 5% of the areas. Of the grasses, all but *Dactylis* are regarded as weeds in richer lowland pastures but they provide valuable grazings in places where the soil is shallow, stony, has poor natural drainage, a high degree of acidity, excessive leaching and low nutrient status. With only a small amount of maintenance such grassland can be upgraded to give a better sward capable of accelerating the soil-forming processes on the parent material below. This can be done by means of lime and phosphorus treatment to encourage growth of *Lotus corniculatus* (birdsfoot trefoil) and *Trifolium repens* (white clover) until these legumes form more than 10% of the sward. This of course gives grazing land of relatively high value, and, because of the nature of the species, for a long season.

The most characteristic form of upland grassland in Britain is that dominated by *Agrostis tenuis* (bent) and *Festuca ovina* (sheep's fescue). *Agrostis–Festuca* grassland is the mainstay of all grazing animals on British mountains and it is said to support more stock per unit area than any other form of mountain pasture. At its best it may contain *Lolium perenne, Poa pratensis* and *Festuca pratensis* in addition to the species listed above. Grazing on the one hand causes a certain amount of stimulation because of treading which encourages tillering and the marked manurial effects of animal droppings. On the other hand grazing becomes selective in that some spp. are eaten while others are not. This often means that spp. which are less palatable tend to persist at the expense of the more palatable. Heavy grazing at first leads to a fall in *Festuca* and a rise in *Agrostis* content; later coarse grasses such as *Nardus stricta* (moor mat grass) which are hardly ever eaten may dominate the sward. Grazing animals remove from grasslands in carcase, wool and hide, elements that are essential for plant growth and this represents a considerable reduction in fertility. It is easy to see that grazing in this respect has the same biological effect as leaching by rainwater. For *Agrostis–Festuca* grassland restoration is simply a matter of applying ground limestone. The growth of the legume component of the sward is stimulated, nitrogen fixation is accelerated, and the nitrogen content of the soil is raised. In the event of a phosphorus deficiency light dressings of ground rock phosphate or basic slag may be given.

In many parts of the world there are vast tracts of land that would be greatly improved by revegetation. For financial and other reasons, it may not be possible to give costly remedial treatment to large areas, and it may instead be desirable to select only a few sites, even in pastoral settings, for the high-maintenance treatment that leads to prime grassland. The remainder could then be given, perhaps as an interim measure, less costly treatment sufficient to produce a lower-fertility but largely self-supporting type of grassland; such land would be ideal for tree planting or amenity purposes, or even some light grazing. In cool, moist places in Africa, Europe and the USA the following species have been successfully used in revegetation schemes on a wide range of waste materials:

Agrostis tenuis
Dactylis glomerata
Deschampsia flexuosa
Festuca arundinacea
F. ovina
F. rubra
Holcus lanatus

4 Woodland

Trees have been successfully planted as saplings or as cuttings, in notches, continuous slits or in holes, either on bare spoil or on spoil closely covered in grasses and herbs. They have also been planted as seeds, either alone or with a grassland seeds mixture. A grass cover *per se* is important on many reclaimed sites, particularly in urban areas, because it masks the raw material and gives a pleasing, finished look to the site in the shortest possible time. It is also important because the sward binds the surface and prevents erosion, and it ameliorates the raw parent material and initiates processes (see p. 148) which lead to the formation of a fertile soil. Many foresters advise that a seeds mixture be sown and allowed to stand on its own for a number of years 'to prepare the ground' for the subsequent planting of trees. It is common experience in spoil-heap reclamation that while trees planted in raw spoil often die back, those in grassland make healthy growth.

Frequently, it is the local climate that determines tree growth rather than the properties of the spoil-heap material, because the latter can often be ameliorated sufficiently (see p. 151) to allow root growth to take place. Thus, the climatic differences which exist say, between the north and south of England, between Pennsylvania and Georgia, USA, and between Denmark and Yugoslavia in Europe, do mean that there could be a wider choice of suitable species in the more favoured areas. In any given area there will be differences from site to site in the degree of exposure to winds and frost, and this will also affect the numbers of suitable species. Further, the local atmospheric pollution may also be a controlling factor because some coniferous species are more susceptible than broad-leaved trees to contaminated air. Finally, no reclamation scheme involving tree planting can succeed in urban areas without adequate fencing or other deterrents to vandalism.

4.1 Establishing the plantation

Age and type of plant

What is chiefly looked for in trees suitable for planting out on poor sites is sturdy transplants having a well developed root system and a high ratio of root collar to shoot length. Too small or too slender specimens are liable to damage, and form poor trees; too large and too stout specimens are difficult to establish. For conifers, good specimens will usually have been grown 2 years in one soil then a further year in another (called 2 + 1 transplants) and measure about 30 to 38 cm (12 to 15 in) tall, although smaller specimens may be preferred in dry exposed places. Some species are used when 1 + 1 transplant and others as 2 + 2 because the important criteria are height and sturdiness rather than age alone. A danger with smaller plants 15 to 23 cm (6 to 9 in) lies in their being unable to withstand the competition from grasses and herbs (see p. 169 below) and on some sites it may be necessary to use taller, older plants up to 46 cm (18 in). Hardwood plants are usually taller than conifers, and in the range 46 cm to 92 cm (18 in to 36 in). It is sometimes an advantage to prune the tallest hardwoods after planting.

Handling of plants

In order to obtain the best results the trees must be quickly transferred from the nursery to the planting site and in numbers that can be planted at once or without excessive delay. During the time spent out of the soil the plant is obviously very vulnerable to drying out and other damage. Much depends on the organization of the whole operation from lifting in the nursery to planting on the site. The aim is to bring sturdy plants with live roots to planting sites but unfortunately there is much evidence that this is not always done. It has been stated that there are often more failures due to dead or damaged roots before planting than to the harshness of the environment after planting. One step towards protecting the trees from drying out is wrapping the bundles in sacking, damp straw or polythene. Another is to ensure that the bundles are stacked in the lorry so that the roots are not in moving air; finally a tarpaulin sheet must be placed over the load. When transport is over long distances and by train and ship, the protection of bundles of trees requires much greater care, over a longer period.

At the plantation some temporary shelter must be available to protect the bundles from direct sunlight and drying winds. Ideally when planting begins only a small number of trees at a time should be removed from the shelter by the planter and carried to the prepared holes in a waterproof bag. It is often thought worthwhile to organize the planting operation so that one man's sole job is to keep a number of planters supplied with fresh trees from the bundle shelter or the heeling-in trench. If the trees cannot be planted within a day or two of reaching the site, steps must be taken to take them out of the packing and to place their roots in contact with moist loam soil where frost and drying winds cannot reach them. This operation (known as 'heeling-in' in England) is best done in prepared trenches in fertile, moist, but free-draining, soil. Ground with a history of waterlogging or of drying out must be avoided.

Planting holes

Slit (or notch) planting would not normally be used on derelict sites where there is no soil or vegatation cover present. Instead planting is done in holes whose diameters and depths depend on the species and/or the size of the root systems. The trees should be placed in the holes and their roots spread outwards and downwards before being firmed in; trees are planted to the depth of the root collar. It is right that operations should be made as simple as possible and it is recognized that some species of tree can often succeed when planted directly into the raw waste material. Nevertheless it is also known that, if the failure rate is to be kept to a low value, the bottom of the planting hole should contain a high proportion of fine material (2.0 to 0.002 mm) in which plant roots may be closely packed. This places the absorbing regions of the roots in close contact with the source of water and mineral salts in solution.

From earliest days it has been acknowledged that some amelioration (even just breaking up the material into fine particles) produces a more satisfactory plantation requiring little replacement of dead trees (beating-up). In pioneer plantings of conifers and hardwoods in 1890 in Cumbria, England, sweepings from hay lofts were thickly spread on the raw shale, and the resulting vegetation helped to bind the surface material and accelerate its breakdown into small particles. Holes were dug for trees and two buckets of topsoil were placed in each. In South Staffordshire, England, in 1903, pits were dug and rough turves were placed in them before the trees were planted. The placing of turves or loam soil in the planting hole is recommended because this material possesses physical and chemical properties conducive to rapid growth of roots. On flat or gently sloping sites this work can be easily carried out, but on steep slopes there are mechanical difficulties which may be eliminated by enclosing the roots with a quantity of loam soil in a hessian bag (sand-bag) before planting. This procedure simplifies transport of material on difficult sites and ensures that tree roots may initially grow in fertile material and then gradually elongate into the raw parent material. The planting holes may be prepared with a spade or a hand auger in light ground; a power-driven post-hole borer fitted to a tractor may be needed in heavy ground. In badly compacted ground a chisel plough (or subsoiler) may be required to rip open the surface before planting can begin. Alternatively small explosive charges may be used to produce cylindrical holes from 38 to 50 cm (15 to 20 in) diameter and 46 to 76 cm (18 to 30 in) deep. Trees planted in holes prepared by this method showed some early advantage because of the amount of fine material produced and the shattering that occurred around the hole.

Spacing

This will depend on the likely growth rate of the species under the given conditions of climate and parent material, and also on how quickly a tree cover is required. Spacing of 0.92 m (3 ft) or 1.25 m (4 ft) is common practice on many reclamation schemes with 1.5 m (5 ft) the widest normal spacing. Generally on poor exposed ground close spacing is favoured. Numbers per unit area at each spacing are as follows: 0.92 m (3 ft): 4850; 1.2 m (4 ft): 2700; 1.5 m (5 ft): 1750. Frequently on a reclaimed site there will be a number of different ground types because of local texture, acidity, exposure (aspect and slope), etc, and it will not be unusual for each such area to have a different species. The pattern of planting carried out at the Littleburn colliery site in Co. Durham in 1956 (see Richardson *et al.* 1971) shows that on a 5.4 ha (13.26 acre) site there were 25 different areas designated and 11 different species were used in the planting. Although this arrangement did not allow very large areas for each species on this single site, when it was repeated on another 30 sites using the same species, the area per species was large enough to allow valid conclusions to be drawn about performance on a wide range of habitats. In order to ensure accurate planting, the boundaries of each area must be shown on a plan and the ground marked out with labelled stakes to guide the planters. Where the areas are large and it is decided to plant a mixture of trees in each of them, special care must be taken to instruct the planters and to stake out the ground for their guidance. If an alternative plant mixture is to be used the British Forestry Commission advises that either each man carries two bags with one species in each and takes a plant alternately from each bag or two men work in the same row but each plants only one species. With group mixtures, where one species is planted in a matrix of another, the advice is to mark the centre of each group with a stake, then plant the groups around the stakes at the desired spacing and finally plant the matrix trees.

Time of planting

It is safest to carry out planting when the tree is dormant or when the rate of growth is small. In temperate regions in the Northern Hemisphere this may be from October to April provided the ground is not frozen. The argument in favour of autumn planting relies on the assumption that young trees can become settled into their new environment during the winter and are therefore able to begin new growth in the spring without any check. However, it seems that there is usually better establishment when the planting is done in the spring and this is the aim with both softwoods and hardwoods in England. It is recognized that in exceptional seasons the timing may have to be revised, and this may have no great effect on subsequent growth provided planting is not carried out in frosty weather or in a cold drying wind and that the parent material is not waterlogged or too dry (see section 2.5).

Beating-up

The aim in all plantations is to avoid any trees dying back, but failures do occur even in fertile soil and they are most likely to be greater on reclaimed land in spite of all steps taken to ameliorate the low fertility. In forestry practice it is not usually considered worthwhile to replace dead plants (called beating-up in England) unless more than 20% failure has occurred. However, on reclaimed sites in the early stages of plant growth 1 to 2 year beating-up should be carried out wherever the appearance of the site is marred by dead trees regardless of the percentage loss. Later on, e.g. after 6–8 years, it is unlikely that a few dead trees here and there will make any lasting effect on the plantation. Beating-up must be performed with great care using good quality plants of the same species and the same spacings as in the original planting.

Weeding

In order to improve quickly the appearance of the reclaimed sites and to stabilize the surface before erosion becomes severe, it is usual to prepare the ground and sow a grass seeds mixture (see section 3.2). This may be done in late summer and then the tree planting can take place the following spring or at a suitable time later. The danger attached to this procedure is that there will be intense competition for water and mineral ions and very often the grasses and legumes are successful and the trees are checked, show poor growth and die back. The owner is in some difficulty. If he drastically undersows (or even omits a seeds mixture) the appearance could be poor and the erosion serious. If he sows generously with adequate fertilizer he eliminates erosion and establishes a grassland which kills off the trees. Where there is a choice the second procedure is best, provided the site can be weeded yearly until the trees grow tall enough to compete successfully. Weeding consists of cutting back (or otherwise killing) all herbaceous and shrubby growth in a radius of 0.45 m (18 in) around each tree.

4.2 Selecting tree species

Tree planting on spoil heaps has quite a long history in the coalfields of Europe and the USA, although for many years the activity was sporadic and on a small scale. Nevertheless, it is from the records made at planting and from the survivors of early plantations that much modern work is based. In England some pioneer planting to beautify acid shale tips was commenced in Cumbria in 1898 and in Staffordshire in 1904; and by 1918 it was possible to draw up tentative lists of species that could flourish in poor, acid ground and polluted air. Because there was no information to guide the planters as to what species would be best to use for a main crop, or even if trees would grow in the raw spoil material, it was decided to plant mixtures of species as follows:

Trees: *Acer pseudoplatanus* (sycamore)
Alnus glutinosa (black alder)
A. incana (grey alder)
Betula spp. *(B. pubescens, B. verrucosa)* (birch)
Fagus sylvatica (beech)
Fraxinus excelsior (ash)
Larix decidua (European larch)
L. leptolepis (Japanese larch)
Picea sitchensis (sitka spruce)
Pinus mugo (mountain pine)
P. nigra var. *austriaca* (Austrian pine)
P. sylvestris (Scots pine)
Populus × *canadensis* var. 'serotina' (black Italian poplar)
Quercus robur (common oak)
Salix spp. (willow)
Ulmus glabra (wych elm)
Shrubs: *Ligustrum vulgare* (privet)
Mahonia aquifolium (Oregon grape)

Rhododendron spp. (rhododendron)
Sarothamnus scoparius (broom)
Spirea salicifolia (spirea)
Symphoricarpos rivularis (snowberry)
Ulex europaeus (gorse)

By far the most successful species were *Alnus glutinosa, Betula* spp., *Larix decidua* and *Pinus sylvestris;* and in this group the tallest specimens reached 8.4 m (28 ft) in 16 years and the average growth rate was 0.43 m (1.4 ft) per year. *A. incana* and *Populus* were less vigorous but together with the shrubs *Sarothamnus* and *Ulex* they counted as successes. The remainder generally failed and only a few scrubby sycamores survived, but sycamore, ash and oak all proved to be useless for the object in view.

Following these early trials, in most countries with reclamation problems, agencies have been developed from which growers can obtain precise information about suitable species for difficult sites. This usually includes advice on planting techniques as well as lists of tree combinations for both rapid and permanent cover. In the United States, for example, the Soil Conservation Service (Department of Agriculture) have a comprehensive system based on the National Plant Materials Centre at Beltsville, Maryland, and twenty regional centres. Here promising native and foreign species, and species found both as natural colonists and as planted specimens, are first increased in numbers and then tested in the field under a wide range of climatic and soil conditions. Those which attain a desired performance are maintained as foundation stocks (as seeds or plants) for the use of commercial growers. The trials usually extended to grasses, herbs and shrubs.

Acid parent material

There is no doubt that *Alnus glutinosa* is an outstanding tree in reclamation work, and it is rapidly becoming the preferred species on spoil banks in the USA, as it has been in Europe for many years. An examination was made of the results of tree planting on acid sites in Belgium, Britain, Czechoslovakia, Denmark, France, Germany, Poland, Yugoslavia and the USA. *A. glutinosa* was very successful in 65% of them, *Betula* spp. in 57%, *A. incana* in 40%, *Pinus sylvestris* and *Robinia pseudoacacia* in 33% and *Quercus borealis* in 21% (this latter tree has very slow growth in the first few years, but it has a good survival record in Europe and the USA where, it is claimed, its growth after 12 years approaches that of conifers).
A. glutinosa is a native tree in Europe southwards from latitude 65°N, growing in low country by stream sides and wet places. I do not know of any example of this tree occurring as a natural colonist of collery waste heaps in north-east England. Nevertheless, it has long been recognized as a species that grows well on poor, acid soils and, as mentioned above, it was one of the species selected for the early Cumbria trials. The tree is a non-leguminous nitrogen fixer and it often has a matted root formation which holds water in the soil, so that even in well drained ground a local area of moisture is brought about. However, it has already been demonstrated (see p. 159) that spoil heaps are by no means arid sites, and, in the ones examined, the soil moisture at 23 cm (9 in) depth was above the permanent wilting point throughout the year. *A. glutinosa* is very hardy; it shows rapid growth, 5.3 m (18 ft) in 10 years, it produces abundant leaf litter and it can succeed on heavy and light land. It tolerates acid and alkaline soil. It is an excellent tree to start a plantation on derelict ground even if other species have to be introduced later. It is an effective nurse crop and its presence greatly improves the parent material.

A. incana extends further north than *A. glutinosa*, almost reaching the Arctic circle. In the south of Europe it grows at 1200 m (4000 ft) in Italy. There is a tendency to form multiple-stemmed trees but this only reduces the growth rate by a third; single-stemmed trees can reach 3–6 m (10–20 ft) in ten years. A third alder, *A. viridis* (green alder), a native of central and south-east Europe, is very hardy and has proved satisfactory in cold damp mine spoils and exposed sites, notably in Denmark and Yugoslavia.

Betula spp. (*B. pubescens*, *B. verrucosa*) are the first tree colonists on colliery spoil in Belgium, Britain, Denmark and Germany and this may be because the large bare surfaces offer the high temperature and light intensity required for germination. The plant has a deeply penetrating root and a high ratio of root length to shoot length; it tolerates acid conditions down to pH = 3.5 and it has a low mineral requirement. Its growth rate is larger than for most broadleaved trees and individuals can reach 4.8 m (16 ft) in 10 years. *Betula* requires careful handling if it is to travel unharmed from nursery to planting site, and this may account for its not being an automatic choice like *Alnus* for acid ground. In the USA the species most used is *B. nigra* (river birch).

Robinia pseudoacacia has been grown widely in the USA and Europe. It has not been planted on a large scale in Britain, but where it has been tried it shows good survival and height growth, reaching 5 m (17 ft) in 10 years. It is a leguminous nitrogen fixer which tolerates low fertility. In suitable climates it survives high and low soil reaction (pH 8.5 to 3.5) and it spreads rapidly to form a closed canopy. It is said to be susceptible to insect and fungus attack and it may be planted with *Alnus* to ensure a continued cover.

In suitable climates certain conifers do well on acid material. For example *Larix decidua*, *Pinus contorta*, *P. nigra* and *P. sylvestris* are used in both the USA and Europe. Because of local conditions of frost and rainfall, the following pine species are used widely in the USA: *Pinus banksiana*, *P. echinata*, *P. resinosa*, *P. rigida*, *P. strobus* and *P. virginiana* (which is said to be the most acid-tolerant of pines).

Amongst the shrub species which tolerate acid conditions there are two which do well in warm open situations in the USA, *Amorpha fruticosa* (a legume) and *Rhus capallina;* the latter has shown promise in trials in England. Two shrubs which are highly rated in both the USA and Europe are *Eleagnus umbellata* and *Robinia fertilis;* they are tolerant of both acid and alkaline material.

The following tree and shrub species are known and reported to tolerate acid spoil material:

Trees: *Acacia baileyana* (acacia)
        A. melanoxylon (blackwood acacia)
        Acer negundo (box elder)
        A. platanus (American sycamore)
        Alnus glutinosa (European black alder)
        A. incana (grey alder)
        Betula nigra (river birch)
        B. pubescens (birch)
        B. verrucosa (silver birch)
        Larix decidua (European larch)
        Liquidambar styraciflua (sweet gum)
        Populus deltoides (cottonwood)
        P. × canadensis (black Italian poplar hybrids)
        Pinus banksiana (jack pine)
        P. contorta (lodgepole pine)
        P. echinata (short leaf pine)
        P. nigra var. *Austriaca* (Austria pine)
        P. nigra var. *calabrica* (Corsican pine)
        P. resinosa (red pine)
        P. rigida (pitch pine)
        P. sylvestris (Scots pine)
        P. virginiana (Virginian pine)
        Quercus borealis (= rubra) (red oak)

> *Robinia pseudoacacia* (black locust)
> *Salix* × *purpurea* (willow hybrids)
> Shrubs : *Amorpha fruticosa* (false indigo)
> *Eleagnus angustifolium* (Russian olive)
> *E. umbellata* (autumn olive)
> *Rhux capallina* (dwarf sumac)
> *Robinia fertilis* (bristly locust)
> *R. hispida* (rose acacia)
> *Sarothamnus scoparius* (broom)
> *Ulex europaeus* (gorse)

Alkaline parent material

Little or no vegetation is supported because of its soil reaction (pH 7.5 to 12.0) Like acid parent material there are usually other inhibiting factors such as poor physical condition, lack of nutrients, organic matter and micro-organisms; the spoil may also have high metal toxicity such as exists in pulverized fly ash (PFA) due to boron. Trials have been carried out on a wide variety of sites in several countries (e.g. on Magnesian Limestone quarry waste, PFA, calcareous strip mine overburden, ironstone mine tailings, etc.). The results show that, after modest amelioration treatment, *Alnus glutinosa*, which is the outstanding plant on acid spoils, grows very satisfactorily on all of them. In suitable climates the following trees and shrubs are known to tolerate a high-pH medium.

> Trees : *Alnus glutinosa* (European black alder)
> *A. incana* (grey alder)
> *Betula verrucosa* (silver birch)
> *Fraxinus excelsior* (ash)
> *Larix decidua* (European larch)
> *L. leptolepis* (Japanese larch)
> *Picea sitchensis* (sitka spruce)
> *Pinus banksiana* (jack pine)
> *P. nigra* var. *austriaca* (Austrian pine)
> *P. resinosa* (red pine)
> *P. sylvestris* (Scots pine)
> *P. virginiana* (Virginia pine)
> *Populus alba* (white poplar)
> *P.* × *canadensis* (black Italian poplar hybrids, e.g. 'Robusta', 'Serotina')
> *Prunus avium* (wild cherry)
> *Robinia pseudoacacia* (black locust)
> *Salix alba* var. *vittellina* (willow)
> *Salix alba* var. *britzensis* (willow)
> Shrubs : *Atriplex halimus* (orache)
> *Colutea aborescens* (black senna)
> *Cratoegus monogyna* (hawthorn)
> *Eleagnus angustifolia* (Russian olive)
> *E. umbellata* (autumn olive)
> *Hippophae rhamnoides* (sea buckthorn)
> *Lespedeza bicolor* (shrub lespedeza)
> *Lonicera maackii* (amur honeysuckle)
> *L. tatarica* (Tartarian honeysuckle)
> *Ribes aureum* (golden currant)
> *Robinia fertilis* (bristly locust)
> *R. hispida* (rose acacia)
> *Symphoricarpos orbiculatus* (coralberry)
> *Ulex europaeus* (gorse)
> *Viburnum dentatum* (arrowwood)

9 Financial control and contract procedure

Ian S. Clark

The various elements of financial control and contract procedure are closely related. To retain control of the cost of a project from the first design and feasibility studies through all the stages to completion of work on site, it is necessary to adopt a process of estimating, tendering and contract documentation which will enable the maximum financial control to be achieved. To this end it is logical to consider the elements of financial control and contract procedure together.

1 Cost planning and control

I do not intend to examine the skills of estimating, cost planning and cost control, but to consider the application of these disciplines to reclamation projects.

1.1 Estimating

Estimating is an essential element of early design work and feasibility studies. Generally, estimates fall into two categories; the first is a simple and sometimes rough estimate based on data analysed from other projects of a similar size, type and function, and the second is a more detailed estimate based on approximate quantities priced at current rates extracted from the contract documents of similar projects.

An enormous quantity of statistical data is available from various sources in the building industry which enable professional consultants to assess relatively quickly the probable cost of a building of a certain size, type and function. Very often this is done by relating the unit cost per place, bed or square metre (depending on the building's function) of a building of a similar size, shape, design, construction and function to that under consideration. This method certainly provides a quick and sometimes fairly accurate assessment of the probable cost, and in many instances is adequate to enable a client to proceed to full documentation and tender enquiries. There is no doubt, however, that an estimate based on approximate quantities consistently provides a more accurate guide to probable cost and in addition provides a better basis for cost planning (see section 1.2).

The emphasis must be on the word probable, even where estimates are prepared from approximate quantities. It is rare for more than half of the tenders received on a competitive basis from a selected list of firms to be within 10% of the lowest tender. Hence on a £100 000 contract, a reasonably satisfactory result would be for three tenders from a total of six to be between £100 000 and £110 000, one possibly at £150 000 and the other two grouped between £110 000 and £130 000. The significance of the above example is that, given identical tender documents, there is still likely to be a fairly wide divergence in tenders received. Market conditions, work load, expertise, profit and overhead elements and even errors in pricing are all factors affecting tender prices.

It is clear therefore that to evolve a complicated and time-consuming tool of precise accuracy in order to evaluate the quantities of the various elements of work required at estimating stage, would be effort wasted against a background of lost precision in applying a monetary value to the elements. It is not intended to imply that a slipshod approach should be made to estimating but that attention to minute detail is often unwarranted, and the degree of accuracy applied to any element can be directly equated to the prominence which that element enjoys in the overall scheme.

You may consider that this is an unnecessary digression into the theory of estimating and cost planning, but it has considerable bearing on the emphasis placed on the elements of an estimate as set out below and is, therefore, worthy of consideration.

Estimates of cost for reclamation schemes are of threefold benefit; they provide a platform for comparative cost calculations for a variety of design solutions, they give an indication of likely expenditure to enable the client to organize finance and apply for grant-aid where applicable, and they also enable assessment of outlay against after-use benefits.

The application of unit costs derived from other projects provides at best a very rough indication of the probable cost; thus analysis of tenders for schemes involving similar site conditions and area will often show a considerable difference in cost per hectare. One of the major factors is invariably the earthworks quantity which will depend on the size and disposition of the pit heap, embankment or other feature to be worked. This quantity can vary from site to site even where the land parcels are of the same or similar area. Certainly statistical data can be extracted from the costs of projects and, provided these are used with intelligent application bearing in mind the differences which would materially affect cost, they can be a useful guide in the early stages of a project's development.

The complexity of many building and civil engineering projects makes cost analysis data a useful tool for estimating where the preparation of an approximate estimate based on rough quantities can be a time-consuming exercise. In general, reclamation schemes are not so complex and the number of main elements is small compared with a building or engineering project; by careful application of the correct emphasis to the detail of the main elements a fairly accurate estimate can be produced quite quickly.

A typical reclamation scheme might in one form or another entail work which can be considered under the following elemental sections:

Preliminary works:	Contractor's site establishment, supervision, operatives' welfare facilities, insurances etc.
Demolitions and site clearance:	Removal of old buildings and general site clearance preparatory to the main work.
Earthworks:	Soil stripping and replacement, bulk shale or other waste material excavations.
Drainage:	Temporary and permanent ditches and piped drains.
Water supply and other services:	New water mains and troughs for pasture, re-routing gas, electric, water, Post Office and other mains.
Surface treatment and planting:	Cultivation seeding and tree planting.
Fences:	Boundary and field fences, protective fences to woodland planting.
Roads and paths:	Access tracks and roads, reinstatement of paths etc.

Preliminary works

These invariably form a small part of the contract since reclamation work does not entail complicated or expensive temporary site establishments like those often required for major building or engineering works. A percentage addition of 5% to the estimated cost of the other sections is generally quite adequate to cover these costs.

Demolitions and site clearance

On the majority of schemes this work will not amount to as much as 10% of the total cost of the scheme and unless there are particularly difficult conditions (e.g. a site honeycombed with shallow foundations with little fill available to provide a covering blanket of adequate depth) a sum of £1000 or £2000 for general clearance will suffice.

Schemes involving large quantities of muck shifting entail the use of heavy plant. These machines make short work of quite large buildings and often the debris is good clean brick and concrete rubble which has a monetary value as hardcore. Isolated concrete slabs and foundations also offer little resistance and are generally cleared with little trouble at low cost.

Caution must be exercised when considering sites previously occupied by heavy industry where large heavily reinforced machine and furnace bases might be encountered. Like the iceberg, an inoffensive-looking pad only just visible at ground level can cause considerable difficulty when fully exposed and found to be dense reinforced concrete. Unless these objects can be covered by an adequate depth of fill and left *in situ* a reasonably low rate of £1.00/m³ for removal of ordinary foundations can become £20.00/m³ and entail blasting with explosives. On this basis the removal of a machine base of even moderate size can cost £1000 or more. Very often the task is made more difficult by previous demolition work which has reduced buildings to ground level and left debris covering potentially difficult areas.

Examination of old plans showing the location and function of the various buildings once occupying the site is often a useful guide to the likely size and problem, if any, of visible or indeed hidden items of this nature.

Whilst strictly not a demolition item, mention should be made here of shaft caps. Again, these do not usually amount to a large part of the works, but old mine and air shafts and the like are often so deep that even when filled it is desirable to place a concrete cap or pad over with a good bearing on surrounding firm strata to counter collapse and subsidence of the landform at some future date. These caps can cost £1000 or more depending on size, but some provision should be made in the estimate if any shafts are known or thought likely to exist.

Earthworks

These can be responsible for 50% or more of the total cost of the project. It is, therefore, imperative where the earthworks play a large part to pay particular attention to the earthworks quantities. Earthworks calculations can be time-consuming, but an advantage can accrue where the scheme proceeds to tender with little alteration and the earthworks calculations, as prepared for the estimate, can be used for the tender documents. The quantities so obtained also provide a check on cut/fill balance and can make the task of comparative cost exercises easier (see section 1.2).

Care must be exercised in assessing the likely difficulties in the earthworks operation, such as ease of loading, method of handling, carting and depositing, haul distance and nature of material. Uphill loading and carting material off site can add considerably to cost. A long haul will also slow production and, therefore, add to the cost, although running conditions must also be taken into account since a good running surface such as a railway embankment can mitigate, to some extent, the effect of a long haul. Hot material requiring special treatment, abrasive material which will cause excessive wear and tear of plant, and slurry which could well require additional or even different plant, all tend to inflate the cost. Where a large quantity is involved, say 1 000 000 m³, a tenth of a penny on a unit rate would make a £1000 difference and here data from previous projects of a similar nature are invaluable in assessing a likely market rate for the job.

This example of a small change in unit rate having marked effect on cost serves well to illustrate the early remarks in respect of emphasis on the elements of an estimate. It is of little importance whether, for example, an existing structure will cost £100 or £200 to demolish, when a mere tenth of a penny on an earthworks rate would add £1000 to the cost.

The probable cost of soil stripping, depositing in spoil heaps and later respreading, is a relatively simple calculation based on the area of soil available times the required depth of strip ascertained from trial pits and post hole auger samples. Here again, loading, method of handling, carting and depositing, haul distance and nature of material will affect the rate. Generally quantities are not very large and, therefore, the total cost of this operation does not figure greatly in the total. However, any requirement to import soil or cart soil off site should be noted since this can add considerably to the cost of the soil operation. A stripping, stacking and replacement operation costing £0.20–£0.30/m³ can quite well become £1.00–£3.00/m³ for imported soil.

Drainage

The proportion of drainage cost can vary considerably from project to project, but estimating on the basis of a linear measure of ditches, piped drains and numbered items for manholes, culverts, silt chambers and headwalls is a relatively simple task.

Some consideration to works at the outfalls from the site is worthwhile. The cost of culverted road crossings for sewer connections, or piped drains to connect to streams or other outfalls, can cost as much and sometimes more than the site drainage itself. While the scheme might provide for relatively inexpensive open ditches, the outfall to take the run-off might have to be a fairly large piped drain which can add considerably to the overall cost.

Water supply and other services

Provision for water main, troughs and water meter are relatively minor items of cost. Usually an allowance of £100–£300 per trough, depending on numbers, will adequately cover this provision. Provision for water supplies to allotments and the like can be dealt with in a similar manner and create few problems.

Diversions of main services can figure more prominently. Estimates of cost for diversions obtained from the appropriate public undertaking are the best guide to probable cost. In some instances diversions are not necessary, but adequate protection must be provided to the pipe cable or equipment. This can be by way of fencing at a set distance each side of the pipe or cable to delineate its route and specially constructed crossing pads to enable plant to cross. While provision of these protective items may not be very costly, the possible effect on the site works must not be overlooked. Restricting plant movement to one or two crossing points over a main cable or pipe can in some instances create considerable disruption to what would normally be a simple earthworks operation, and in turn reflect in the unit rate for earthworks.

Surface treatment and planting

The calculation of areas for surface treatment is usually straightforward, but the cost per hectare will depend a great deal on after-use proposals, soil conditions, availability of top- and subsoil, and finished gradients.

After-use proposals affect the cost of surface treatment in that a light sowing of grass seed for temporary stabilizing of a site designated for industrial development will be far less costly than the heavier sowing and fertilizer treatments for a site designated for pasture, agriculture or public open space. Availability of soil and the nature of the waste material will affect the requirements for sewage sludge, lime, basic slag and fertilizers. Steep slopes requiring stabilizing solutions will be more expensive than areas with gentle gradients.

The cost of planting will depend on the species, density and method of planting. The range is great, from whip planting at a few pence each to standard or semi-mature trees at several pounds each.

An important factor not to be overlooked both for seeding and planting is the cost of maintenance and establishment work. Allowance should be made for cutting and fertilizing the grass during the contract maintenance and defects period, and subject to responsibility for the land after this period, an allowance should also be made for beating up, pruning, weeding etc as required, to planted areas.

Fences

These are best assessed by a linear measure of the fencing requirements, since the type of fence and quantity can vary extensively depending on the development proposals; hence incorporation of a derelict railway embankment into part of a country walk can involve a much larger quantity of fence per hectare than, say, a reasonably square and compact area of land reclaimed for agriculture use.

The cost of the fence per linear metre will obviously depend on the type of fence; post and rail cost more than twice as much as post and wire. Allowance must be made for gates and stiles, rabbit-proof netting for forestry areas, and protective fences for ditches in pastures.

Difficulty is sometimes experienced when driving fence posts into hard ground, usually on the boundaries of the site next to areas of fairly intense demolitions (such as a row of terrace houses). Because it is not possible to provide a good fill cover, or to effectively grub up all the foundations along the site boundary line, extra costs can be incurred in excavating the post holes and backfilling around post holes in concrete. Generally the extra cost of fences erected on such ground is insignificant at the estimating stage, unless a large proportion of the fencing is so affected.

Roads and paths

The requirements can vary from merely grading and compacting the waste material to define a track, to reinstatement of a road to full Ministry of Transport specification. The cost will therefore vary according to the particular requirement.

Bridle paths requiring an ash surface can often be provided quite cheaply by utilizing burnt shale or similar waste material from the site, rather than importing blast furnace or similar slag at a much higher cost.

Other miscellaneous items

Other items such as contingencies, professional fees, land acquisition costs, administrative costs, aerial and other surveys etc can be included as required.

Reference was made above to the use of rates contained in tenders for similar projects. It is well to note, however, that some allowance must be made for possible increase in costs and market conditions when taking rates from any but current projects.

Seasonal variations in market trends can also affect rates; very often winter rates for bulk muck shifting on a firm self-draining shale can be a good deal lower than the summer rates when demand for all types of earthwork is greater.

Appendix 1 gives an example of an estimate at 1975 rates that might be prepared for a typical pit-heap reclamation scheme in north-east England.

1.2 Cost planning

Cost planning can be described as the discipline by which the design of a project is evolved according to the brief requirements at the optimum cost in terms of capital outlay, after-use management cost and financial return or benefit.

Application of any cost-planning technique must be within the framework of the design brief. It is only on rare occasions that initial or capital cost is the main criterion. Indeed, if cost was the main criterion, it is conceivable (for example) to reshape a conical pit heap, in order to achieve gradients that would be reasonably stable with the minimum of earthworks, drainage and fencing, but the end result would very likely be visually unacceptable, have no after-value or development potential and possibly be costly to maintain because of excessive erosion.

More often than not, site location and planning requirements determine whether the site is to be reclaimed for housing, industry, agriculture etc (this is more fully considered in Chapter 3), and the after-use requirements will be an important factor in determining cost. The waste material may be such that on a site designated for housing, for example, the toxicity is high or the load-bearing capabilities are poor so that the bulk of the material will have to be removed from site, a costly operation on most occasions. Industrial sites require fairly large flat areas which again can result in more earthworks and more expense.

There are, however, no hard and fast rules; it may be that a nearby derelict quarry can be filled by the material from the proposed housing site, thereby reclaiming two sites for little more than the price of one. It can also be that the existing land is ideally suited to formation into large flat areas with associated mounding and embankments and therefore ideal for an industrial site.

A detailed cost plan develops in two stages. The first is considering the factors mentioned above during the initial design/development stage, weighing and costing all the alternative possibilities to find the most economic solution to the design brief. The second is considering the most economic layout in keeping with the requirements for landform, drainage etc.

A site to be reclaimed for agriculture will, on the face of it, give its maximum after-use return if the whole site area can be reclaimed for agricultural use (subject to shelter-belt requirements). But the cost of achieving the required gradients might be prohibitive because of the vast amount of additional earthworks required, thereby making the financial return uneconomic against outlay. The introduction of a reasonable proportion of forestry planting, while resulting in a lower after-use return, could drastically reduce the initial capital cost by reducing the earthwork quantities to an acceptable level. An optimum level of cost against return is thereby achieved.

Within the second stage of the cost-planning work there is also the consideration of individual design/cost problems relating to particular areas of the site. Detailed earthwork calculations carried out at the estimating stage are of benefit when considering the effect of possible landform changes in a specific area. Overlays of alternative sections can be compared with the initial section to assess the effect on cut and fill quantities. Comparative cost exercises on varying gradients of slope are often required; the effect on cut/fill, drainage, surface treatment, planting and fencing are all variables in this calculation. In a cut situation an increase in gradient might reduce earthworks, but introduce complications of erosion necessitating cut-off ditches, ground stabilizing solutions and perhaps the introduction of forestry planting together with associated fencing.

It is well to note that in seeking the ideal design/cost solution, the requirements of the brief are not forgotten—nor the visual impact or effect on the after-use overlooked. The cost plan is a useful element in economic design development, providing it is used correctly and not allowed to dominate other essential elements to the detriment of the finished scheme.

2 Pre-contract procedure

This section deals with the procedure up to and including receipt and acceptance of a tender. When a suitable scheme has been devised at an acceptable level of cost, the accuracy or otherwise of the estimate can be put to the test by seeking tenders.

To some extent the type of contract and the tender procedure to be adopted will influence the rates used for the estimate in that an 'open' tender could well result in a more competitive price than a 'select' tender, and a competitive tender a lower price than a negotiated tender.

Before examining the form of the tender documents and the procedure to be adopted, it is as well to consider briefly the types of contract.

2.1 Types of contract

Contracts for building and civil engineering works fall into two categories, incentive and risk-bearing contracts, and cost-reimbursement contracts.

Incentive and risk-bearing contracts are those in which the contractor is awarded the contract, either in competition or by negotiation, and priced against the background of market prices ruling at the time. The rates are fixed in terms of work content, subject to certain qualifications laid down in the contract, and any operation taking a longer or shorter period than estimated by the contractor is his own risk. The contractor has a high risk and a high incentive to lower his costs and thereby increase his profits.

Cost-reimbursement contracts are those in which the contractor is paid his prime cost of labour, plant, material and certain overheads plus either a percentage or fixed fee for site management, overheads and profit. In this case the contractor has a low risk and low incentive to decrease cost—indeed quite the reverse in the case of a percentage fee.

A third type which falls between the previous two is the target contract which, while primarily a cost-plus-fee contract, has a set monetary target; any saving between final cost and target is shared in an agreed proportion between contractor and employer. This does provide some incentive to the contractor to reduce costs.

The most suitable type of contract will depend largely upon the nature of the work. A project with a large degree of uncertainty in the difficulties to be encountered could attract such high rates to cover risk that a cost-reimbursement contract would be a more economical proposition. Reclamation projects generally fall into the category of fairly low risk with certain elements being in the high-risk category (e.g. hidden foundations as described in section 1.1). Where an item cannot be easily described or quantified a large proportion of any rate or price quoted will be a contingent for the risk involved. It is prudent, in such instances, to relieve the contractor of the burden of excessive risk by including either a provisional sum for work which cannot readily be described or quantified or, where the nature of the work is known but the quantity in doubt, by including provisional quantities for items to be measured as work proceeds. Cost-reimbursement, or 'fixed-fee' contracts as they are often called, are being used more in the building industry, and indeed there is one large well-known firm of contractors in the U.K. which has adopted this type of contract for most of its building operations.

Reclamation projects, while utilizing specialist skills in earthmoving and landscaping techniques, are not commonplace to the same extent as building and similar construction work. In many parts of the country there is still a lack of information on firms with the necessary skills prepared to undertake the work and the cost levels of the various elements involved. There is no doubt that adoption of a competitive tender procedure is a relatively safe and easy way of ascertaining market conditions, and the number and capabilities of interested firms, and establishing a general level of prices; these prices then become recognized by both employers and contractors as the market rates for the area, to which outside organizations are attracted or deterred from entering as the case may be.

2.2 Competitive tenders

Competitive tenders can be classified as 'open' or 'selective'. The term 'open tender' is used here to mean tenders sought by public advertisement. In the short term the system has the advantage of providing a good indication of the scope, nature and price range of the market. In the long term the system tends to suffer from the lack of selectivity and to make the market stale by attracting the cut-price firms who after executing one contract disappear, but in the meantime discourage more reputable firms.

The term 'selective tender' is used here to mean tenders sought from a select list of firms known to be interested in undertaking the work and having the necessary capabilities. This system has the advantage of providing the desirable control to maintain a healthy market, free of cut-price merchants and firms with inadequate capabilities. There is the disadvantage in the early stages of having to acquire a knowledge of firms' capabilities, and of whether the tenders received are reasonable or representative of the true market conditions for the area. To some extent this knowledge can be acquired by public advertisement, inviting applications from interested firms to be included on a select list and then checking the applicant's capabilities and previous performance. There is no guarantee however that selection in this manner will establish reasonable price levels.

An ideal system for an organization or authority embarking on an extensive reclamation programme is to adopt the 'open tender' initially and, after a prescribed period depending on the number of jobs turned over, select a list of firms who have proved their capabilities. This procedure will also establish a recognizable market price.

The adoption of a selected list of contractors from 'open tender' experience does not preclude the addition of new firms to the list. In fact, this is essential to maintain a healthy and competitive market and reduce the possibility of a price-ring being established.

It is advisable to divide the list into sections related to plant and management capabilities. The work broadly falls into two categories: projects of a pure landscaping nature involving little earthworks or grading requiring heavy mechanical plant, and projects of a civil engineering nature involving earthworks requiring the use of heavy mechanical plant. Within these two categories further sub-divisions are possible depending on the size and turnover of the firms involved.

The number of firms in each category or sub-division should be sufficient to avoid the necessity of inviting the same firm to tender for several schemes which could give that firm more than its fair share, or indeed overload that firm so that performance on one scheme might be to the detriment of another.

Care is necessary to ensure that firms selected from the list are genuinely interested, have plant, operatives and management available, and that there is a sufficient number invited to provide an adequate element of competition. This does not guarantee the lowest possible tender, but providing care is taken in selecting the tenderers, it does ensure a competitive and reasonable tender from a firm known to have the required capabilities and standards of workmanship.

An organization contemplating an extensive programme of reclamation over a long period could adopt a three-phase procedure to some advantage: first, establishing market conditions by 'open tender'; second, introducing 'selective' tendering once market conditions have been satisfactorily tested and established; and third, introducing serial or continuation contracts to reduce contract risk and promote incentive cost reductions by planned capital investment in plant.

The introduction of serial or continuation contracts would only be feasible where a good deal of forward planning is possible so that a detailed programme of work can be established for the projects in any particular series. The contractors invited to participate would have to be carefully selected. Experience of individual performances gained from the initial 'open' and 'selective' procedures would greatly assist this selection. The number and value of schemes offered would have to be such as to offer the necessary incentive for capital investment and a good guarantee of continuity of work to reduce the risk of unemployment or a 'stop/go' situation.

The tender procedure requires careful consideration. Initially, an element of competition should be introduced for each series, either by inviting selected contractors to tender for the first project in the series and negotiating the remaining projects in the series upon the successful tenderers' rates and prices, or as an alternative (and perhaps more preferable) by seeking from the selected contractors a management and on-cost fee expressed as a percentage of lump sums approximating the value of each project in the series together with a schedule of rates for the major items of work.

The disadvantage of negotiating on the basis of one project is that it might not be typical or representative of the remainder in the series, whereas a schedule of rates can be carefully compiled to be representative of all the major items of work in each scheme. Some method of adjustment for price fluctuations would be required so that scheduled rates could keep pace with market trends. The Price Adjustment Formula published by the National Economic Development Office might well serve this purpose. Safeguards would need to be provided for employer and contractor alike; for the former, to safeguard performance and workmanship by the provision of termination of a series in the event of standards not being maintained, and for the latter to terminate a series in the event of delays between projects disrupting continuity. Other factors would have to be considered, such as form of contract and nomination for specialist works, but in principle such a procedure could work well and have the advantages of maintaining a rolling programme, allowing early initiation of the contractor's expertise and providing a stable cost structure free from day-to-day market fluctuations.

2.3 Tender documents

Tender documents usually comprise the drawings, details of the conditions of contract, specification and/or bills of quantities and have a threefold function:

- to present the tenderer with all the pertinent information for him to acquire a clear understanding of all matters which might affect his tender and performance of the contract;
- to provide a document which can be readily priced by the tenderer;
- to form a clear and precise reference manual for use during the execution of the works.

The information contained in the documents should be comprehensive and free from ambiguities. Ideally the documents should not only provide the vehicle for tendering, but also present the various elements in a form that assists the execution of the project in terms of workmanship and financial control. The effectiveness of any cost-planning work will depend on the cost control exercised during the course of the works. A properly prepared specification and bill of quantities will greatly assist this process as well as being an aid to the calculation of interim payments and the value of variations.

While not essential, it is neater if tender and contract information can be bound in one document. In this form a document might contain:

Instructions and general information for tenderers

Form of tender

Form of agreement

Form of bond

Form of contract

Specification

Bill of quantities

The precise form that the documents take will largely depend upon the type of contract to be used. Reclamation projects generally fall into two categories, those of a landscaping nature with minor earthshaping, rather than mass excavations, and those of a civil engineering nature with a large amount of earthmoving, drainage and the like.

2.4 Instructions and general information for tenderers

This section is a general introduction and provides information such as names of persons whose permission is to be sought before entering lands or property, directions regarding pricing the bill or specification, details of proposed method of correcting contractors' pricing errors, information regarding return of tenders, site location and brief description of the works.

It is advisable to limit the contents of this section to matters of information only, perhaps drawing the tenderers' notice to some specific item for which due allowance must be made in his price, but avoiding the insertion of items which have a monetary value and are more properly included in the specification and/or bills of quantities.

2.5 Form of tender and form of agreement

The form of contract largely determines the wording of these sections. If it is not the intention for the fully priced tender document to be returned, arrangements must be made to provide the tenderers with separate forms of tender. The appendix attached to the form of tender, and containing information on bond percentage, time for completion, liquidated damages, period of maintenance etc is dealt with in section 2.6.

2.6 Form of contract

Two forms of contract are currently popular for contracts with predominance of landscape work: the Conditions of Contract for use in connection with Works of Civil Engineering Construction agreed between the Institution of Civil Engineers and Federation of Civil Engineering Contractors (commonly known as the ICE Conditions of Contract), and the Conditions of Contract (1969 Edition) issued by the Institute of Landscape Architects. I do not propose to consider the legal effectiveness, merits or otherwise of these contracts, since there are many excellent commentaries by legal experts already published, but rather to consider the specific application of these contracts to reclamation, and appropriate additions and amendments to suit the particular requirements of reclamation projects. The following references are to the fifth edition of the ICE Conditions of Contract issued in June 1973 and the first edition of the Conditions of Contract issued by the ILA.

The 1973 edition of the ICE Conditions of Contract contains a number of amendments which correct anomalies arising under the fourth edition (January 1955), and incorporates amendments resulting from various statutes in respect of metrication, tax fluctuations and value-added tax. The ILA Conditions of Contract were modelled on the RIBA Form of Building Contract, but to date none of the various amendments made to the latter have been incorporated in the ILA form nor have the amendments resulting from the various statutes referred to above been recorded or included.

It is understood that a revised edition of the ILA form is currently being considered by the Institute, but until a revised edition is issued this form, unless suitably amended, is limited in scope and perhaps only suitable for relatively small reclamation projects.

Other than specific amendments to conditions of contract to conform with the client's requirements, such as a local authority's 'standing orders', there are certain aspects of reclamation projects which necessitate amendments or additions to the contract, or at least require consideration as to whether an amendment or addition is desirable.

Sub-letting (ICE clause 4, ILA clause 14)

It is advisable, because of the specialist nature of certain elements of reclamation, to ascertain at the time of tender which sub-contractors, if any, the tenderer proposes to use in the event of being awarded the contract. This information can be of value when assessing tenders, particularly where the capabilities of a named sub-contractor are known from previous experience.

A suitable amendment would read as follows:
'The contractor shall provide in writing on the form headed "sub-contractors" attached as an appendix to the form of tender the names of bona-fide sub-contractors and indicate those items of work as listed in the bills of quantities to be undertaken by the sub-contractors. Such names listed shall be deemed to have been approved by the engineer and no sub-contractor other than those named shall without written consent of the engineer be allowed to undertake these or any other works listed in the bills of quantities.'

Another possibility is to include a list of approved firms for a specific section of the works and require the tenderer to seek rates from one or more of these firms.

Sureties and guarantee bond (ICE clause 10, ILA clause 37)

It is a fairly common requirement that a bond agreement is made with a firm named by the employer. While it is prudent to retain such a clause as a safeguard for due completion of the works, where an 'open' tender procedure is adopted or where little is known of the firms tendering, the necessity for the clause is reduced when the firms are taken from a select list and details of the firm's financial background and reputation are known and considered acceptable. Any firm not satisfying the standards set for inclusion on the select list would not be invited to tender.

Noise and disturbance (ICE clause 29, ILA clause 17)

Reclamation work frequently involves noise and pollution which can cause considerable irritation and disturbance to adjoining owners or occupiers, particularly in residential areas. Noise can be controlled to some extent by the insertion of a clause making the fitting of efficient silencers to machines mandatory and in very difficult conditions, e.g. a site close to a hospital, by restricting working to specific times. Pollution will generally be air- or water-borne. Dust thrown up by the movement of heavy plant over fine shale can be carried a considerable distance and can cause annoyance in surrounding residences; toxic chemicals in the waste material may come into contact with water carried by a drainage system or indeed be washed by the simple action of rain to mix with and contaminate streams and watercourses.

A suitable amendment incorporating these requirements might read as follows: 'All mechanical plant or wagons employed on these contract works shall be fitted, if normally required, with efficient silencers and the contractor shall take all reasonable steps at all times to reduce the amount of noise to the minimum required for any particular operation he may be engaged upon so as to avoid any undue annoyance and disturbance to local residents. The contractor shall also take all reasonable steps by watering or otherwise to abate any nuisance which may arise through wind action blowing about dry materials or from the working of plant or machinery in very dry ground conditions.'

Mineral and materials of commercial value (ICE clause 32, ILA clause 35)

On those sites where the material to be worked is known to contain, or thought likely to contain, materials of commercial value, it is advisable to extend these clauses to include duff coal, coke, breeze and other materials or minerals of commercial and economic value and the fact that, in the event of such materials being found, the engineer may order them to be removed either by the contractor or a specialist nominated at any time by the engineer.

Commencement of the works (ICE clause 41, ILA clause 21)

The ICE Conditions of Contract provide for commencement 'on or as soon as is reasonably possible after the date for commencement of the works to be notified by the engineer'. While it is incumbent upon the contractor to commence the works at such time as to enable completion to be achieved within the time stated or date required by contract, nevertheless there are times when a protracted commencement can jeopardize later work critical to a season of the year (e.g. seeding or planting). A situation can arise where the main works, such as earthworks, drainage, and fencing, are completed within the time required but little leeway is left for an autumn seeding. In such an event failure to keep to the programme might well be laid at the contractors' feet and the work finished in the following spring at no extra cost. Nevertheless, the delay could in some instances cause inconvenience to the employer.

Any time specified for commencement after the engineer's instruction must be reasonable in relation to the time required for consideration of tenders; hence if a period of three months is required for consideration of tenders it would be unreasonable to ask the contractor to commence work within two days of the instruction. It can be argued that a stated period is of little more benefit than a 'reasonable' period in that failure of the contractor to comply with the stated period leaves the employer in the same position. However, a clearly stated period leaves all parties in no doubt of the intention and provides the engineer with the facility of pressing for compliance with his instructions immediately the period is exceeded.

The ILA form provides for specific possession and completion dates to be inserted but here again there is no requirement for immediate commencement other than the implication asserted by the provision to 'begin the works forthwith and regularly and diligently proceed.'

When the completion of certain operations is critical (e.g. to enable seeding and/or planting to commence and finish at specific times) the contractor can be required to frame his programme around specified dates.

A typical amendment might read:

'The programme of the works shall be such that all necessary engineering operations are completed to enable grass seeding to commence not later than 1 August and be completed by 31 August.'

The amendment would apply to clause 14 ICE Conditions, and clause 21 ILA Conditions.

Sectional and partial completion (ICE clause 48, ILA clause 21)

'Section' must not be confused with a trade or elemental section of work such as earthworks or drainage. Sectional completion denotes the completion of all work, i.e. earthworks, drainage, fencing, seeding etc, within a defined area.

The ILA Form of Contract makes no specific provision for sectional completion, so in the event of this requirement occurring an amendment, possibly similar to the standard clause 16 'Partial Possession by Employer' in the RIBA Form of Contract, would be needed.

Unless there is such a requirement it is advisable to delete all reference to sectional completion so as to indicate clearly to a tenderer that substantial or practical completion applies to the whole of the works.

A complication can arise where a project includes both seeding and planting work and where there is a fairly large gap between seeding completion (possibly in March or April) and planting completion (possibly October or November). To avoid a protracted maintenance period on seeded areas, sectional completion could be introduced, since it is often in the employer's interest to take over the maintenance of an area after the expiration of the alloted defects period rather than continue to supervise the contractor in this work.

Maintenance and defects (ICE clauses 48 and 49, ILA clauses 13 and 31)

Contractors will often seek to persuade an architect or engineer that the work is substantially or practically complete, particularly on a reclamation scheme where the earthworks and drainage amount to 90% of the whole. In the later stages of a project of this nature, where the bulk of the remaining work might be sub-contracted, the contractor's interest and attention to supervision and control can flag. Certification of substantial completion and the release of retention monies on 90% of the value leaves little to promote any incentive for completion of the remaining 10%. Invariably, of course, this work is the most critical to the employer's programme for the proposed after-use.

The words 'substantial' and 'partial' are very often not considered precise enough in the legal sense to satisfy authorities on contract law, but they are generally accepted as indicating a degree of completion to permit occupation and use of the works by the employer, albeit the liability for certain minor items of work and possibly defects remains to be discharged by the contractor. It is reasonable, therefore, to take the view that a reclamation project is not substantially or practically complete until the completion of all the work including the seeding, fencing etc. At this stage the project should be ready for occupation by the employer and for the maintenance period to commence. In the event of a relatively small area being incomplete at this time it might be unreasonable to withhold the completion certificate unless the area has any special significance in the employer's after-use programme. Substantial completion could be certified subject to the contractor's undertaking to complete this remaining work during the defects period.

Another factor to be considered here is establishment work required during the defects period. Generally a contractor is only responsible for completion of any outstanding work and remedying defects during the maintenance period, but where grass seeding and planting forms part of the contract there is almost certain to be a requirement for fertilizer dressings, grass cutting, pruning etc. The contractor's responsibility for this establishment work and the time for commencement of the defects period can be covered by an amendment to ICE clause 49 or ILA clause 13 on the following lines:

'The contractor shall be responsible for the maintenance of the site for a period of twelve months, from the date of completion of the seeding operations, within which time he shall carry out all establishment works described in the specification and itemized in the bills of quantities within 14 days of receiving written instruction to commence such establishment works.'

Special conditions

Some authorities prefer to insert additional clauses in respect of site accommodation, works area and other preliminary matters in the amendments to condition of contract rather than the specification or preliminaries to the bills of quantities. This is a matter of individual preference but matters relating specifically to the provision of temporary or permanent works are generally best kept in the specification or preliminaries.

Appendix to conditions of contract

An appendix is attached to the form of tender in the ICE Conditions and to the Conditions of Contract in the ILA Conditions, but the matters dealt with are broadly the same. The appendix presents no specific problems peculiar to reclamation projects, but care must be exercised in selecting a date for completion which enables any seasonal work to be undertaken at the appropriate time. Also, the period for maintenance must be of adequate length to ensure that the appropriate establishment work can be carried out. A twelve-month period which ensures the inclusion of a whole growing season is preferable.

The reference to sectional completion in the ICE conditions can be deleted unless the provision is specifically required for the reasons previously mentioned.

2.7 *Specification and bills of quantities*

The specification and bills of quantities are complementary and therefore best considered together. The specification should describe the various elements of the works and contain a comprehensive description of the materials and workmanship, avoiding unnecessary repetition of information contained in the drawings and bills of quantities. The bill-of-quantity items should be concise but in sufficient detail to make the intention clear without repeating information contained in the specification. Ideally, to ensure that all the documents are mutually explanatory of one another and to avoid ambiguities, the specification and bills of quantities should be prepared in unison.

The precise form of these documents will depend on the form of contract. Clause 11 of the ILA Conditions of Contract refers to the bills being in accordance with the Standard Method of Measurement of Buildings Works, whilst clause 57 of the ICE Conditions of Contract refers to bills prepared in accordance with the Standard Method of Measurement of Civil Engineering Quantities. The former tends to produce a document on the traditional lines of a building contract containing preliminaries, trade preambles and fully described and accurately measured quantities, while the latter produces a document containing a detailed specification with approximate quantities in keeping with civil engineering practice.

As previously stated the size and nature of the project tends to dictate the form of contract, but the most important requirement common to both is to produce a document which is clear and concise in description and quantity.

It is convenient and indeed desirable to produce the specification and bills of quantities in sections corresponding to those contained in the estimate, thereby making the task of comparing tenders with estimate relatively simple, and enabling any major discrepancy in cost or work content to be pinpointed. It also provides the facility of a pre-tender check to ensure that items in the estimate have not been missed in the tender document and *vice versa*.

Some authorities favour the use of the Specification for Road and Bridge Works produced by the Department of the Environment, the Scottish Development Department and Welsh Office (1969), obtainable at Her Majesty's Stationery Offices. While this document forms a useful foundation to build on for an organization contemplating reclamation for the first time, it is specifically produced for roadwork contracts and therefore requires considerable amendment to apply to the special requirements of reclamation projects.

Authorities and organizations embarking upon a fairly extensive reclamation programme are well advised to produce a standard specification which can be amended as required to suit the particulars of any scheme. The following is an examination of the framework of such a specification with more detailed consideration of the major elements and relevant information affecting the measurements and descriptions in the bills of quantities. The sections used are those listed in the typical estimate contained in appendix 1 and cover the most common elements of reclamation work.

Preliminary works

This section of the specification should contain items relating to the following:

- Site office requirements for the engineer and his representatives, including telephone, office equipment, heating, lighting etc; also any restrictions or special requirements in respect of offices for the contractor's site staff.

- Information and requirements in respect of traffic control, temporary roads and maintenance of existing roads.

- Information and requirements in respect of statutory and other services.

- Any special requirements regarding the 'form of statement' (ICE Conditions clause 60 (1) only). The facility is available to direct a contractor as to the form his monthly applications should take and how variations, dayworks, sub-contractors' invoices and claims should be presented in these applications and in the final account. The adoption of a standard system is of benefit where a number of schemes are running concurrently with different contractors involved and also some benefits accrue from the cost-control aspect by requiring a contractor to present this information in a regular and orderly manner.

The preliminary section of the bills of quantities should contain reference to these items to enable the contractor to enter their monetary value. Reference should also be made to insurances, works areas, water supply, operatives' welfare facilities, guarantee bond and other clauses in the conditions of contract relevant to the project which could conceivably have monetary value. In addition items such as contingencies, protection and temporary works can be included in this section (e.g. fencing to prevent livestock from straying, or protection of existing vegetation to be retained).

Demolitions and site clearance

In addition to the usual specification clauses in respect of protection of adjoining property, removal of debris, grubbing up tree roots etc, the following matters require special attention:

- The after-use or future development will have a bearing on the amount of demolitions required. A site reclaimed for agriculture will not require foundations and other obstructions removed below the depth (normally about 1 m) of subsequent cultivations. Obviously large bases and slabs close to finished ground level should be broken and dispersed because they are likely to have a detrimental effect on drainage.

- Bases, rubble, walls and other remains in deep fill areas (5 m and over) can be left *in situ* and only broken down and compacted if unstable.

- Burning of combustible materials on site should be prohibited where colliery waste or other combustible materials are evident.

- A clear indication should be given where the demolition of a building or structure is to include grubbing-up foundations and whether the material is to be carted and tipped off-site or in deep fill.

- Provision should be made for breaking up hidden foundations where the site is known or expected to contain such items. Again, unless after-use dictates otherwise, the requirement need only be to break these to 1 m or so below finished surface.

Often very large machine bases resist attack by even the biggest machines. In such cases the carefully controlled use of explosives can reduce an obstinate base to a manageable size very quickly and at a moderate cost. Where such problems are known or expected to exist, it is wise to include a specification clause in respect of the use and control of explosives, clearly indicating that their use would only be with written authority of the engineer and then only under direction of a properly qualified person, and all liabilities for damage, loss, injury etc, are to rest entirely with the contractor.

The provision in the bills of quantities for removal of hidden foundations can be either a provisional sum for the work to be carried out under the direction of the engineer, or provisional quantities for the various materials likely to be encountered.

Shaft caps

Caps can be required for a variety of purposes, including disused mine shafts, drift workings, air shafts and other deep pits which, because of their depth and indifferent fill, are difficult or even impossible to leave in unsafe condition without capping.

The specification should contain the following information:

- any particular statutory or other requirement which the contractor will be required to observe (the National Coal Board for example issue information sheets containing details for capping mine shafts, setting out minimum diameter and thickness, concrete strengths and reinforcement requirements);

- concrete strengths and method of placing, reinforcement and formwork requirements;

- the position of the cap, whether at ground level, rock head or other level;

- demolition if any to top of shaft;

- compaction of ground to receive cap;

- safeguards for workmen and public;

- waterproofing cap, i.e. bitumen paint;

- compaction of fill over cap and period of curing prior to filling over;

- restriction of the use of heavy plant over cap until adequately covered by fill;

● marking position of cap at finished gound level.

The bills of quantities should contain the various items required, including excavation, demolitions, compaction of base and any blinding, the concrete cap, reinforcement shuttering, waterproofing, marker post and air vent if required. Where the capping level is to be ascertained by investigation, the excavation (i.e. measured net or otherwise) should be stated so that the contractor can make an appropriate allowance for working space.

Earthworks

The main items to be specified under this section are as follows:

(a) *The type and state of the materials likely to be found*, e.g. shale, bricks, boulders, clay, soil, earth, slag and so on and whether these materials are wet, dry fused or in any other state which could affect the contractor's tender.

(b) *The method of handling, deposition and compaction*, e.g. 'the materials in the filling areas shall be deposited in layers not exceeding 300 mm in thickness and shall be well compacted by the passage of the earthmoving plant and equipment over the site'. Where a specific bearing capacity is required this should be stated.

(c) *Any restrictions to the method of achieving the final landform* such as working from the lowest to highest contours and marrying-in at boundaries. If any particular area requires very accurate contouring this should be stated, but in general a requirement should be included stipulating that all areas be finished to the required level to a clean line with even transitions in grade, the surface being free from irregularities and depressions to facilitate proper surface drainage.

(d) *Any specific requirements for handling certain materials* such as hot or burning shale, slurry or fused material.

Arguments can occur in respect of the classification of hot or burning material. Temperature alone is not a criterion since a very small pocket of hot material at 200°C covering an area of a few square metres would present no difficulty, but on the other hand material with a temperature of 150°C covering an area of 1000 m² (1200 yd²) would present difficulties and above-average wear and tear on machinery.

Typical clauses to cover this situation can be framed on the following lines:

Material shall be designated as *hot material* when the temperature registers 120°C at a depth of 0.60 m below the surface at the time of working over an area. No additional payment shall be made for the excavation of such material for isolated volumes of less than 250 m³. The engineer will determine what materials shall be designated hot and his decision shall be final. Material designated by the engineer as hot shall be excavated in layers not exceeding 0.15 m thick and shall be spread and compacted in a layer not exceeding 0.10 m in thickness in areas well away from the excavation area or in areas as directed by the engineer and shall be covered with a layer of not less than 0.60 m compacted thickness of colliery waste with a low combustion factor. The contractor shall make provision for adequate air cooling of plant during excavation of hot material and shall allow in his pricing for all costs connected therewith. The engineer shall be informed immediately if, in the opinion of the contractor, hot material is encountered.

Material shall be designated as *burning material* when the temperature registers in excess of 290°C over an area of at least 750 m² at a depth of 0.60 m below the surface at the time of working the area. No additional payment shall be made for the excavation of such material for isolated volumes of less than 150 m³. The engineer will determine what material shall be designated burning and his decision shall be final. Material designated by the engineer as burning shall be excavated in layers not exceeding 0.15 m thick and shall be spread in layers not exceeding 0.10 m thick in areas as directed by the engineer. After the temperature of the material has dropped to below 200°C, measured at a depth of 0.10 m below the surface, the materials shall be re-excavated and spread in layers not exceeding 0.10 m thick in areas well away from the original excavation area or in areas as directed by the engineer, and each layer shall be covered with a layer of not less than 0.60 m compacted thickness of colliery waste with a low combustion factor. The contractor shall make provision for shift working until the heart of the burning material is removed or until such time as the engineer decides the condition of the material permits the resumption of normal working hours, and the contractor shall allow in his pricing for all costs connected therewith.

Slurry material occurring in any but very small quantities is usually mixed with shale at ratio of 2 : 1 or 3 : 1 and spread in thin layers (usually around 300 mm; 11.8 in). A clause should be inserted stipulating these requirements and giving any restrictions there might be on areas for spreading. Where slurry is in ponds it is prudent to lay down the method of working or at least draw the contractor's attention to the possibility of bund walls being breached or surge occurring if the material is not handled in the correct manner. It is sometimes helpful, where doubt exists as to the nature and extent of the material, to require a preliminary trial pit or trench across the slurry to ascertain water content and other properties which might affect the mode of operations.

Boulders or fused slag will require breaking or burying. A typical specification clause might read: 'Boulders and masses of fused slag shall be buried in deep fill and shall in no circumstances be buried less than 1 m below the finished surface. This material shall be placed in a manner to avoid aggregations causing voids which may lead to subsidence of the fill material over'.

All these materials which differ from the normal waste material can be expressed in the bills of quantities as items of provisional quantities 'extra over' the bulk earthwork items to enable tenders to indicate the extra rate required for handling such material in compliance with the specification.
(e) *The grading and initial cultivation work comprising the following typical clauses:* After completion of earthwork operations the surface shall be graded out to smooth line and contour to the engineer's satisfaction. Those areas of shale to be covered by soil are to be left the required amount lower so that when the soil has been replaced the surface marries in with adjoining shale areas. The colliery shale and subsoil surfaces shall be rooted to their full depth using heavy subsoil cultivators or rooters at not more than 0.60 m centres in the direction of the contour or to a slight fall as directed by the engineer. All stone, wood and other hard material over 150 mm in any dimension shall be removed and buried not less than 1.00 m below the colliery shale surface, the surface then to be 'scrubbed' or lightly graded to remove irregularities and depressions.
(f) *Subsoil and topsoil stripping and replacing,* stating: location and depth of soil to be stripped and spread; cultivations, stone picking and grading requirements; restrictions to stripping and replacing during bad weather and tracking of heavy plant after spreading; siting of spoil heaps so as not to impede the working or drainage; preparation of stacking areas including stripping of topsoil and grading to required levels prior to stacking; weeding requirements.

Care should be taken to provide an allowance for bulking or compaction in solid and waste materials. The compaction element of a loosely deposited shale can have a considerable effect on quantities. While any allowance is often at best a guess, no allowance at all can result in radical design changes during the execution of the works.

Drainage

The specification for drainage works on reclamation schemes generally follows conventional civil engineering practice. There are, however, three matters worthy of more detailed consideration: compaction of shale on line of ditches, backfilling ditches, and maintenance.

Some shales compact well and ditch erosion is minimal, but where erosion is likely to be excessive the ditch profile can be preserved to some extent by compacting the shale prior to excavating the ditch. A typical specification for such an operation might read: Where ditches are constructed in colliery shale the material on the line of the ditch shall be compacted for a distance of 1.5 m each side of the ditch centre line by four passes of a 7-tonne roller at a depth of 450 mm below the surface and a further four passes at finished surface level.

To prevent excessive erosion during grass and vegetation establishment, temporary contour ditches are frequently utilized. These ditches are backfilled, usually during the maintenance period, when the grass has become established. Inevitably the profile of these ditches is enlarged by erosion and periodical cleaning so that the cubic content per linear metre is as much as double the original. A contractor will very often advance the argument that the specification required him to dig a ditch of a certain cross-sectional area and backfill the same ditch at a specified time, but not to backfill a ditch of twice the cross-section. It is important therefore to make the specification clear to the effect that the contractor's prices are to include for additional stone as may be required to backfill the ditches during the maintenance period over and above the cubic content of those ditches as dug, so that due allowance is made for profile changes arising through erosion and cleaning. If there is any doubt whether erosion will take place or not—the reverse is sometimes true in that the ditches fill with silt—a provisional cubic quantity can be inserted in the bill of quantities and the contractor paid for the actual amount used.

Reference is made above to maintenance work. The surface erosion particularly during the establishment of vegetation is often excessive during the twelve months following completion and necessitates regular cleaning of silt from ditches, watercourses, silt traps etc and periodic general inspection of the whole system to ensure correct functioning. While the contract imposes a duty on the contractor to remedy defects, silting and general wear and tear are not defects as such, although it might be argued that failure to maintain the system properly could result in damage or defects occurring. To avoid misunderstanding and possible arguments over the legal interpretation of contract maintenance, it is advisable to specify the maintenance work required during the contract-maintenance and defect-liability period and include an item in the bills of quantities to define the contractor's responsibility and enable him to insert his rate for the work. A typical clause might read: 'Carry out all necessary maintenance of the drainage system after construction and during the maintenance period including de-silting ditches, drains, manholes and catchpits, removal of obstructions and periodical examination of the system to ensure correct functioning and that all reasonable precautions are taken to reduce flooding and erosion to a minimum'.

Water supply and other services

Re-routeing of main services, cables equipment etc are usually executed by the public or statutory undertaking responsible. An estimate from the appropriate body can be inserted in the bills of quantities as a P.C. sum for nomination by the engineer.

Agricultural specifications are usually appropriate for water supplies to cattle troughs and the like, but consideration should be given to the material specification, particularly metals, where corrosive shales or soil are evident.

Surface treatment and planting

There are three ways of dealing with this section. The first is to specify the work as for the other sections and leave the contractor free to choose either to execute the work himself or sub-let to a specialist; the second is to specify a list of approved specialists from which the contractor is to seek prices and include in his tender; and the third is to include a p.c. sum for the work to be carried out by a firm (or firms) to be nominated by the engineer.

There is another alternative and that is to delete this work completely and let a separate contract with a specialist firm but this is not a recom-' mended procedure unless there is to be a time lag between completion of the other work and commencement of seeding and planting operations. This splitting of the work into two contracts can be advantageous where the waste material has a high toxicity and when it is wise to leave the regraded surface for a period prior to seeding, allowing the weather to leach out some of the toxic chemicals. Unless there is this time lag, letting concurrent but separate contracts is likely to create contractual problems in respect of conflicting responsibilities for the site and the works.

The criterion for the selection of the most suitable alternative is the nature of the work required. In the case of a project predominantly of a landscaping nature where the tenderers specialize in seeding and planting work, there is very little advantage to be gained in nominating other specialists to do the work. On the other hand, for contracts predominantly of an earthshifting nature where the tenderers are civil engineering contractors, selection of specialist firms to tender for the seeding and planting work is preferable. Whether this is by way of nomination of an approved list or a p.c. sum depends on the employer's preference, but where there are relatively few specialists in an area where a large amount of work of this nature is being carried out a system of nomination by p.c. sum has the advantage in the greater degree of selectivity which can be exercised to prevent one firm cornering the market and perhaps taking on more work than it can handle efficiently.

The issue of a list of approved firms is a quite satisfactory system providing the list has a sufficient number of firms to ensure that contractors can get a reasonable response from their enquiries and obtain competitive tenders. The system has the advantage in that, while the firms are approved by the employer, they are not nominated in the sense that the contractor selects the firm as his sub-contractor for which he assumes full responsibility rather than a nominated sub-contractor for which the employer has certain responsibilities (ICE clause 59 and ILA clause 28).

Irrespective of the system adopted a specification will be required. Reclamation work poses problems in specification writing for cultivations and seeding work. The nature of the surface material upon completion can be vastly different from the existing condition prior to work commencing. The chemical properties will affect fertilizer requirements, and physical properties will affect the amount and type of cultivations required. The specification, therefore, should, together with the billed items, have a degree of flexibility. To achieve this flexibility the specification and bills of quantities for cultivation and seeding work should contain the following information:

- If the work is to be let as a nominated sub-contract the tender document must contain full details of the conditions of the main contract and any initial cultivation and stone-picking operations to be carried out to the shale and soil surfaces.

- Lime and fertilizer treatments specified should either give details of the type and spreading rates where a fairly good knowledge of soil conditions is available, or include a provisional sum for the supply of lime fertilizers from an approved merchant with various spreading rates measured as provisional quantities. The provisional sum can be calculated on a rough estimation of the likely type and quantities of lime, basic slag, fertilizer etc required, payment being made against invoices received from the suppliers. The sub-contractor's profit, attendance, handling and spreading charges can be stipulated as being covered by the rates set against 'spread only' quantities (see the example given in Appendix 2. Sufficient allowance should be made for fertilizers etc required during the maintenance period and an item inserted for soil tests on samples of the finished soil and shale surfaces so that the correct treatments can be determined.

- A description of the cultivations required for each type of material or designated area stating the number of passes required for each type of cultivation. This ensures that all the tenders are on the same basis and gives the engineer full control to vary any single element if conditions so warrant, without losing track of the overall cost (see Appendix 2).

- The composition and sowing rates for the various grass seed mixes to be used.

- Grass cutting and other work to be carried out during the contract maintenance period (see Appendix 2).

The example in Appendix 2 is not intended as a recommended treatment for any particular material but serves to illustrate the framework upon which the contractor can build his price and provide the engineer with the facility to add, omit or rearrange operations as site conditions dictate.

The stone-picking items do give rise to problems in that the nature of the material encountered, varying from hard stony shales to fine friable shales, will have a marked effect on the amount of stone picking required and therefore the cost. It is impossible to cover all possibilities and remain fair to both contractor and employer, but it must be remembered that contracts do provide for circumstances where the nature of the work is of a character beyond that reasonably foreseeable at date of tender. One must therefore be prepared to vary the requirements where conditions make it impossible to achieve the desired result.

Fences

This section conforms to specification and billed quantities for agricultural, road and general fencing, conforming to BS1722.

Three items which are worthy of note are 'hard dig', 'clearing fence line' and post and wire fences on soft shales.

The specification should clearly delineate between digging for fence posts which is deemed to be included in the billed rates and that which would be considered as hard dig over and beyond that reasonably foreseen. Holes in shales or hard stony material should not, it is submitted, be given any special consideration providing the specification clearly expresses this intention, but holes dug in or through old foundations or in rock where the use of a pneumatic drill is required should form the bases for an 'extra over' rate.

Difficulty sometimes arises at boundaries where marrying-in has occurred to undulating or rough ground. The specification should indicate that the rates for fences in such situations should provide for blading and levelling to remove such irregularities and ensure the fences follow the landform to a regular line.

A post and strained wire fence can sometimes be troublesome when the straining effect on undulating areas tends to pull posts in or out of the ground. This in turn slackens the line wires. An effective counter measure is to provide substantial posts let well into ground in the bottoms of dips and on to tops of rises. These steady the fence and prevent movement up or down.

Where part of the fencing work attracts grant it is helpful to divide the bills into the appropriate section, and even where there is no such necessity division of the fencing into sections such as boundary, woodland, field, public open space and the like assists location for interim valuations, variations and final account work.

Roads and paths

Little of this section has problems peculiar to reclamation but, again as for fences, where certain elements are grant-earning, such as reinstatement of tracks and bridle paths, separation of these elements aids later calculations and grant submissions.

2.8 Assessment of tenders and reports

Assessment of tenders for reclamation projects follows conventional lines. In addition to the normal arithmetical check and notification and agreement to the method of adjusting such errors, some care should be taken to examine rates and ensure those for large quantities, such as bulk muckshift, are reasonable. It is preferable, if in doubt, to check with a tenderer to ensure he has taken full account of the specification and site conditions. Inevitably errors in pricing will occur and are the contractor's risk, but a substantial error on a large quantity, while possibly presenting the employer with an attractively keen price, will more than likely lead to considerable problems, at worst leading to bankruptcy of the contractor and at best a delayed and possibly ill-managed job of poor quality, which in the end is to no-one's advantage.

The decision to accept or reject a tender must rest with the employer but he should be given a full appraisal of all pertinent matters by his professional advisers.

3 Post-contract procedure

This section deals with the procedure after acceptance of a tender, namely the execution and completion of the work. The concern of the employer and his professional advisers during the execution of the works is supervision and cost control.

3.1 Supervision

As for any other project, whether building or civil engineering, the word 'supervision' is used in a broad sense to mean:

- monitoring the day-to-day progress;
- ensuring the contract documents are being correctly interpreted and strictly followed;
- approving methods of operation and programme of events;
- issuing additional information and drawings as may be necessary to clarify any aspect of work;
- serving notices and issuing instructions regarding variations to the works or suspension of the works or the removal of defective work etc;
- assessing the value of variations and certifying interim payments on account;
- assessing delays and granting extension as appropriate;
- certifying practical or substantial completion;

- preparing lists of defects and supervising their correction;
- compiling the measurements for the final account to secure final payment to the contractor.

The main aim of all this activity is to control the conversion of the design information into reality and so ensure the final project fulfils the employer's brief requirements in terms of both function and cost.

While the day-to-day supervisory problems are no different from any other landscape or engineering project, there are a number of matters which are worthy of special note, as follows.

Final shape The question of tolerance in finished levels should be agreed with the contractor prior to commencement; plus or minus 300 mm (12 in) is probably a reasonable compromise, providing all areas remain free-draining. However, it should be noted that some engineers prefer a certain amount of final shaping by eye rather than strict adherence to the contours shown on the earthworks drawing. This is largely a matter of personal preference, but the intention should be made clear to the contractor at the outset.

Compaction It is virtually impossible to budget accurately for a balance of cut and fill because of the variable compaction factor. Most waste tips are loose when deposited and therefore compact after spreading when traversed by heavy machines. With this in mind it is advantageous to include in the specification directions for the order of works so that any slack or excess is accommodated in a chosen area and hence avoid the embarrassment of having to double-handle some of the fill to achieve a balance. The specification clause giving effect to this requirement might read: 'The construction of the new landform shall be commenced from the lowest contour and be continued to the highest'. This clause does sometimes give rise to queries from contractors who would prefer to work downhill. However the logic is in the fact that the bulking/compaction element can be judged as the earthworks proceed so that any slack or surplus can be accommodated by revision to the highest, less critical contours. It is advisable to clarify this matter at the outset so that the contract earthworks operations provide a degree of flexibility with the minimum effect on cost.

Site survey Many existing condition surveys are produced these days from aerial surveys which are quite adequate for the average reclamation project. However, changes can occur (e.g. borrow pits or dumping) which can change the original shape even between tenders being sought and work starting. It is advisable for both engineer and contractor to agree, by spot checks or a more detailed survey if necessary, that all levels and features are acceptable as shown prior to work commencing and thereby avoid the possibility of arguments later in the contract.

Preservation of existing vegetation, trees etc It is advisable to ensure the contractor clearly understands which areas, plants or other features are to be retained. It is not unusual for a contractor to be mistaken in his selection of species and remove the wrong plants. This comment has more relevance to a civil engineering than a specialist landscape contractor.

Hidden foundations Any items such as machine bases or other hidden obstructions will be dealt with in the usual way, the contractor informing the engineer or his representative who will take note of the size and nature of the obstruction for the value to be assessed against the provisional quantities provided in the bills. Not infrequently however the obstructions take the form of fairly large isolated pockets or pits of rubble from building demolitions. The composition can vary and include brick, stone, concrete and even steel. Short of putting the whole operation on a daywork basis there is no straightforward answer, but a random sample system can be usefully employed. A mutually agreed area is selected as a random sample and the cubic content of excavation agreed, work is commenced and plant records kept. From this information a rate can be calculated and expressed as 'extra over' the general earthworks rates. This rate is then applied throughout to all obstructed areas. This system, while not foolproof, can if sensibly evolved reimburse the contractor for the extra difficulty without removing all incentive to maintain efficiency and output. A check must be kept to ensure the random sample remains representative.

Top- and subsoil quantities It is advisable to establish the quantities of top- and subsoil strip by a before-and-after survey and avoid arguments in respect of compaction factors which can be considerable on good arable topsoil when deposited in spoil heaps.

Final survey Ideally the survey of the finished shape should be done prior to soiling. This enables the engineer to discover any errors in the final shape requiring correction before the soil is replaced and provides more accurate information to calculate the bulk earthwork quantities.

Water supplies Particular care should be taken to ensure adequate depth of water services where they cross ditches. The erosion of ditch bottoms in shale materials can be considerable and all too frequently water service pipes are left fully exposed and spanning between the ditch sides. In this position they become vulnerable to damage by frost, livestock and vandals.

Fertilizing and seeding Where various rates and mixtures are specified for different areas very close supervision is advisable, first to ensure the contractor or his sub-contractor is fully conversant with the requirement and secondly to see that various applications and seed mixes are applied to the areas designated. It is astonishing how often a seed mix for say, a public open space, finds its way onto woodland and *vice versa*.

Fences A cursory check of fence lines does not always reveal inherent defects or failure to comply with the specification. The use of shorter than specified intermediate posts may not be apparent nor indeed too important in normal ground but in some soft shale materials soon leads to sagging fence lines. The failure to fix ratchet winders to line wires might be excused on the grounds that the modern high-tensile wire used can be highly tensioned and does not sag even when severely distorted, but removal of a section of a fence for any reason thereafter creates difficulty in respect of re-tensioning.

3.2 Cost control

A detailed cost-planning service in the early days of a project loses all its value unless rigorously pursued during the contract period.

The essential element of cost control is the monitoring of variations and changes as work proceeds on site together with a projection of the effects that any changes might have on subsequent work so that the financial implication can be ascertained and the employer advised.

The elements in reclamation work which have the most marked effect on cost are unsuitable materials in the excavations, such as slurry, hot material, fused slag etc, and drainage problems. The more detailed the initial site investigation the less likelihood of unpleasant surprises in earthwork costs but this element is essentially vague and up-to-date records in terms of site measurement are essential to keep the employer apprised of his financial commitment.

Drainage problems are generally less severe in their cost implications, but an underground spring or inaccessible blocked culvert can create problems, and while a relatively inexpensive ditch might alleviate the problem, the additional run-off at the outfalls from the site can create greater difficulties. A fairly generous provision for work to outfalls can be of considerable help in such cases (see section 2.7 under *Drainage*).

4 Grant-aided projects

The types of grant available and operations likely to rank for grant are considered in detail in Chapter 1.

Where grant aid is to be sought for a scheme it will assist applications and approvals if the documents starting with the estimate are prepared in a form that is acceptable to the authority or department from which grant aid is sought, and are itemized to show clearly those elements which are grant-aided and those which are not.

Mention is made in earlier sections of this chapter of this fact and it is very often worthwhile to ascertain information on grant-aided works for any particular scheme so that the estimates and subsequently the bills of quantities can be drafted in a form whereby the aided and non-aided works are readily separated. It is not essential and not always desirable to produce separate sections for grant-aided and non-grant-aided works since this can lead to a disjointed document, but separation of items so that they can be easily abstracted is helpful. A good example is fencing where perhaps the internal field fencing is not grant-earning. Here the field fences, with their straining posts, stiles and gates can be put under the heading of 'field fences' thereby making extraction of cost a simple task.

An important function in the cost-control process is updating cost and advising the appropriate body of cost changes to grant-aided work. Where an authority or Government department has authorized expenditure of public money on a project, it is right and proper to keep that authority or department fully informed of the cost implication of variations and where any major difficulty is encountered, which would increase the costs beyond authorized limits, the authority or department should be advised prior to the issue of instructions for the additional work.

Appendix 1 Typical estimate for the reclamation of derelict land

		Unit cost (£)	Total cost (£)
Demolitions and site clearance			
Pull down and remove fences	4 500 m	0.10	450.00
Pull down and remove building 29 × 8 × 4 m high complete with heavy concrete floor	Item		400.00
Ditto partly demolished brick structure 7 × 2 × 1 m high	Item		50.00
Ditto brick structure with concrete roof and floor slab 6 × 3 × 3 m high	Item		50.00
Ditto arched brick structure 5 × 2 × 1.5 m	Item		100.00
Ditto brick structure on heap 3.5 × 3 × 2.5 m high	Item		50.00
Break up remains of machine base 1 × 2 × 1 m	Item		20.00
Break up concrete slabs, roads and the like	800 m²	1.00	800.00
Pull down and remove brick wall	90 m²	0.50	45.00
Remove sundry debris and rubbish	Item		500.00
			£2 465.00

		Unit cost (£)	Total cost (£)
Shaft caps			
Provision for investigating mine shafts and capping as required	3	700	2 100.00
			£2 100.00
Earthworks			
Excavate to remove topsoil and deposit in stockpiles	26 000 m³	0.16	4 160.00
Excavate topsoil from stockpile and spread over forestry areas (av. 200 mm)	8 000 m³	0.16	1 280.00
Excavate waste material and deposit on adjoining areas	422 000 m³	0.12	50 640.00
Extra over last for removing slurry and burying in thin layers	40 000 m³	0.41	16 400.00
Ditto burning material	3 000 m³	0.31	930.00
			£73 410.00
Drainage			
Permanent open ditch	1 070 m	0.60	642.00
Temporary ditch backfilled during maintenance period	490 m	2.00	980.00
Ditch crossings	3	160.00	480.00
Catchpits and headwalls to ditches	2	160.00	320.00
750 mm outfall pipe to stream	60 m	30.00	1 800.00
Headwall to last	1	200.00	200.00
Connection of catchpit to existing manhole in road	Item		400.00
			£4 822.00
Water supply			
Excavate for and lay water main	220 m	0.50	110.00
Cattle troughs and stopcocks	2	55.00	110.00
			£220.00
Seeding and planting			
Initial cultivations, removal of stone and grading	19 ha	80.00	1 520.00
Cultivate and seed shale areas	15 ha	450.00	6 750.00

		Unit cost (£)	Total cost (£)
(*As last*) new soiled areas for woodland planting	4 ha	400.00	1 600.00
Provision for two-year establishment period of grass on shale	15 ha	200.00	3 000.00
Woodland planting	9 ha	520.00	4 680.00
Provision for five-year establishment period for woodland planting	9 ha	260.00	2 340.00
			£19 890.00

Fences

Post and wire fence	4 890 m	1.50	7 335.00
Post and wire fence with netting	2 035 m	2.00	4 070.00
Field gates	2	40.00	80.00
Field gates to woodland areas	3	45.00	135.00
			£11 620.00

Roads and paths

Reinstate farm track 3 m wide	200 m	3.00	600.00
Bridle path in compacted red shale 1.2 m wide	100 m	0.15	15.00
			£615.00

Summary

Demolitions and site clearance	2 465.00
Shaft caps	2 100.00
Earthworks	73 410.00
Drainage	4 822.00
Water supply	220.00
Seeding and planting	19 890.00
Fences	11 620.00
Roads and paths	615.00
Preliminaries 5% on items 1–8	5 757.00
Contingencies 5% on items 1–9	6 045.00
Total estimated cost	£126 944.00

Note The estimated cost of £126 944.00 does not include professional fees, land acquisition, legal and administration costs.

Appendix 2 Example of typical cultivation and seeding specification and bill items for a reclamation project

The following is an example of the main framework for a specification and bill of quantities for a 10 ha (25 acre) site reclaimed to provide 7 ha (17 acres) of agricultural land and 3 ha (8 acres) of woodland. The available soil and subsoil is spread on the agricultural area and the woodland area remains bare shale.

Specification clauses

Description of site

Before commencement of cultivation and seeding the following initial cultivations and soiling operations will have been completed by the general contractor:

(a) Surface of colliery shale in all areas ripped to a depth of 600 mm (24 in) with a heavy subsoil rooter at 600 mm centres along the contours.

(b) All stones etc of 150 mm (6 in) diameter or over removed and buried.

(c) Surface of shale graded and scrubbed.

(d) Subsoil spread to specified thickness on all areas except woodland.

(e) Subsoil ripped to its full depth, i.e. 300 mm (12 in).

(f) Stones etc of 150 mm (6 in) diameter or over removed from surface subsoil.

(g) Surface of subsoil graded or scrubbed.

(h) Topsoil spread to specified thickness on all areas except woodland.

(i) Stones etc of 50 mm (2 in) diameter and over removed from surface of topsoil.

(k) Surface of topsoil graded or scrubbed.

Lime and fertilizers (provisional item)

The sub-contractor shall allow the provisional sums included in the bills of quantities for the sampling and analysis of the soil and the supply of lime and fertilizers over the total area.

Before starting cultivations the sub-contractor shall make arrangements for the sampling and analysis of the soil to determine the type and rate of application for lime and fertilizers and shall deliver and spread the lime and/or fertilizers over the site to the instructions of the engineer.

Cultivations—soiled areas

The sub-contractor shall undertake the following operations over soiled areas in the order shown (average total depth of soils expected to be 400 mm; 16 in).

1 Spread ground limestone as specified.

2 Chisel plough 150 mm (6 in) deep (one pass).

3 Spread basic slag as specified.

4 Disc harrow (two passes).

5   Heavy harrow (one pass).

6   Remove all stones, wood, metal and other deleterious material larger than 50 mm (2 in) diameter brought to the surface.

7   Scrub (one pass).

8   Distribute compound fertilizer as specified.

9   Light harrow (one pass).

10   Roll with Cambridge roller (one pass).

11   Sow grass seed as specified.

12   Light harrow (one pass).

13   Flat roll (one pass).

Cultivations—shale areas

The sub-contractor shall undertake the following operations over shale areas in the order shown:

1   Spread ground limestone as specified.

2   Chisel plough 150 mm (6 in) deep (one pass).

3   Spread basic slag as specified.

4   Disc (one pass).

5   Remove all stones, other deleterious materials larger than 50 mm (2 in) diameter.

6   Scrub (one pass).

7   Spread dried sewage sludge as specified.

8   Heavy harrow (one pass).

9   Distribute compound fertilizer as specified.

10   Roll with Cambridge roller (one pass).

11   Sow grass seeds mixture as the prescribed rate.

12   Light harrow (one pass).

13   Flat roll (one pass).

Grass seed mixtures

1 Grass seed mixture 'A'

    30 kg Perennial Ryegrass S23
    14 kg Cocksfoot S143
     7 kg Timothy S48
     3 kg Meadow Fescue S53
     3 kg Creeping Red Fescue S59
     7 kg White Clover S100
     3 kg Red Clover S123
    ─────
    67 kg/ha (60 lb/acre)
    ─────

This mixture shall be used on all pasture areas at the rate of 67 kg/ha (60 lb/acre).

2 Grass seed mixture 'B'

    40 kg Red Fescue S59

9 kg White Clover S184
9 kg *Festuca tenuifolia* (certified strain)
9 kg *Agrostis tenuis* (certified strain)

67 kg/ha (60 lb/acre)

This mixture shall be used on all woodland areas at the rate of 67 kg/ha (60 lb/acre).

Cultivations and grass seeding—general

No lime, seed, fertilizer, basic slag, or dried sewerage sludge shall be applied or cultivations carried out when ground or other conditions are unsuitable. The engineer's decision shall be final.

The prices of cultivations, treatments and operations, where indicated in the foregoing, shall be based on the number of passes of the machine or cultivator specified. Additional passes, cultivations or amendments to the specification will be paid for in accordance with the items marked 'provisional'.

Prices for the removal of stones etc shall include the removal off-site, or burying not less than 900 mm (35 in) below the finished surface, of all materials of the size limit stated brought to the surface by these cultivations, notwithstanding that such materials conform to the description of materials to be removed during the initial cultivations.

No fertilizer or seed is to be sown until the engineer has approved the seed bed.

The sub-contractor will be required to produce all delivery notes for lime, seed, basic slag and compound granular fertilizers for inspection and recording.

The lime, fertilizer and seed shall be supplied by a merchant approved by the engineer. The seed shall be mixed to the required specification at the merchant's works and delivered to site in sealed bags clearly marked with the code reference for the mixture.

The contractor must ensure that all machinery and implements used in establishing and maintaining the grass sward are properly guarded in accordance with the Agriculture (Safety, Health and Welfare Provisions) Act 1956 and Regulations made thereunder.

Establishment period

The sub-contractor shall maintain all the grassland for a period of 12 months commencing from the date of completion of the sowing of the grass seed and carry out the following work:

(a) Supply, deliver and spread ground limestone and fertilizer as specified by the engineer and within two weeks of receiving written instructions (see provisional sum included in bills of quantities).

(b) Prior to the first cutting of the grass remove all stones, wood, metal and other deleterious matter of 50 mm (2 in) diameter and over, and before completion of the establishment period remove all such similar materials that have worked to the surface. All such materials to be removed from the site.

(c) The sub-contractor shall cut and mulch the grass when 100 mm (4 in) in height reducing the height to 50 mm (2 in). Avoid root pulling and cutting in wet weather.

(d) The sub-contractor shall throughout the remainder of the establishment period cut and mulch the seeded areas according to growth and shall allow for a cut to take place as often as the grass produces a further 100 mm (4 in) of growth from the previous cut and prevent the grass from seeding.

(e) It is anticipated that mowing will be required every 12 to 14 days during the height of the season but only once every 20 to 22 days at the start and finish. The sward should enter the dormancy period with a growth of no more than 100 mm (4 in) height.

All cutting and mulching shall be undertaken using a Sapper Bamford B6 flail mower or Lupat Flailmaster or other machine to be approved by the engineer. The sub-contractor will be required to prevent the mulched grass from collecting in rows or rills or in any other way deleterious to the growing sward.

During the establishment period the sub-contractor shall direct his attention to establishing a good sward of this specific mixture free from pernicious and other weeds. In doing so the sub-contractor shall apply approved weed-killer at the direction of the engineer.

Bills of quantities descriptions

Soil sampling and analysis

Provide the provisional sum of £50.00 for soil sampling and analysis.

Lime compound fertilizer and basic slag

The type and rate of application of lime, fertilizer and basic slag will depend largely upon the results of the soil analysis.

All charges for taking delivery, unloading, storing and transporting on site, profit and all other charges in connection with the supply of limestone, compound fertilizer and basic slag must be included in the items for the spreading of these materials. The prices for 'spread only' items shall therefore include all such charges.

Provide the provisional sum of £1600.00 for the supply of lime compound fertilizer and basic slag for application during cultivation of the seed bed and establishment period.

Cultivations and seeding—soiled areas

Chisel plough, disc, heavy harrow, remove all stones, etc, scrub, light harrow, roll, light harrow and roll as specified.	7 ha
Spread only ground limestone at a rate of 12.50 tonnes/ha (5 tons/acre).	7 ha
Extra over last for a rate of 25.00 tonnes/ha (10 tons/acre) (provisional).	7 ha
Spread only basic slag at a rate of 0.63 tonnes/ha (0.25 tons/acre).	7 ha
Extra over last for a rate of 1.25 tonnes/ha (0.5 tons/acre) (provisional).	7 ha
Spread only compound granular fertilizer at a rate of 0.25 tonnes/ha (0.10 tons/acre).	7 ha
Extra over last for a rate of 0.50 tonnes/ha (0.20 tons/acre) (provisional).	7 ha
Supply and broadcast seed as specified at a rate of 67 kg/ha (60 lb/acre) (Mix A).	7 ha

Cultivations and seeding—shale areas

Chisel plough, disc, remove all stones etc, scrub, heavy harrow, roll, light harrow, and flat roll.	3 ha
Spread only limestone at a rate of 12.50 tonnes/ha (5 tons/acre).	3 ha
Extra over last for a rate of 25.00 tonnes/ha (10 tons/acre) (provisional).	3 ha
Spread only basic slag at a rate of 0.63 tonnes/ha (0.25 tons/acre)	3 ha
Extra over last for a rate of 1.25 tonnes/ha (0.50 tons/acre) (provisional).	3 ha
Supply, deliver and spread, dried sewage sludge at a rate of 5.00 tonnes/ha (2.0 tons/acre).	3 ha
Extra over last for a rate of 10.00 tonnes/ha (4 tons/acre) (provisional).	3 ha
Spread only compound granular fertilizer at a rate of 0.25 tonnes/ha (0.10 tons/acre).	3 ha
Extra over last for a rate of 0.50 tonnes/ha (0.2 tons/acre) (provisional).	3 ha
Supply and broadcast seed as specified at a rate of 67 kg/ha (60 lbs/acre) (Mix B).	3 ha

The following cultivation work all provisional

Chisel plough (one pass—to a depth of 200 mm; 8 in)	3 ha
Disc (one pass).	3 ha
Heavy harrow (one pass).	3 ha
Light harrow (one pass).	3 ha
Roll (one pass).	3 ha

Establishment period

Remove all stones, etc, and other deleterious matter 50 mm (2 in) diameter and over prior to first cut over soiled areas.	7 ha
(As last) but over shale areas.	3 ha
Cut and mulch grass as specified over soiled areas (first cut).	7 ha
(As last) but additional cuts (5 No. provisionally).	35 ha
Cut and mulch grass as specified over shale areas (first cut).	3 ha
(As last) but additional cuts (5 No. provisionally).	15 ha

10 Development and maintenance organizations

Jill Foister

1 Introduction

Organizations supervising agricultural and woodland management generally may be considered as development organizations, because the build-up of soil fertility and soil structure is normally a direct result of good management techniques. However, particularly careful application of these techniques is necessary where reclamation stites are concerned. On the other hand, maintenance operations apply in the management of public open space, where post-contract work mainly involves the preservation of a certain status quo. In many urban situations in particular, vandalism and excessive wear on grass areas mean that continual replacements of plants and groundcover are necessary. When considering newly reclaimed land for public open space, therefore, considerable adjustments do need to be made and careful supervision is required in order that fertility is increased and a less vulnerable soil structure is developed.

In Co. Durham,* agricultural and woodland uses are considered to be the most suitable, when incorporating correct management techniques, for building up fertility at the least cost to the public. The sites under these temporary uses represent a reservoir of land which can be appropriated or sold for any suitable use which might present itself in the future. It is important, therefore, that organizations undertaking management should have the necessary technical expertise to bring about a situation of increasing fertility in such a way that possible future uses are not jeopardized.

Depending upon the use or uses to which the land is put, the management of local authority sites is either taken over at the end of the contract maintenance period by departments specializing in landscape management, such as estates or parks departments, forestry units, etc, or alternatively it may be leased, rented or sold to appropriate organizations on a commercial basis which usually takes into account the fertility status of the land. In this chapter, techniques of management have been studied with reference in particular to work in Northumberland and Durham, where several sites were visited. Alternative organizations for carrying out the management of land reclaimed from pit heaps are discussed although reference is also made to precedents that have been set in other fields of reclamation.

*Grateful acknowledgements are made to the several local authorities mentioned in the text for information on the management of reclamation sites, especially in Durham and Northumberland.

2 Agricultural grassland management

The value of pasture grasses in improving soil structure has been shown to depend on two main factors: the weight of root material produced, and the strength of the roots (Russell 1950). On reclaimed sites, the density

Figure 67. A reclaimed
landscape six years after
completion of the contract.
The site is used for casual
recreation and the maintenance of the grass is by
occasional rough mowing,
with the vegetation between
the young trees cut down
twice a year. The young
trees are inspected for any
damage or loosening of the
stakes at regular intervals
(courtesy University of
Newcastle upon Tyne
Landscape Reclamation
Research Project).

of the sward, especially of the bottom growth, is also very important,
particularly for preventing erosion and gullying on slopes, for decreasing
temperature fluctuations at the surface, and for building up the humus
content and the micro-organism population in the shale.

2.1 Effects of grazing animals on sward development and soil structure

The grazing habits of different animals vary considerably in their effect on
sward development.

Cattle use their tongues to collect their food and thus do not close-graze
the sward (Moore 1950). Although they are not over-selective in their
grazing, like most animals they will choose the best grasses wherever
possible. Those species most beneficial to the development of the soil
structure can be encouraged with careful management, correct stocking
rates being particularly important. If grazing is too light, for instance,
coarser species are avoided and allowed to increase. Any uneven growth
of this sort must be cut or topped off after grazing.

Sheep, on the other hand, do graze closely and prefer the bottom
grasses. This directly encourages root development and the formation of
a close, dense sward. Species such as perennial ryegrass, rough- and
smooth-stalked meadow grasses, crested dogstail and wild white clover
are normally allowed to develop with close grazing. Cocksfoot, requiring
room for development, is either grazed out or left in coarse tufts and in
the latter case topping-off is an essential practice.

Horses are extremely selective, avoiding coarse grasses and also areas
which they reserve for their dung. Parts of the field are, as a result, over-
grazed whilst others become coarse and tufted.

Grazing also has a direct physical effect on soil structure. During wet
weather the shale surface of reclaimed areas becomes very susceptible to
poaching or treading by the grazing animals. This is especially the case
when, as on many of these sites, bottom growth is not particularly well
developed. Heavier animals such as cattle and horses can be a problem
in this respect and careful management must ensure that beasts are not
left on the shale pasture areas during periods of risk. Strip grazing with
complementary topping-off of uneven growth is necessary if poaching is
to be avoided.

Grazing by horses of land reclaimed from opencast coal workings has, on the other hand, had 'disastrous' results according to the Ministry of Agriculture (North-East Region). In some counties sheep, which do not have such a significant poaching effect, and 3–12-month-old calves, are the only animals considered suitable for grazing reclaimed land. In Nottinghamshire, for instance, sheep are very much favoured and one site at Kirby Colliery was initially stocked with them even though it is well away from the main sheep-grazing area.

Certain other factors may also affect the choice of animals to graze a site. Reclamation is very often carried out in fringe areas where, increasingly, problems relating to the proximity of built-up areas may dictate the use of the sites. Sheep-worrying by stray dogs is a well-known hazard although there is some argument that this problem could be partly solved by adequate fencing.

2.2 Adjustment of grazing programme to part-time use of reclaimed sites

The period of grazing on reclaimed sites has to be strictly controlled owing to the vulnerability of the sward and soil structure. If the ground is too wet it may be necessary to wait for a complete growing season after reclamation before grazing, and to take a hay or silage crop. This course is preferred on the opencast sites in the north east. It has the disadvantage, however, that the bottom species of the sward tend to suffer at the expense of the taller grasses, and the land does not benefit from manuring. Generally, animals are put to graze the land as soon as conditions allow. In Stirling, for example, grass sown in the spring may be let on a grazing licence from August to October. At Big Waters in Northumberland, cattle were on the site six months after sowing in the spring, but were taken off after a short period.

2.3 Management of early reclamation sites

In the past, most derelict land was reclaimed for agriculture by local district authorities on the assumption that the minimum treatment was necessary to produce the intended result, i.e. a grass sward suitable for grazing, and techniques of reclamation and management were limited. On

Figure 68. A completed part of the Windy Nook, Felling, reclamation site (Tyne and Wear County) showing adequate maintenance with the ditch in an unobstructed condition and the growth of grass kept within reasonable limits by machine cutting as there was no grazing maintenance on this site (courtesy University of Newcastle upon Tyne Landscape Reclamation Research Project).

early sites which were visited in Durham, insufficient drainage, inadequate grading of the final surface and, in some cases, inappropriate seed mixes have led to considerable problems. It is almost impossible to carry out essential operations such as the topping-off of unevenly grazed pasture and the effective application of manure and fertilizers. Arrangements for grazing these sites were usually made on a short-term (seven-year) lease with a local farmer who took full control of the management of the land. The difficult nature of the sites, together with the short period of lease, meant that the farmers had little incentive to improve the grass sward.

Today it is realized that, as has been shown, grazing in itself represents a very sound method of encouraging both the bottom growth and root system of grasses to aid the development of soil structure, provided that certain adjustments are made to allow for the vulnerability of reclaimed sites. Thus, adequate rather than minimum treatment is the recommended procedure. Several county authorities, including Durham, now have specialized reclamation units which carry out soil sampling and recommend fertilizer treatments, as well as directing general management policies on sites owned by the county council. They also offer advice to district councils on the management of sites, but direct control over these is necessarily limited.

2.4 Present-day tenancy arrangements

Most local authorities lease or rent grassland sites to local farmers on a very temporary basis initially and may rètain a good deal of control over their management. Certain criteria are regarded as important by the reclamation units in Northumberland and Durham in judging applications for grazing a site:

- the farmer's experience and standard of farming;

- his type of farm;

- his interest in shale reclamation and the building-up of fertility on reclaimed sites;

- his willingness to co-operate with the Council;

- that he has or will have sufficient stock to graze the land;

- that he has available land for the stock during periods when there is a risk of poaching the shale.

The degree of control that local authorities have over the management of these sites is determined largely by the terms under which the land is occupied. For instance in Durham, for the first four years after reclamation or until the soil structure has developed sufficiently well, a 364-day grazing and mowing licence holds. The licence is subject to one month's notice and the County Council has right of entry at any time for purposes in connection with management. On sites where occupation tenancies are in force (i.e. where existing farmland has been included in reclamation schemes), normal agricultural tenancy conditions hold. In Northumberland the 364-day licence applies for the grazing of upgraded farmland, whereas a six- to-seven-month tenancy holds on reclaimed shale surfaces. In both of these cases the contract agreement sets out specific conditions with which the licensee must comply. These include:

- that the land must not be used for any purpose other than for grazing animals owned by the licensee;

- only cattle and sheep shall be used for grazing the land which shall not be entered or in any way used by horses, ponies, donkeys, asses, goats or poultry;

- any instructions given by the local authority with regard to the management of the land and the way in which the right granted by the contract agreement should be exercised must be complied with;

- all artificial fertilizers, weed sprays, etc which may be supplied by the local authority must be applied in accordance with instructions from that authority.

Under these terms, the County Council pays for the supply of all fertilizers and lime that may be required and a nominal rent is charged.

In order to specify the necessary treatments, the reclamation units in both Northumberland and Durham carry out regular detailed checks on soil fertility and sward composition. They supervise fertilizer applications on sites directly under their control and give advice on management techniques to the farmer on an informal basis.

In many cases, however, a local district authority will carry out reclamation works, or else will supervise the management of the land either bought or leased from the County Council after restoration. The county reclamation units often can work only in an advisory capacity, and management is sometimes unsatisfactory. A disadvantage in these circumstances appears to be the short period of tenancy. The farmer concerned has little incentive to manage the reclaimed site when he is not sure that he will reap the benefits of his efforts in the future and, in the absence of sufficient control over fertilizer applications from the local authority, sward development obviously suffers. In many cases the farmer would prefer a longer tenancy of at least seven years after an initial period of, say, one year during which time the future potential of the site might be assessed.

Another problem relating to the short tenancy arrangements is the difficulty in planning the provision of buildings which may be necessary if the additional land comprises a large proportion of the total farm unit. This may lead to imbalance in the farm structure or to unsatisfactory management of the developing sward. At Roddymoor and Brancepeth Colliery sites, both in Co. Durham, occupation agreements are in force and normal agricultural tenancies operate. Long-term planning is thus feasible and the buildings needed for overwintering the increased stock can be provided under grant from the Ministry of Agriculture (see section 2.6). This takes time, however, and meanwhile the reclaimed land may be undergrazed.

Many local authorities feel that a certain period should elapse before any decision can be made on the long-term management conditions. In Stirling, after three years, the land is sold to the farmers concerned, whereas in Northumberland it is intended that farmers should be given agricultural tenancies when an acceptable soil structure has developed. At that time the farmers themselves should have considerably benefited from the advice given at present by the reclamation units. In Durham also, agricultural tenancies are arranged after a period of four years, but if the land is not considered fit the 364-day licence is continued.

The question of the possible future use of reclamation sites for arable land should be mentioned at this point. Along with the stony nature of shale, the basic problem is that of the vulnerability of the soil structure. This has been severely damaged in certain cases where ploughing has been attempted many years after reclamation. However, in opencast restoration where there is a cover of topsoil and subsoil, cereals and potatoes have been grown specifically to ameliorate soil conditions, and in a shale situation the policy of ploughing-in a pioneer crop could be considered as an initial mulching technique. Many local authorities in counties where arable farming is predominant say that they will plough up whenever the conditions are suitable although it has been estimated that this may be at least seventy years after reclamation.

2.5 Agricultural fertilizer subsidies

Subsidies on fertilizers and basic slag are no longer available from the Ministry of Agriculture, except for hill farm areas. There is still subsidy, however, on lime which varies according to the fineness of the lime and its calcium content. This is explained in a leaflet on subsidies available from the Ministry of Agriculture. Transport costs for delivery of lime are subsidized at a set rate of 16p/tonne for the first 8 km (5 miles) and 1p/tonne for every 1.6 km (1 mile) over that distance, and a rate for spreading the lime is also included. Once again there is a limit (60% of the net cost) to the amount of subsidy payable.

In Northumberland and Durham the farmers licensing the reclaimed sites are instructed by the county reclamation sections to obtain and arrange for the application of the necessary treatments. In such situations the local authority reimbursed the subsidized cost to the farmers.

2.6 Agricultural grants for further work

Under the Farm Capital Grant Scheme 1973 (and the 1970 scheme which continues to cover certain items for hill farms), a variety of works are eligible for grant which may be necessary during the initial period of establishment. These are set out in leaflet FCG issued by the Ministry of Agriculture, Fisheries and Food, as follows:

Schedule of eligible works and facilities

Item 1   Provision, replacement, improvement, alteration, enlargement or reconditioning of permanent buildings (excluding living accommodation and buildings designed and intended for specialized horticultural use), silos, bulk dry stores, yards, loading platforms, ramps or banks.
(Note: Grant may be payable on specialized horticultural buildings under the Horticulture Capital Grant Scheme or the Farm and Horticulture Development Scheme.)

Item 2   Provision, replacement or improvement of systems for disposal of farm waste.

Item 3   Provision, replacement or improvement of facilities for the supply of electricity or gas for agricultural purposes.

Item 4   Field drainage, including under-drainage and ditching.
(Note: The reconditioning and restoring of an existing field drainage system is eligible only if the system has not previously been grant-aided).

Item 5   Provision, replacement or improvement of facilities for the supply of water.

Item 6   Provision or improvement of farm flood protection works: protection or improvement of river banks.

Item 7   Provision, replacement or improvement of roads, fords, bridges, culverts, railway crossings, creeps, piers, jetties or slips.

Item 8   Provision, replacement or improvement of pens, dips, stells or other facilities designed and intended for use in connection with the gathering, treatment or feeding of sheep or cattle or for sheltering them in periods of adverse weather but not for in-wintering.

Item 9   Orchard grubbing.

Item 10   Provision, replacement or improvement of wirework for hop gardens (as from 23 July 1974 applications for grant for hop wirework are being dealt with under the Hop Gardens (Replanting and Restructuring) Scheme).

Item 11   (Applies to Scotland only).

Item 12   Any work or facility incidental to the carrying out or provision of any work or facility specified in the preceding paragraphs of this Schedule or necessary or proper in carrying it out or providing it or securing the full benefit thereof.

The standard rate of grant is now 20% of the approved expenditure. There are certain exceptions which may apply to reclaimed land as follows:

Field drainage (Item 4)   maximum   55%
                           minimum   25%
Remodelling works   50%

The grant may be based on:

● the actual cost (a test will be made to ensure that it is not unreasonably high—if it is, grant may be reduced); or

● standard costs for certain work, or

● a combination of both the above.

Further details are given in the leaflet as to methods of application for grants.

In order to qualify for grant on the range of items listed, a farmer must be able to show that the business is capable, after the grant-aided work has been carried out, of yielding to any person reasonably skilled in husbandry a net annual income of at least £1870. Thus, if underdrainage is required after reclamation works have been carried out, there may be certain delays until the land is legally recognized as a part of a viable farm unit and the grant can be applied for. There may, therefore, be some argument for works such as this to be included under grant for the reclamation contract itself.

2.7 Alternative management organizations

It has been shown that one of the main problems of using private farmers to manage reclamation sites is that a substantial area of additional land may create an imbalance in the structure of the existing farm which will affect the efficiency of the management of the sward. As an alternative, farming by co-operative groups would have the advantage of a more flexible management structure. It is pointed out by several county authorities that such an arrangement would be considered if any such organization applied for tenancy of a site. The grazing of stock owned by the local authorities themselves has also been considered in certain areas, e.g. in Nottinghamshire. As long as a large enough area was involved, the movement of stock off the sites when required could be co-ordinated. In this way long-term planning by individual farmers would not be necessary for efficient management and the arrangement would be particularly useful where agriculture is to be only a temporary use. Usually, however, pit-heap reclamation sites are too small and their distribution too scattered for such an arrangement to be practicable.

In areas of opencast restoration the Ministry of Agriculture's Divisional Land Commissioners supervise management work on land owned or leased by the National Coal Board, for the initial five years. During this time fencing and drainage are carried out and the land is then sold back to the original owner. The National Coal Board, however, does not at present carry out the reclamation of colliery waste heaps, and sites in Northumberland and Durham have generally been too small to make supervision of their management by the Ministry of Agriculture feasible. An advantage in such supervision would be the degree of direct control that the Ministry would have over operations carried out during the initial period of establishment. However, plans for future management would need to be considered at an early stage to ensure satisfactory development.

The local authorities are in the best position to ensure co-ordination between the short- and long-term uses of the sites. The use of private farmers to manage the land, on short leases in order to control operations, may, however, lead to problems of imbalance in farm structure (see section 2.4). There is thus a need for co-ordination between the various departments and a higher degree of forward planning.

Figure 69. Lack of adequate maintenance on this site has led to blockage of the path drains, loss of the shrub cover planted on the banks, and the growth of vegetation over the path.

3 Management of woodland areas

3.1 Supervision by local authorities

One of the main aims of management of woodland areas is the development of strong root systems which will improve and protect the soil structure and also produce wind-firm trees. This is an important criterion in the choice of young stock, and several local authorities including Northumberland, Fifeshire, Stirling and Nottinghamshire have established nurseries where plants are grown from seed or bought in as young seedlings to be grown on.

It is important that management operations are supervised so that the techniques used relate to the particular problems of reclamation. In most counties, work is carried out by forestry units, which may be supervised by reclamation sections as in Northumberland and Nottinghamshire, or else by specialist forestry firms under contract as in Durham and the West Riding of Yorkshire. In Northumberland, the county's direct labour unit provides a small amount of local employment, mostly for redundant miners.

Certain management operations—in particular, weeding and beating up—are essential not only to encourage root development but also to ensure the survival of trees on the reclaimed shale surfaces.

Weeding This may be necessary between the plants to eliminate competition from weeds and grasses especially as one of the commonest forms of planting is screefing, followed by notching small whips into grass-covered shale. The extent of weeding required will depend largely on the seed mix specified for the forestry areas. In Northumberland low-maintenance grasses have been used after experience on two sites where perennial ryegrass was sown. On one particular site, weeding is required twice during the growing season and here granular herbicides are being considered in preference to hand and machine techniques.

Beating up Planting on reclamation sites generally requires a far heavier beating-up programme than normal forestry establishment owing to the problems of shale material, including low pH, deficiency of nutrients and susceptibility to drought. Other factors affecting the number of trees lost are competition from weeds and grass in more fertile areas, the presence of predatory animals such as voles and rabbits, exposure and vandalism. In Northumberland again, the problem of competition on one site where plants were notched into the soil was so acute that it was replanted completely using forestry-ploughing techniques.

3.2 The supervision of woodland by economic management

Sites which are particularly hostile to the growth of vegetation without considerable amelioration have been able to support only a very limited range of species. The survival of trees by careful choice of species, planting methods and management policy is more important than any doubtful economic returns that may be forthcoming in the future. However, once the trees are established, the possibility of management along economic lines should not be ruled out in certain situations. In areas where large-scale forestry already exists, local authorities are aware of this potential. Stirling County Council have only small amenity woodlands, planted on reclamation sites, but they would consider the commercial possibilities of these woodlands, or additional planting, in the future. The reclamation section of Nottinghamshire County Council also intends to supervise the coppicing by their forestry units of ash, sweet chestnut and sycamore on some of their sites.

The success of economic management will be affected by the species planted, and their spacing.

Species The species most frequently planted on reclamation sites, such as alder, willow and birch, do not have much economic potential. However, pines such as Scots, Corsican and Lodgepole have done extremely well on shale and may very well be considered as forest trees in this situation, as may sycamore which represents the most useful of the hardwoods which will grow on shale. The greatest commercial benefits appear at present to be from either specialist stock such as Christmas trees or else coppice such as have been mentioned.

Spacing An average of 1.8 m (6 ft) spacing is recommended by the Forestry Commission to facilitate efficient management. Planting in rows means that plants are easily found during weeding operations. In Durham and the West Riding of Yorkshire this spacing is used, while in Northumberland 1.5 m (5 ft) is used.

In opencast restoration areas, the NCB pay the Forestry Commission as agents for establishment work. After five years the Forestry Commission either acquire the land (if suitable in terms of slope, drainage and consolidation) or else continue to act as agents. Up to date they have not been interested in supervising management on reclaimed pit heaps. The main factors against it are the relatively small areas of planting involved and the scattered nature of the sites. The Forestry Commission would only consider areas larger than 8–12 ha (20–30 acres) and attached to existing sites that they already supervise. They are, however, willing to offer advice, and certain grants are available for privately managed forests (see section 3.3).

Certain of the farmers leasing reclaimed land for grazing said that they would be interested in managing woodlands to the extent that they could take cuts for silage between trees planted adjacent to their farms. This would serve to keep the grasses short and so encourage tillering, although it would not eliminate competition due to grasses growing round the base of the plant. However, with careful design of access, slope and planting distances (which would have to be more in the region of 2.4 m (8 ft) to allow machine mowers in) such use would allow a certain economic benefit to the farmer.

3.3 Forestry grants

Costs of management of planted areas on the reclamation sites have been substantial. At Big Waters they amounted to £60/ha (£25/acre) in 1971, totally £500 per year, mainly due to the amount of weeding required. There is no grant available to cover these costs, although grants for economically managed woodlands do exist. (See Chapter 1, section 2).

Thus such grants are not available for forestry planting on reclaimed sites where economic factors are not, as yet, considered. Grants of this kind may provide the incentive to establish reclamation planting along more economic lines.

3.4 Management of woodland for amenity and conservation

Several county authorities are now aware that the management of reclaimed sites for both amenity and conservation requires special supervision. A great deal more research needs to be carried out, however, to determine the most efficient methods of establishment. Shrub layer development, pioneer planting and the introduction of suitable amenity species are fields in which the Durham reclamation unit is particularly interested.

Local conservation bodies may be able to advise on the particular techniques required to encourage wildlife. In both Yorkshire and Northumberland local naturalists' trusts are consulted on various aspects of woodland management. In Northumberland it is hoped to lease suitable

Figure 70. Although vandalism is often a reason why a maintenance organization loses heart, failure to keep a high standard of maintenance in turn encourages vandalism.

areas such as Big Waters to the Northumberland and Durham Naturalist Trust. It may be that in such situations other specialist recreational bodies would be interested in sharing management, such as the maintenance of watercourses by angling clubs.

4 Control of reclamation site management

The need for control over the management of reclaimed sites at the end of contract maintenance and during the vulnerable establishment period cannot be overstressed. It has been shown in this chapter that various specialist organizations such as private farmers, forestry contractors and forestry units of the local authorities are used to carry out management work. In such cases, strict supervision by reclamation units is necessary in order that the aims of the reclamation work are fulfilled.

Such control is even more important in urban public open-space areas where there is often neither the incentive of immediate economic return, nor the money available in the form of grants or subsidies, to carry out satisfactory management.

The supervision of public open space is generally handed on after reclamation to the normal maintenance sections of the local authorities, i.e. estates or parks departments, and in certain situations a city parks department will carry out reclamation work itself. The management of sites for recreational use presents particular problems. The pressure of use on a newly established surface, for instance, can lead to serious damage, including the complete breakdown of any developing soil structure and subsequent erosion. Not only must care be taken to control excessive use of the sites, but treatments must relate to the fertility status of the shale.

Most city parks departments do not have the facilities or staff available for proper supervision of these shale areas. Often no sampling is done and any seeding and fertilizer treatment tends to be according to a fertilizer standard practice for all open space areas.

It is most important for the development of the sites that supervision is continued after the contract period, either according to instructions laid down by the designer and passed on in the form of management plans, or else by a specific reclamation unit similar to that operating within some county councils.

5 Contract arrangements

Considering the limited availability of financial support for management work after reclamation, a revision of the existing contract arrangements may be called for. It is not practicable with the present arrangement of contracts to extend contractual responsibility over a period of years, which would be the logical division, and which would in fact have to be a variable period according to factors affecting individual sites. Accordingly, a period which is short enough to be acceptable from the point of view of contractors but is, more importantly, long enough to ensure that the ecological balance is tending to stability rather than instability, must be selected. This selection is bound in some respects to be arbitrary, but this quality should be minimized as far as possible by a scientific approach to the conditions of individual sites.

5.1 Rational planning of treatments

Where a standard procedure is adopted for site development such a procedure must cater for a wide variety of circumstances. Seeding and fertilizer rates, for example, must allow for the worst conditions among the range to be found upon the site. On a large site this range may be very wide and the adoption of a relatively small number of tests of soil conditions may lead to the application of greatly differing quantities of fertilizer on different areas as the conditions change. Clearly it will not be possible to differentiate between treatments on the basis of the minute changes which will be found through a site, but variations which occur can be plotted and a rationalized plan of treatments devised for definable sections of the site.

This work must be capable of being carried out by a contractor without too much difficulty, but if properly planned will obviously create the

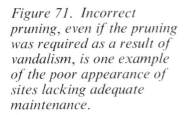

Figure 71. Incorrect pruning, even if the pruning was required as a result of vandalism, is one example of the poor appearance of sites lacking adequate maintenance.

conditions in which a balanced ecology will be promoted more satis-factorily than with less discriminating methods. The effect of this initial care will be felt at all stages of the development of the site. Where such a procedure is not adopted aftercare may become an extremely complex problem and initial deficiencies take many seasons to correct.

5.2 *Aftercare as an integral part of reclamation*

While careful planning of the initial reclamation work undoubtedly makes the aftercare more straightforward, it cannot, because of the nature of landscape development, obviate it completely. A broad generalization may be made that the greater the degree of site work done at the initial stage of reclamation the less will be the work required at the stage of establishment. The removal of all surface material and importation of good quality topsoil to cover a site may result in the quick establishment of a new ecological balance but this will still require some maintenance and will from an economic point of view involve an extremely high level of expenditure. Two points emerge from the study of landscape reclama-tion work. The first is that a landscape project cannot be considered in the same way as a building contract, or an engineering contract. It is not a finite process which is completed at any one point in time. To measure a landscape development by the same criteria as are adopted for building and civil engineering contracts is therefore a basic misconception about the nature of landscape.

The second point is that once this concept of landscape reclamation as a continuing process is accepted the planning approach to landscape projects may have to be radically altered. The presently adopted system of a short-term contract followed by a limited period of establishment might be supplanted by an entirely different form of development contract which might last for a number of years. The advantages of such an arrangement appear to be that by ensuring control of the development during crucial early years it may be possible to reduce quite considerably the capital outlay involved in initial development work, though this may to some extent be offset by additional establishment costs. The need for speedy establishment before handing over to some other party is removed, as is the need to over-specify to allow for the likely failure of the maintaining authority to carry out the necessary establishment operations to ensure the proper development of the site. Both of these aspects could reduce costs considerably and at the same time increase the likelihood of completely satisfactory development.

5.3 *Precedents for longer maintenance periods*

A number of precedents for the acceptance of a longer period of maintenance than is at present normally written into landscape contracts can be quoted. As has already been stated in Chapter 1, the National Coal Board Opencast Division undertakes the restitution of the excavated areas after the extraction of coal. The earthmoving part of the restoration is carried out by the Opencast Division or its agents and the cultivation and aftercare is carried out under the direction of the Ministry of Agriculture's Divisional Land Commissions. The restoration of opencast sites so as to be 'reasonably fit for use as agriculture land' is written into the 1958 Opencast Coal Act (6 and 7 Eliz. 2) in which the two authorized purposes of the Act, are, briefly, to make possible the working of coal, and the restoring of land.

The Act further requires that applications made for the opencast extraction of coal from a site should set out the programme for reclamation in sufficient detail for the Minister to come to an informed decision. It has been the practice for the Coal Board to include a period of five years for controlled aftercare before the site is returned to commercial agriculture. This period is not fixed, and in a number of cases it has been extended at the discretion of the Land Commissioner to seven years where the success of reclamation after five years has not been satisfactory.

The work undertaken by the landscape section of the Ministry of Public Buildings and Works remains always with the jurisdiction of the Ministry itself for the purposes of maintenance and a close liaison is possible between designers and the maintenance branch. Control by the means of detailed maintenance instructions is maintained over a period of ten years and in these circumstances an extension to the actual development contract to cover a longer establishment maintenance period is not necessary.

5.4 Case for new methods of procedure

There may be a case for a complete rethink of all landscape projects on the basis of this approach. This would result in new forms of landscape contractual procedure designed to promote contracts spanning a number of years each, and in turn call for new types of landscape contractor who could organize their work to the greater degree of maintenance work and the longer timescale which would be involved.

References

Agnew, A. F. and Corbett, D. M. 1973. Hydrology of a watershed containing flood control reservoirs and coal surface mining activity, South Western Indiana. In *Ecology and Reclamation of Devastated Land*, ed. R. J. Hutnik and G. Davis, vol. 1, pp. 159–173. New York: Gordon and Breach.

Appleton, J. H. 1970. *Disused Railways in the Countryside of England and Wales.* 11 pp. Countryside Commission.

Ashraf, M. 1969. Studies on the biology of Collembola. *Revue d'Ecologie et Biologie du Sol*, vol. 6, pp. 337–347.

Baker, F. C. 1970. The reclamation of derelict land. A report presented to the Countryside in 1970 Conference.

Barley, K. P. and Kleinig, C. R. 1964. The occupation of newly irrigated lands by earthworms. *Australian Journal of Science*, vol. 26, pp. 290–291.

Barr, J. 1969. *Derelict Britain.* 240 pp. London: Penguin Books.

Bauer, A. M. 1965. Simultaneous excavation and rehabilitation of sand and gravel sites. University of Illinois, National Sand and Gravel Association Project No. 1.

Baweja, K. D. 1939. Studies of the soil fauna with special reference to the recolonization of sterilized soil. *Journal of Animal Ecology*, vol. 8, pp. 120–161.

Beaver, S. H. 1946. *Derelict Land in the Black Country.* 43 pp. Ministry of Town and Country Planning.

Beaver, S. H. 1961. The reclamation of industrial waste land for agricultural and other purposes. *Problems of Applied Geography* (Warsaw).

Bibby, J. S. and Mackney, D. 1969. *Land Use Capability Classification.* Technical Monograph No. 1. The Soil Survey of England and Wales.

Blakely, R. D. 1964. *Reference List for Reclamation of Strip Mine Areas.* US Dept of Agriculture.

Booy, M. E. 1975. Botanical studies in land reclamation after magnesian limestone quarrying. M. Sc. thesis, University of Newcastle upon Tyne.

Bowden, K. L. 1961. *A Bibliography of Strip Mine Reclamation, 1953–1960.* University of Michigan, Dept of Conservation, Ann Arbor.

Bradshaw, A. D., Fitter, A. H. and Handley, J. F. 1973. Why use topsoil in land reclamation? *Surveyor*, 25 May, pp. 39–41.

British Standards Institution. 1971. *Building Drainage.* British Standard Code of Practice 301: 1971. London: BSI.

British Waterways Board. 1972a. *Waterway Environment Handbook.*

British Waterways Board. 1972b. The Leeds and Liverpool Canal—Retention and Improvement.

Buahin, G. K. A. and Edwards, C. A. 1964. The recolonization of sterilized soil by invertebrates. *Report of Rothamsted Experimental Station 1963*, pp. 149–150.

Burges, A. and Raw, F. 1967. *Soil Biology.* 532 pp. London: Academic Press.

Bush, P. W. 1969. Derelict lands studies at the University of Leeds : 1. Spoiled lands to the south east of Leeds—the stages in an air photo study of derelict land. In *Proceedings of the Derelict Land Symposium*, ed. W. G. Collins, pp. 21–28. Guildford: Iliffe Science and Technology Publications.

Caruccio, F. T. 1973. Characterization of strip mine spoil by pyrite grain size and chemical quality of existing ground water. In *Ecology and Reclamation oj Devastated Land*, ed. R. J. Hutnik and G. Davis, vol. 1, pp. 193–226. New York: Gordon and Breach.

Carruthers, I. A. and Canvin, R. W. 1966. Planning the restoration of an open cast coal site. *Operational Research Quarterly*, vol. 18, pp. 399–405.

Chadwick, M. J. 1973. Amendment trials of coal spoil in the north of England. In *Ecology and Reclamation of Devastated Land*, ed. R. J. Hutnik and G. Davis, vol. 2, pp. 175–188. New York: Gordon and Breach.

Chadwick, M. J. and Goodman, G. T. 1975. *The Ecology of Resource Degradation and Renewal*. 480 pp. Oxford: Blackwell.

Civic Trust. 1964. *Derelict Land*. 70 pp. London: Civic Trust.

Clark, D. 1949. *Plane and Geodetic Surveying*. 4th edn, revised and enlarged by J. Glendenning, vol. 1, pp. 374–413. London: Constable and Co.

Clouston, J. B. 1967. The Durham Motorway, landscape study. *Methods of Landscape Analysis, Symposium Report*, pp. 11–19. London: Landscape Research Group.

Clouston, J. B. 1974. Practical experiences derived from rehabilitation of derelict land and re-utilization of disturbed mining areas in a bituminous coal district in SVR. In *Green Mine Spoil Heaps in the Ruhr*, pp. 123–134. Essen: Siedlungsverband Ruhrkohlenbezirk.

Collins, W. G. and Bush, P. W. 1969. The definition and classification of derelict land. *Journal of the Royal Town Planning Institute*, vol. 55, no. 3, pp. 111–115.

Commonwealth Bureau of Soils. 1965. *Bibliography on Spoil Banks Soils and their Reclamation*. No. 1027, CBS, 20.

Conover, H. S. 1953. *Public Grounds Maintenance Handbook*, pp. 271–312. Knoxville, Tennessee: Tennessee Valley Authority.

Cornwell, S. M. and Stone, E. L. 1968. Availability of nitrogen to plants in acid coal mine spoils. *Nature*, vol. 217, pp. 768–769.

Cowan, R. J. 1961. Ironstone workings and land restoration. *Chartered Surveyor*, vol. 94, pp. 83–89.

Curtis, W. R. 1973. Effects of strip mining on the hydrology of sand mountain watersheds in Appalachia. In *Ecology and Reclamation of Devastated Land*, ed. by R. J. Hutnik and G. Davis, vol. 1, pp. 147–157. New York: Gordon and Breach.

Daily, K. M. An investigation in the size, shape, character and boundaries of spaces in the landscape with reference to optimum favourable environmental conditions. Town and Country Planning Library, University of Newcastle upon Tyne, Departmental Study (undated).

Davies, W. M. 1973. Bringing back the acres: sand and gravel. *Agriculture*, vol. 70, pp. 133–138. Ministry of Agriculture.

Davis, B. N. K. 1963. A study of the microarthropod communities in mineral soils near Corby, Northants. *Journal of Animal Ecology*, vol. 32, pp. 49–71.

Deely, D. J. and Borden, F. Y. 1973. High surface temperatures of strip mine spoils. In *Ecology and Reclamation of Devastated Lands*, ed. by R. J. Hutnik and G. Davis, vol. 1, pp. 69–79. New York: Gordon and Breach.

Department of the Environment. 1974. *Survey of Derelict and Despoiled Land: Guidance Notes*. London: HMSO.

Doubleday, G. P. 1970. Preliminary report on the soil forming potential of the shale on the Windynook Whitehills site, Felling. 2 pp. University of Newcastle upon Tyne.

Doubleday, G. P. 1971a. Colliery shales as soil forming materials in north east England. Ph.D. Thesis, University of Newcastle upon Tyne.

Doubleday, G. P. 1971b. Soil forming materials: their nature and assessment. In *Landscape Reclamation*, vol. 1, ch. 8, pp. 70–83. Guildford: IPC Science and Technology Press.

Doubleday, G. P. 1972. Development and management of soils on pit heaps. In *Landscape Reclamation*, vol. 2, ch. 4, pp. 25–35. Guildford: IPC Science and Technology Press.

Doubleday, G. P. 1973. Topsoil sometimes still the best answer in reclamation. *Surveyor*, 31 August, pp. 31–32.

Doubleday, G. P. 1974. The reclamation of land after coal mining. *Outlook on Agriculture*, vol. 8, no. 3, pp. 156–162.

Downing, M. F. 1967. Study tour of landscape reclamation sites in the Lancashire coalfields. Interim Report No. 2, Landscape Reclamation Research Project, University of Newcastle upon Tyne. 40 pp.

Downing, M. F. 1970. Written report: reclamation scheme for land at Windynook Quarry, Whitehills Washery Heap, Upper Heworth Colliery etc. Submitted to Felling UDC. University of Newcastle upon Tyne. 4 pp.

Downing, M. F. 1971. Landform design. In *Landscape Reclamation*, vol. 1, ch. 4, pp. 32–42. Guildford: IPC Science and Technology Press.

Drift, J. van der. 1951. Analysis of the animal community in a beech forest floor. *Tijdschrift voor Entomologie*, vol. 94, pp. 1–168.

Dunger, W. 1968. Die Entwicklung der Bodenfauna auf rekultivierten Kippen und Halden des Braunkohlentagebaues. *Abhandlungen und Berichten der Naturkundesmuseum, Gorlitz*, vol. 43, no. 2, pp. 1–256.

Dunger, W. 1969a. Fragen der naturlichen und experimentellen Besiedlung kulturfeindlicher Boden durch Lumbriciden. *Pedobiologia*, vol. 9, pp. 146–151.

Dunger, W. 1969b. Über den Anteil der Arthropoden an der Umsetzung des Bestandesabfalles in Anfangs-Bodenbildungen. *Pedobiologia*, vol. 9, pp. 366–371.

Edwards, C. A. 1974. Macroarthropods. In *Biology of Plant Litter Decomposition*, ed. C. H. Dickinson and G. J. F. Pugh, vol. 2, pp. 533–554. London: Academic Press.

Edwards, C. A. and Fletcher, K. E. 1971. A comparison of extraction methods for terrestrial arthropods. In *Methods of Study in Quantitative Soil Ecology: Population, Production and Energy Flow*, ed. J. Phillipson. IBP Handbook no. 18, pp. 150–185. Oxford: Blackwell.

Edwards, C. A. and Heath, G. W. 1963. The role of soil animals in breakdown of leaf material. In *Soil Organisms*, ed. J. Doeksen and J. van der Drift, pp. 76–85. Amsterdam: North Holland.

Forestry Commission. 1963. *Industrial Waste Land and its Afforestation and Reclamation: a Bibliography of British References.*

Forestry Commission. 1968. *Grants for Woodland Owners.* London: HMSO.

Frazer, C. K. and Lake, J. R. 1967. *A Laboratory Investigation of the Physical and Chemical Properties of Burnt Colliery Shale.* RRL Report 125. Road Research Laboratory, Crowthorne, Berks.

Furness, J. F. 1954. Tipping in wet pits. *Municipal Journal*, 6 August, pp. 1811–1817.

Gadgil, P. D. 1964. Soil biology in the Lower Swansea Valley. Study Rep. No. 10, University College, Swansea. 31 pp.

Game Conservancy. 1964. *Wildfowl Management on Inland Waters.*

Gemmell, R. P. 1973. Colliery shale revegetation techniques. *Surveyor*, 6 July, pp. 27–29.

Goodman, G. T. and Bray, S. 1975. *Ecological Aspects of the Reclamation of Derelict and Disturbed Land.* 35 pp. London: Natural Environment Research Council.

Hackett, B. 1960. Basic design in landform. *ILA Journal*, no. 49,
pp. 7–9.

Hackett, B. 1971. *Landscape Planning*. 124 pp. Newcastle upon Tyne:
Oriel Press.

Hackett, B. 1972. *Landscape Development of Steep Slopes*. 143 pp.
Newcastle upon Tyne: Oriel Press.

Hale, W. G. 1967. Collembola. In *Soil Biology*, ed. A. Burges and F. Raw,
pp. 397–411. London: Academic Press.

Harding, D. J. L. and Stuttard, R. A. 1974. Microarthropods. In *Biology of
Plant Litter Decomposition*, ed. C. H. Dickinson and G. J. F. Pugh,
vol. 2, pp. 489–532. London: Academic Press.

Haywood, S. M. 1973. Landscape. *The Quarry Managers Journal*, March.

Hebblethwaite, R. L. 1973. Landscape assessment and classification
techniques. In *Land Use and Landscape Planning*, ed. D. Lovejoy,
pp. 17–50. Aylesbury, Bucks: Leonard Hill.

Hodgson, D. R. and Townsend, W. N. 1973. The amelioration and revegeta-
tion of pulverized fuel ash. In *Ecology and Reclamation of Devastated
Land*, ed. R. J. Hutnik and G. Davis, vol. 2, pp. 247–272. New York:
Gordon and Breach.

Hutnik, R. J. and Davis, G. 1973. *Ecology and Reclamation of Devastated
Land*, vol. 1, xiv + 504 pp., and vol. 2, xiv + 538 pp. New York:
Gordon and Breach.

Hutson, B. R. 1972. The invertebrate fauna of a reclaimed pit heap. In
Landscape Reclamation, vol. 2, ch. 8, pp. 64–79. Guildford: IPC
Science and Technology Press.

Hutson, B. R. 1974. The invertebrate fauna influencing soil development
on industrial reclamation sites. Ph.D. Thesis, University of Newcastle
upon Tyne. 359 pp.

Jacobs, C. A. J. 1972. *Derelict Land in Denbighshire*. DCC Ruthin.

James, A. L. 1966. Stabilizing mine dumps with vegetation. *Endeavour*,
vol. 25, pp. 154–157.

Janetschek, H. 1970. Environments and ecology of terrestrial arthropods
in the high Antarctic. In *Antarctic Ecology*, ed. M. W. Holdgate,
pp. 871–885. London: Academic Press.

Johnson, C. 1966. Practical operating procedures for progressive
rehabilitation of sand and gravel sites. University of Illinois, National
Sand and Gravel Association, Project no. 2, 1964–1965.

Johnson, G. A. L. 1961. Lateral variation of marine and deltaic sediments
in cyclothemic deposits with particular reference to the Visean and
Namurian of Northern England. *C. r. 4 Int. Congr. Strat. Carb.
Heerlen, 1958*, vol. 2, pp. 323–330.

Krause, R. R. 1973. Predicting mined-land soil. In *Ecology and Reclamation
of Devastated Land*, ed. R. J. Hutnik and G. Davis, vol. 1, pp. 121–
131. London: Gordon and Breach.

Kühnelt, W. 1961. *Soil Biology with Special Reference to the Animal
Kingdom*. 397 pp. London: Faber.

Lake, J. R. 1968. Unburnt colliery shale: its possible use as roadfill
material. 5 pp. Crowthorne: Road Research Laboratory.

Lake, J. R., Frazer, C. K. and Burns, J. 1966. A laboratory investigation
of the physical and chemical properties of spent oil shale. *Roads and
Road Construction*, vol. 44, no. 552, pp. 155–159.

Land Use Consultants. 1970. Stoke on Trent reclamation programme.
ILA Journal, no. 90, pp. 14–22.

Land Use Consultants. 1971. A planning classification of Scottish landscape
resources. Occasional paper no. 1, Countryside Commission for
Scotland.

Lofty, J. R. 1974. Oligochaetes. In *Biology of Plant Litter Decomposition*,
ed. C. H. Dickinson and G. J. F. Pugh, vol. 2, pp. 467–488. London:
Academic Press.

Loots, G. C. and Ryke, P. A. 1967. The ratio Oribatei: Trombidiformes with reference to organic matter content in soils. *Pedobiologia*, vol. 7, pp. 121–124.

Luxton, M. 1967. The zonation of saltmarsh Acarina. *Pedobiologia*, vol. 7, pp. 55–56.

MacCartney, J. C. and Whaite, R. H. 1969. *Pennsylvania Anthracite Refuse:* a survey of solid waste from mining and preparation, USAT. Bureau of Mines, Washington.

Macdonald, P. I. 1969. Derelict land studies at the University of Leeds: a rational approach to the study of derelict land and the principles of definition and classification. In *Proceedings of the Derelict Land Symposium*, pp. 29–33. Guildford: Iliffe Science and Technology Publications.

Macfadyen, A. 1963. The contribution of the microfauna to total soil metabolism. In *Soil Organisms*, ed. J. Doeksen and J. van der Drift, pp. 3–17. Amsterdam: North Holland.

McHarg, I. L. 1968. *Design with Nature*. 197 pp. New York: Natural History Press.

McNay, L. M. 1970a. Mining and milling waste disposal problems: where are we today? *Proceedings of the Second Mineral Waste Utilization Symposium*, pp. 125–129. Chicago: US Bureau of Mines/IIT Research Institute.

McNay, L. M. 1970b. Surface mine reclamation, Moraine State Park, Pennsylvania. Information circular no. 8456, US Department of the Interior, Bureau of Mines.

Maurer, R. 1974. Die Viefalt der Kafer- und Spinnenfauna des Wiesenbodens und Einflussbereich von Verkehrsimmissionen. *Oecologia (Berl.)*, vol. 14, pp. 327–351.

May, J. T. *et al.* 1973. Some characteristics of spoil material from kaolin clay strip mining. In *Ecology and Reclamation of Devastated Land*, ed. R. J. Hutnik and G. Davis, vol. 1, pp. 3–14. New York: Gordon and Breach.

Meijer, J. 1974. A comparative study of the immigration of Carabids (Coleoptera, Carabidae) into a new polder. *Oecologia (Berl.)*, vol. 16, pp. 185–208.

Middleton, R. E. and Chadwick, O. 1955. *A Treatise on Surveying*. Revised by B. J. Munton. 6th edn, vol. 1, pp. 386–396. London: E.F.N. Spon.

Milne, A. 1959. The centric systematic area-sample treated as a random sample. *Biometrics*, vol. 15, pp. 270–297.

Ministry of Agriculture, Fisheries and Food. *Farm Capital Grant Scheme 1970 and 1973*. Explanatory leaflets. London: HMSO.

Ministry of Agriculture, Fisheries and Food. 1971. *The Restoration of Sand and Gravel Workings*. London: HMSO.

Ministry of Agriculture, Fisheries and Food. 1972. *Farming Restored Opencast Land*. Advisory leaflet 510. London: HMSO.

Ministry of Health. 1939. *Report on Restoration of Land Affected by Iron Ore Working*. London: HMSO.

Ministry of Housing and Local Government. 1955a. *Explanatory Memorandum on the Ironstone Restoration Fund*. London: HMSO.

Ministry of Housing and Local Government. 1955b. *Technical Memorandum No. 3: Mineral Working*. London: HMSO.

Ministry of Housing and Local Government. 1956. *Technical Memorandum No. 7: Derelict Land and its Reclamation*. London: HMSO.

Ministry of Housing and Local Government. 1957. *Derelict Land: a Select List of References*. Bibliography no. 107. London: HMSO.

Ministry of Housing and Local Government. 1958. *Technical Planning Memorandum: Pulverized Fuel Ash*. London: HMSO.

Ministry of Housing and Local Government. 1959. *Colliery Spoil Heaps*. Circular 26–29. London: HMSO.

Ministry of Housing and Local Government. 1960a. *Local Employment Act: Rehabilitation of Derelict Neglected or Unsightly Land*. Circular 30/60. London: HMSO.

Ministry of Housing and Local Government. 1960b. *The Control of Mineral Working*. London: HMSO.

Ministry of Housing and Local Government. 1961a. *Pollution of Water by Tipped Refuse*. London: HMSO.

Ministry of Housing and Local Government. 1961b. *Technical Committee on the Experimental Disposal of House Refuse in Wet and Dry Pits: Report*. London: HMSO.

Ministry of Housing and Local Government. 1963. *Bibliography No. 107: a Select List of References*. London: HMSO.

Ministry of Housing and Local Government. 1965. *Bibliography No. 107: Addendum*. London: HMSO.

Ministry of Housing and Local Government. 1967a. Explanatory leaflet on grants for the reclamation of derelict, neglected or unsightly land under the Industrial Development Act 1966 and the Local Government Act 1966. London: HMSO.

Ministry of Housing and Local Government. 1967b. Circular 17/67 (10 March 1967). Industrial Development Act 1966. Local Government Act 1966. Rehabilitation of derelict neglected or unsightly land. Industrial Development Act 1966. Water and sewage schemes. London: HMSO.

Ministry of Housing and Local Government. 1967c. *Refuse Storage and Collection*. London: HMSO.

Ministry of Housing and Local Government. 1970a. *The Protection of the Environment*. London: HMSO.

Ministry of Housing and Local Government. 1970b. *Derelict Land*. London: HMSO.

Ministry of Town and Country Planning. 1946. *The Restoration Problem in the Ironstone Industry in the Midlands*. London: HMSO.

Ministry of Town and Country Planning. 1948. *Advisory Committee on Sand and Gravel: Report No. 1*. London: HMSO.

Ministry of Town and Country Planning. 1949. *Country Planning: Reclamation of Mined Land*. Bibliography No. 84. London: HMSO.

Ministry of Town and Country Planning. 1953. *Advisory Committee on Sand and Gravel: Report No. 18*. London: HMSO.

Ministry of Transport. 1969. *Specification for Road and Bridge Works*. London: HMSO.

Moore, H. I. 1950. *Grassland Husbandry*. 141 pp. London: Allen and Unwin.

National Coal Board. 1967. *Plant Growth on Pit Heaps*. Research pub. No. 42. 24 pp.

Neumann, U. 1971. Die Sukzession der Bodenfauna (Carabidae (Coleoptera), Diplopoda und Isopoda) in den forstlich rekultivierten Gebieten des Rheineschen Braunkohlenreviers. *Pedobiologia*, vol. 11, pp. 193–226.

Nielsen, C. O. 1967. Nematoda. In *Soil Biology*, ed. A. Burges and F. Raw, pp. 197–211. London: Academic Press.

O'Connor, F. B. 1967. The Enchytraeidae. In *Soil Biology*, ed. A. Burges and F. Raw, pp. 213–257. London: Academic Press.

Oxenham, J. R. 1966. *Reclaiming Derelict Land*. 204 pp. London: Faber.

Penning Rowsell, E. C. 1973. Alternative approaches to landscape appraisal and evaluation. Middlesex Polytechnic at Enfield, Planning Research Group, Report no. 11. 49 pp.

Phillipson, J. 1971. *Methods of Study in Quantitative Soil Ecology: Population, Productive and Energy Flow*. IBP Handbook No. 18. 297 pp. Oxford: Blackwell.

Professional Institutes Council for Conservation. 1974. *Dereliction of Land*. 22 pp. London: PICC.

Research Committee on Coal Mine Spoil Revegetation in Pennsylvania. 1965. *A Guide for Revegetating Bituminous Strip Mine Spoils in Pennsylvania.*

Reynoldson, T. B. 1943. A comparative account of the life cycles of *Lumbricillus lineatus* Mull. and *Enchytraeus albidus* Hessle in relation to temperature. *Annals of Applied Biology*, vol. 30, pp. 60–66.

Rhee, J. A. van. 1969. Development of earthworm populations in polder soils. *Pedobiologia*, vol. 9, pp. 133–140.

Richardson, J. A. 1956. The ecology and physiology of plants growing on colliery spoil heaps, clay pits and quarries in County Durham. Ph.D. Thesis, University of Durham.

Richardson, J. A. 1957. Derelict pit heaps and their vegetation. *Planning Outlook*, vol. 4, no. 3, pp. 15–22.

Richardson, J. A. 1958. The effect of temperature on the growth of plants on pit heaps. *Journal of Ecology*, vol. 46, pp. 537–546.

Richardson, J. A. 1975. Physical problems of growing plants on colliery waste. In *The Ecology of Resource Degradation and Renewal*, ed. M. J. Chadwick and G. T. Goodman, pp. 275–285. Oxford: Blackwell.

Richardson, J. A. and Greenwood, E. F. 1967. Soil moisture tension in relation to the colonization of pit heaps. *Proc. University of Newcastle upon Tyne Phil. Soc.*, vol. 1, no. 9, pp. 129–136.

Richardson, J. A., Shenton, B. K. and Dicker, R. J. 1971. Botanical studies of natural and planted vegetation on colliery spoil heaps. In *Landscape Reclamation*, vol. 1, ch. 9, pp. 84–99. Guildford; IPC Science and Technology Press.

Riley, D. and Barber, S. A. 1969. Bicarbonate accumulation and pH changes at the soybean *(Glycine Max (L) Merr.)* root–soil interface. *Soil Sci. Soc. Amer. Proc.*, vol. 33, pp. 905–908.

Roberts, H. E. and Stothard, J. N. 1968. Use of computers for road design. *Journal of the Institution of Civil Engineers*, paper no. 7133, pp. 105–127.

Roots, B. I. 1956. The water relations of earthworms. II. Resistance to desiccation and immersion and behaviour when submerged and when allowed choice of environment. *Journal of Experimental Biology*, vol. 33, pp. 29–44.

Russell, Sir E. J. 1947. Agricultural restoration of mining and quarrying sites. *Agriculture*, vol. 54, pp. 49–51.

Russell, Sir E. J. 1950. *Soil Conditions and Plant Growth*. 411 pp. London: Longmans.

Salt, G., Raw, F. and Brian, M. V. 1948. The arthropod population of pasture soil. *Journal of Animal Ecology*, vol. 17, pp. 139–150.

Sand and Gravel Association, 1967. *Pit and Quarry Textbook*. 239 pp. London: MacDonald and Co.

Satchell, J. E. 1967. Lumbricidae. In *Soil Biology*, ed. A. Burges and F. Raw, pp. 259–322. London: Academic Press.

Satchell, J. E. 1974. Litter: interface of animate/inanimate matter. In *Biology of Plant Litter Decomposition*, ed. C. H. Dickinson and G. J. F. Pugh, vol. 1, pp. xii–xliv. London: Academic Press.

Scoular, J. D. 1966. The use of heavy earthmoving machinery and plant. Landscape Reclamation Seminar. University of York, Institute of Architectural Studies. 13 pp.

Seelye, E. E. 1963. *Design: Data Book for Civil Engineers*, vol. 1. New York: John Wiley.

Shenton, B. K. 1968. Afforestation of pit heaps in County Durham. University of Newcastle upon Tyne, Landscape Reclamation Research Project, Report no. 5, Parts 1–9.

Simonds, J. O. 1961. *Landscape Architecture*. 244 pp. London: McGraw-Hill.

Southwood, T. R. E. 1966. *Ecological Methods*. 391 pp. London: Methuen.

Sports Council. 1973. *Rickmansworth Gravel Pits*.

Stockdill, S. M. J. and Cossens, G. G. 1966. The role of earthworms in pasture production and moisture conservation. *Proc. N. Z. Grassl. Assn., 1966*, pp. 168–183.

Stout, J. D. 1974. Protozoa. In *Biology of Plant Litter Decomposition*, ed. C. H. Dickinson and G. J. F. Pugh, vol. 2, pp. 385–420. London: Academic Press.

Stout, J. D. and Heal, O. W. 1967. Protozoa. In *Soil Biology*, ed. A Burges and F. Raw, pp. 149–195. London: Academic Press.

Street, H. E. and Goodman, G. T. 1967. Revegetation techniques in the Lower Swansea Valley. In *The Lower Swansea Valley Project*, ed. K. J. Hilton, pp. 71–110. London: Longmans.

Taylor, M. C. 1973. Conservation of industrial monuments. *Journal of the Royal Town Planning Institute*, vol. 59, pp. 225–232.

Thomas, M., Ranson, S. L. and Richardson, J. A. 1973. *Plant Physiology*, 5th edn. 1062 pp. London: Longmans.

Thornton, I., Atkinson, W. J., Webb, J. S. and Poole, D. B. R. 1966. Geochemical reconnaissance and bovine hypocuprosis in Co. Limerick, Ireland. *Irish J. Agric. Res.*, vol. 5, pp. 280–283.

University of Newcastle upon Tyne. 1971, 1972. *Landscape Reclamation*, vols. 1 and 2. Guildford: IPC Science and Technology Press.

Wallwork, J. A. 1967. Acari. In *Soil Biology*, ed. A. Burges and F. Raw, pp. 363–395. London: Academic Press.

Wallwork, J. A. 1970. *Ecology of Soil Animals*. 283 pp. London: McGraw-Hill

Wallwork, J. A. 1974. *Derelict Land*. 333 pp. Newton Abbot: David and Charles.

Walsh, G. B. 1910. Coleoptera of the Grangetown slag heaps. *Naturalist, Hull*, vol. 35, p. 339.

Warner, R. W. 1973. Acid coal mine drainage effects on aquatic life. In *Ecology and Reclamation of Devastated Land*, ed. R. J. Hutnik and G. Davis, vol. 1, pp. 227–237. London/New York: Gordon and Breach.

Webb, J. S. and Atkinson, W. J. 1965. Regional geochemical reconnaissance applied to some agricultural problems in Co. Limerick, Eire. *Nature*, vol. 203, pp. 1056–1059.

Webb, J. S., Thornton, I. and Fletcher, K. 1968. Geochemical reconnaissance and hypocuprosis. *Nature*, vol. 217, pp. 1012–1016.

Weddle, A. E. 1969. Techniques in landscape planning. *Journal of the Royal Town Planning Institute*, vol. 55, pp. 387–389.

Westoll, T. S. 1968. Sedimentary rhythms in coal bearing strata. In *Coal and Coal Bearing Strata*, ed. Murchison and Westoll, pp. 105–123. Edinburgh: Oliver and Boyd.

Whyte, R. O. and Sisam, J. W. B. 1949. *The Establishment of Vegetation on Industrial Waste Land*. Commonwealth Agricultural Bureaux, joint pubn. No. 14. 78 pp. Aberystwyth: CAB.

Whyte, W. S. 1969. *Basic Metric Surveying*. 312 pp. London: Butterworth.

Williamson, P. and Evans, P. R. 1973. A preliminary study of the effects of high levels of inorganic lead on soil fauna. *Pedobiologia*, vol. 13, pp. 16–21.

Wood, R. F. and Thirgood, J. V. 1955. *Tree Planting on Colliery Spoil Heaps*. Forestry Commission research pubn. No. 17. 18 pp.

Young, C. P. 1973. *Estimated Rainfall for Drainage Calculations in the United Kingdom*. Department of the Environment, Transport and Road Research Laboratory, Report No. LR595.

Zevi, B. 1964. The modern landscape dimensions of landscape architecture. In *Shaping Tomorrow's Landscape*, vol. 1, *The Landscape Architect's Role in Conservation*, pp. 16–19. Amsterdam: Djambatan.

Index

Pollution *continued*
  water supplies, of, 26, 38, 70, 84, 115, 184
Polypropylene matting, in preventing erosion of watercourses, 75, 82
Potassium, as plant nutrient in soil, 96, 101, 102, 113, 152, 155
  increased levels in burned shale, 100
  lacking in china clay waste, 85
  promoting growth of clover, 154
  promoting winter hardiness of clover, 102
Professional Institutes Council on Conservation, 20
Pyrite in soil, 28, 32
  geochemistry of formation, 87, 88
  oxidation of, 71, 92, 102, 151
  weathering of, 91, 103, 109, 111, 112

Quarries,
  filling of, 13
  pits left following abandonment, 8
  waste from, 85, 86, 97
Quartz, 85, 89

Railway lines, derelict, 3, 11, 12, 13, 45, 50, 52, 177
  restoration of, 1, 42
Rape, growth of, 107
Ray-Go Ram 75 compactor, 64
Reclamation units, local authority, 208, 209, 215
Recreation, as after-use of reclaimed land, 40–42, 44, 57
  canals, for, 1, 4
  railways, for, 1
Refuse, 13, 28
  anthracite, 17
  basis for horticulture, as, 40
  unsuitability for filling wet pits, 7
Regrading, 4, 15, 40, 41, 51, 52, 53–69, 79, 98, 115, 120, 148
Rhizobium, nitrogen fixation by, 155
Rhododendrons, growth on china clay spoil heaps, 28
Roads, 38
  access to site, for, 174
  derelict, 12, 13
  on site, 11, 30, 177, 194
Robinia pseudoacacia, 171, 172
Roddymoor Colliery site, 37, 48, 63, 107, 110, 134, 136, 138, 139, 209
Run-off, 79
  coefficient of, 73
Ryegrass, perennial, 123, 161, 163, 201, 206
  nitrogen, effect on yield, 107
  pH, effect on yield, 108
  phosphorus, effect on growth, 105
  potash fertilizers, effect on growth, 101

St Anthony site, 42
Salinity of soil, 32, 92, 110, 134, 136, 139
  effect of weathering, as, 90

grazing animals and, 111
measurement of, 95, 109
resulting from weathering of iron pyrite, 91
Sand and gravel working, 26, 42, 80, 85, 97
Sandheaps, 8, 100
Sand-tray models, 47
Science Museum Fund, 3
Scottish Development Department, 187
Scrapers, 60–64, 157
Seeding, 115–118, 177, 192, 198, 215
  correct time of year for, 157–158
  cost of, 198
  mixtures, 162–165, 193, 201
    Cockle Park, 163
  scheduling as part of overall reclamation sequence, 184, 185
  sequence of operations, 120–123
  soil properties and, 156–159, 192
  specification for, 200–203
  woodland, for, 166, 169
Services affecting site, 30, 34
Shaft caps, 30, 175, 188, 198
Shale, as main component of colliery waste, 86
Sheep, 164, 207, 208
  effects of grazing, 111, 206
  scouring of, 111
Shovel, mechanical, 60, 61
Shrubs, 29, 49, 169
  acid-tolerant, 171, 172
  alkaline-tolerant, 172
  preventing erosion, 2
Siderite, 87
Siderotil, 91
Silica, 85
Silt, 77, 79, 82, 84, 91
Ski slope, as after-use of reclaimed site, 47
Slate,
  formation of, 85
  weathering of, 89
Slurry, 60, 62, 67, 196
  disposal of, 5, 62, 176, 190, 198
  moisture content of, 27
Slurry lagoons, 10, 27
Soil, 26, 85–125
  acidity, *see* Acidity in soil
  aeration of, 109, 113, 126, 145
  alkalinity, 172
  analysis of, 93, 94, 150, 155
  calcium in, 150, 151
  chemically inert, 85, 100
  chemistry, 87
  classification of, 55, 67
  compaction during earthmoving, *see* Compaction
  depth, 27
  drainage, *see* Drainage
  fauna, *see* Fauna, soil
  fertility, 46, 155, 156, 157, 163, 168, 205, 215
    development of, 100